COLLECTIONS

OF

THE PROTESTANT EPISCOPAL

Historical Society,

FOR THE YEAR

1851.

PUBLISHED BY ORDER OF

THE EXECUTIVE COMMITTEE

OF THE SOCIETY.

NEW YORK:
STANFORD & SWORDS, PUBLISHERS.

1851.

R. CRAIGHEAD, PRINTER AND STEREOTYPER,
112 FULTON STREET.

Officers of the Society.

President.
The Rt. Rev. T. C. BROWNELL, D.D. LL.D.

Vice-President.
The Rev. FRANCIS L. HAWKS, D.D. LL.D.

Secretary.
The Rev. B. FRANKLIN.

Treasurer.
FREDERICK S. WINSTON, Esq., 60 Cedar street, New York.

Executive Committee.

The Rev. WM. BACON STEVENS, D.D., Penn.
" " PHILIP SLAUGHTER, Virginia.
" " A. B. PATERSON, N. Jersey.
" " J. H. HOBART, N. York.
" " W. I. KIP, D.D., N. York.
" " T. W. COIT, D.D., Conn.
" " T. C. PITKIN, Conn.
Mr. JOHN ALEXANDER, Md.
" SAMUEL H. HUNTINGDON, Conn.
" ROBERT BOLTON, Jun., N. Y.
" G. M. WHARTON, Penn.
" E. A. NEWTON, Mass.
" G. L. DUYCKINCK, N. Y.

Corresponding Members.

Mr. R. H. Gardiner, Gardiner, Maine.
Rev. Charles Burroughs, D.D., Portsmouth, N. H.
" Joel Clapp, D.D., Bellows Falls, Vt.
" J. A. Hicks, D.D., Rutland, "
" Samuel B. Babcock, Dedham, Mass.
" J. H. Eames, Providence, R. I.
" N. S. Richardson, New Haven, Conn.
" Alfred Stubbs, New Brunswick, N. J.
" S. C. Brinckle, New Castle, Del.
" W. D. Wilson, D.D., Geneva, W. N. Y.
" F. H. Cuming, Grand Rapids, Mich.
" C. W. Fitch, Piqua, Ohio.
" Mr. J. M. Moore, Madison, Ill.
" Samuel Chase, D.D., Robin's Nest, Ill.
" Benj. Akerly, Milwaukee, Wis.
" S. Davis, Green Bay, "
" Alfred Louderback, Davenport, Iowa.
" E. G. Gear, Fort Snelling, Minn.
" F. J. Clerc, St. Louis, Mo.
" William Vaux, Fort Laramie.
" J. N. Norton, Frankfort, Ky.
" Charles Tomes, Nashville, Tenn.
" W. C. Stout, Fayetteville, Ark.
" Charles Gillette, Houston, Texas.
Mr. George S. Yerger, Vicksburgh, Miss.
Col. Isaac Croom, Greensborough, Ala.
Rev. C. Hanckel, D.D., Charleston, S. C.
" C. Wallace, " "
" T. J. Young, " "
" J. A. Sheppard, Scuppernong, N. C.

The corresponding members are agents of the Protestant Episcopal Historical Society in their several dioceses. Where no corresponding member is elected the member or members of the Executive Committee in that diocese performs the duties.

Direct Church papers, donations of books, pamphlets, manuscripts, &c., to the Rev. Benj. Franklin, Philadelphia. Subscriptions and moneys to F. S. Winston, Esq., Treasurer, 60 Cedar street, N. Y.

TABLE OF CONTENTS.

PREFACE.

The Executive Committee of the Protestant Episcopal Historical Society have, at length, the pleasure of presenting to its members the first volume of its collections.

That it has not sooner appeared is less the fault of the Committee than of some of the members of the Society. The former adopted as a rule, to which they have inflexibly adhered, to contract no debt which they had not the means of paying at any moment when it might be demanded. Hence they were unwilling to print until they had funds in hand to pay for the work. Some of the members, from inattention, delayed their payments for a time, and the Committee waited to receive them. The volume is as large as their means enabled them to make it.

The Committee indulge the hope that it will not, in its contents, disappoint the reasonable expectations of the Society. It will be found to present the record of past events only; interesting, as they hope and believe, to all the members of the Church alike. It is made up of the early documents themselves, with but two exceptions. Those two consist merely of a condensed summary of the facts connected with two past events of historical interest to churchmen (occurring in colonial times), chronologically arranged, and embodying the substance of many scattered documents. These two were prepared by two members of the publishing Committee. Nearly the whole of the book consists of that which has never before been published, and a part of it presents probably the best history extant of the earliest labors in America of the venerable Society for Propagating the Gospel.

The book will afford to the members of the Church a specimen of the general nature of the materials, which (should the Society be sustained) will compose the future volumes of the series. The materials at the disposal of the Committee are abundant enough for many such volumes as this; and some of them are of deep interest, and indeed importance to the Church. To Churchmen, therefore, we must look for support. The historical student or antiquary who is not a churchman, may here and there be found to attach a value to such a publication as ours; but the number of such is not large, and, therefore, our support must be derived from Protestant Episcopalians, alive to the importance of preserving the documentary history of their portion of the Church of Christ. Our subscription list of members is at present small; it consists of but little more than three hundred names; but among those are to be found that of every bishop, as well as those of many of the oldest and most influential clergy. Had the Society some twelve or fifteen hundred members, the Committee would pledge themselves to publish annually *four* volumes like the present, to a copy of which each member would be entitled by virtue of his annual payment of two dollars.

The present members of the Society are, for the most part, derived from the ranks of the clergy. The laity have not yet had their attention drawn to the subject; and, in fact, most of them are probably ignorant of the existence of the Society. The Executive Committee would, therefore, respectfully solicit the co-operation of the conductors of Church periodicals, in making known to the laity the plans and purposes of the Society; and would ask also for the efficient aid of our numerous parochial clergy, in causing the Society to be known in their respective congregations. If each clergyman would procure but a few lay members, the Society might pursue its work on a larger scale, and more than repay to every member the amount of his annual subscription.

The Committee deem it proper to say that the management of the affairs of the Society costs nothing. It has no paid agent, and the services of every officer are gratuitously rendered.

It only remains to add that the following gentlemen compose the Publishing Committee who have prepared the present volume:

Rev. F. L. Hawks, D.D., LL.D.
Rev. Wm. B. Stevens, D.D.
Rev. W. I. Kip, D.D.
Rev. Benj. Franklin.
Robert Bolton, Jr.
Geo. L. Duyckinck.

KEITH AND TALBOT.

The Society for Propagating the Gospel in Foreign Parts was established in England, by charter, bearing date the 16th day of June, 1701.

One of the first acts of the Society was to send to the English Colonies on this continent a missionary to make personal examination, by travelling over the then several governments of British America that now constitute a part of the United States.

The individual selected was the Rev. George Keith, whose Journal is hereafter presented, and of whom a slight sketch will form a suitable introduction to the record of his labors.

George Keith was born at Aberdeen, in Scotland; not, however, of Quaker parents. At what time he became a member of the Society of Friends, we have not been able to discover. He was possessed of learning, having been very well educated, and his talents were of a high order. His mind was acute and logical, and his temper fearless. In truth, the greatest defects in his character resulted from the indulgence of his temper. He was irritable and overbearing at times, and his language was not always regulated by Christian gentleness. He was, however, we think, honest in avowing and following the convictions of his understanding, but we fear he can scarcely be said to have been an amiable man, inasmuch as he frequently appears to have courted rather than shunned controversy.

The first account we have of his appearing in this country, places him in East Jersey in 1682. He was then a Quaker and held the office of surveyor general. In 1689 he removed to Philadelphia, on the invitation of some wealthy families, who desired him to become tutor to their children. He discharged the duties of this situation faithfully and skilfully. He also (as old Gerard Croese informs us) "at the same time exercising his preaching faculty among an unlearned and ignorant company of people, as for the most part their preachers were, excelled them all, appearing as a bright luminary, and outshining all the rest of that order among them; and by his opportune diligence and industry in all the parts of his ministerial office, he rendered himself beloved of them all, especially the more inferior sort of people."

Keith became a writer as early as the year 1665. His first productions were all in favor of the Quakers. His zeal led him with a fearless spirit to cast himself into the very midst of those among whom he well knew Quakerism had reaped what it deemed a glorious martyrdom. He here boldly threw down the gauntlet, and challenged to theological combat the chosen champions of Puritanism. He thus commenced his "Solemn call and warning from the Lord to the people of New England to repent."

"The burden of the word of the Lord that came unto me on the twenty-first day of the fourth month, 1688, in the town of Boston, in New England, to declare it unto Boston and its inhabitants, and to the inhabitants of New England," &c. A copy of this he posted in the most conspicuous place in the town, and followed it by a letter addressed to "James Allen, Joshua Moody, Samuel Willard, Cotton Mather, *called* preachers in Boston."

In this he charged them with preaching false doctrine, and challenged them to public disputation. Their answer is characteristic of men who felt their power, and at the same time resented the insult offered to their dignity.

"Having received a blasphemous and heretical paper, subscribed by one George Keith, our answer to it and him is, if he desires conference to instruct *us*, let him give us his arguments in writing, as well as his assertions; if to inform *himself*, let him write his doubts; if to cavil and disturb the peace of our churches (which we have cause to suspect) we have neither list nor leisure to attend his motions; if he would have a public audience, let him print; if a private discourse, though he may know where we dwell, yet we forget not what the apostle John saith, Epis. 2, 10th verse." *

To this Keith was not backward in preparing a reply in the shape of another letter more severe than the first, and as if the present controversy were not enough, he turns to the past and evokes new elements of contention in "a brief answer to some gross abuses, lies, and slanders, published some years ago by Increase Mather, late teacher of a church at Boston, in New England, in his book called, An essay for the recording of illustrious providences, &c., and by Nath. Morton in his book called New England's Memorial."

In 1691 Keith was again in Pennsylvania, and now commenced his dispute with the Quakers, which ended in his separation from them, after having been a preacher among them for twenty-eight years. The Quaker writers charge him with ambition and desire to assume undue authority, under a mistaken impression of his own influence. It is, however, but just to Keith to say, that he denied this, and charged his adversaries with a departure from the

* "If there come any unto you, and bring not this doctrine, receive him not into your house, neither bid him God speed."

original doctrines held by the society. Without entering into the particulars of the controversy, suffice it to say that twenty-eight leading members issued against him what they called " A testimony of disownment," in 1692. Keith repaid this with a similar testimony against the twenty-eight, signed by himself and a "considerable party," including "some wealthy and influential members of the society," who adhered to him. Keith and his friends were called Christian Quakers; he charged his opponents with Deism.

Soon after this, in 1694, he went to England and was there admitted to holy orders in the established church.

In April, 1702, he sailed for America on a mission of observation, and the Journal which follows commences with this voyage. In August, 1704, he reached England and became rector of Edburton, in Sussex, where he ended his days.

The authorities for the above sketeh are General History of the Quakers, by Gerard Croese, Proud's Pennsylvania, Keith's churches in New England brought to the test, Keith's Journal, Allen's Biographical Dictionary, Gordon's Pennsylvania, Review of Bishop Doane's Sermon at the Consecration of St. Mary's Church, Burlington, December 23d, 1834.

As a suitable introduction to the official report by Mr. Keith, contained in his " Journal," the publishing committee have prefixed thereto several documents hitherto unpublished, and consisting principally of letters written by Mr. Keith and his companion, the Rev. Mr. Talbot, furnishing a very full account of the general aspect of the colonies in a religious point of view, and together with the detailed report in the " Journal " itself, affording probably the most complete picture that can now be obtained of the precise condition of the Protestant Episcopal Church in America when the venerable society here commenced its labors.

The following letter it is supposed gave rise to the measures which ended in the appointment of Mr. Keith as the first missionary of the Society to America.

A Letter from Mr. George Keith to the Secretary of the Venerable Society about the State of Quakerism in North America.

" Worthy Sir :—

" According to your desire I send you this short Memorial of the State of Religion in such parts of North America where I have travelled, and which I can give of my own knowledge, especially in relation to Quakerism and some other things by letters from my friends there.

"In Pennsylvania, when I came to live there, which was in the year 1689, by the number of men and women that used to come to the yearly meetings from the several parts of that province, and from the West and East Jerseys, we did commonly reckon there might be at least fifteen hundred Quakers, two hundred of which might perhaps belong to the West and East Jerseys.

"After the breach that began in the year 1691, betwixt a party of Quakers that joined with me in opposing some of their errors (especially their notion of the sufficiency of the light within every man to salvation without anything else) and another Party that joyned with Thomas Lloyd then Deputy Governor of Pennsylvania and a great Preacher among the Quakers, all the Meetings in those Provinces abovementioned were broken, and they set up Separate Meetings one from another, on the account of different Principles of Religion (especially in relation to the notion aforesaid of the Sufficiency of the light within, without any thing else, which I and my Friends judged a plain opposition to Christianity, and an Establishing of Deism in its place) so that when I came from Pennsylvania to England, which was in the year 1694, I left behind me fourteen or fifteen Meetings in Pennsylvania, West and East Jerseys, that met apart from the Quakers (on the account of their opposition to their Errors) to the number of above Five hundred persons.

"Since there hath been a Church of England Congregation set up at Philadelphia, the Chief Town in Pennsylvania, a considerable number of those that did come off with me on the account of the Quakers Errors are joyned with the Church of England, both Men and Women of good account, and others of them keep up their Separate Meetings, particularly one at Philadelphia, and some of them have joyned themselves with the Anabaptists in those Parts, as I have had particular Information by letters from my friends there, year after year.

"It would be of great service, as I judge, if one or two more Church of England Ministers were sent to Pennsylvania; it is not to be doubted, but they would not only get hearers, but such as would join with them to make up Congregations, one whereof might be at New Castle, which is forty miles below Philadelphia, by the River Delaware, the other at the Falls by the same River, about thirty miles above it.

"In West Jersey that lyes on the east side of Delaware River, I have several friends that joyned with me in the Separation from the Quakers, especially about Croswicks, which is about Fifteen or Sixteen miles from Burlington (the chief Town in West Jersey lying by Delaware River); if a Church of England Minister were sent thither it is not to be doubted but he would be received and joyned with, both by some of my friends and some other sober persons. The most proper place to set up a Church would be at Burlington, and another at Croswicks abovementioned.

"In East Jersey I have several friends that came off with me in the Separation from the Quakers, and so continue, and as I have been informed by a worthy gentleman, Colonel Morris, formerly my scholar, who has a family and a good estate in that Province, and is now in London, (being lately come from East Jersey, who knows my friends there) they are well prepared to receive a Church of England Minister among them, and it is not to be doubted but he would have several other persons to joyn with him to set up a Church Congregation; the fittest places to set up a Church Congregation are Amboy and the Falls in Shrewsbury, near where Colonel Morris has his house and estate, for though Amboy has few Inhabitants, yet People would come to it from Woodbridge and other places thereabouts.

"The people of East Jersey who are not Quakers, are generally Independents, having originally come from New England, but the young generation might easily be brought off to the Church, if they have any Church set up among them.

"East Jersey has six or seven considerable Towns in it, as Shrewsbury, Middletown, Woodbridge, Piscataway, Elizabeth and Newark Town; the Inhabitants, generally all English that came originally from New England, about Thirty years ago; and Bergen, inhabited generally with Dutch, all Calvinists who have a Dutch Minister.

"There is not one Church of England as yet in either West or East Jersey, the more is the pity; and except in Two or Three Towns there is no face of any public worship of any sort, but People live very mean like Indians. In New York there are but few Quakers, and some that were, are come off and joyned with the Church there. One Mrs. ——, a friend of mine, is lately deceased, but before her death, was baptized, and had the Lord's Supper administered to her, and got her Children baptized, whereof I had a late Account in a letter from one of my friends there, now a zealous Churchman.

"In Long Island there are not many Quakers; it is a great place and has many Inhabitants, English and Dutch; the Dutch are Calvinists and have some Calvinistical Congregations; the English some of them Independents, but many of them no Religion, but like Wild Indians; there is no Church of England in all Long Island, nor in all that great Continent of New York Province, except at New York Town.

"The places where the Quakers have their greatest Meeting in Long Island are Flushing and Oyster Bay, in both which places I have been several times at their Meetings.

"In Road Island where I have been several times, there are many Quakers and Anabaptists, but never had a Church of England until of late.

"In all the Continent of New England there is no Church of England I think, but at Boston, I have travelled through much of it, but never heard of any but that one. Few Quakers are at Boston. There are some at Sandwich, some at Piscataway and other scattered Places, but very few.

"It seems a good expedient to me that such Ministers as go over into these parts that I have named, should not constantly reside in one place at present, but preach at several places through the whole Province, which they may safely now travel through from one end to another, with little charge or difficulty.

"And that a considerable number of little books, such as the Pastoral Letter, and those against Swearing, Drunkenness, and Sabbath breaking were sent to be spread among them. And if a little book were printed by some able man, to show the sin of Schism, to persuade to the Communion of the Church of England, and sent among them, it would be of good service.

"I remain,

"Worthy Sir,

"Your humble servant,

"GEORGE KEITH."

For the more perfect understanding of the relation of Mr. Keith's missionary labors, we here insert a general view of the state of religion in the colonies about the time of his visit.

An Account of the State of Religion in the English Plantations in North America, by Col. Dudley, Governor of New England.

The Plantations on the Shore of America as they lye from South to North may be thus accounted:

South Carolina contains Seven thousand Souls, will admit and support three Ministers.

North Carolina, Five thousand Souls, alike three Ministers, and both stand in need of Schools.

Virginia, Forty thousand Souls, was by the Lord Culpepper divided into about Forty Parishes with an Established Maintenance by Act of Assembly, but are not fully supply'd, and the Maintenance hurt by disuse, but will be always encouraged by Colonel Nicholson the present Governor.

Maryland, Twenty five thousand Souls in twenty six parishes, I suppose well supply'd by the care of Dr. Bray.

Pensilvania and the Lower Counties annext, Fifteen thousand Souls, will well support Four Ministers; one at Philadelphia, and one in each County, with dependant Schools upon each.

West Jersey, Two thousand Souls most Quakers, may yet have one Minister, at present, supported from England.

East Jersey Six thousand Souls in about Seven Towns and Parishes, may at present support Two Ministers, the rest being Dissenters.

Connecticut, Thirty thousand Souls, about thirty three Towns, all Dissenters, supply'd with Ministers and Schools of their own persuasion.

Naraganset or Kings Province, Three thousand Souls, without any Ministry or public form of Religion, may have two Ministers, and might well Support them.

Road Island and Providence Plantations, Five thousand Souls in Seven Towns, at present under a Quaker Government; but might have Two Ministers and Schoolmasters, at first subsisted from hence, at least one of them.

Massachusetts or New England, Seventy thousand Souls, in Seventy Towns, all Dissenters, that have Ministers and Schools of their own persuasion, except one Congregation of the Church of England at Boston, where there are two Ministers.

New Hampshire, Three thousand Souls in Six Towns, all Dissenters, that have Ministers and Schools of their own persuasion.

Province of Mayn, Two thousand Souls in Six Towns (the rest of that great Province being in ten years past wasted and driven off by the Indians) are all Dissenters, and have Ministers and Schools of their own.

In the three last Colonies and Connecticut, by an early law providing for Ministers and Schoolmasters, I am of opinion there are no Children to be found of ten years old, that do not read well, nor men of Twenty that do not write tolerably.

The Ministers to be sent from England to any of the abovesaid Colonies, must be men of good learning, sound morals, and should not be very young; and where there is not the view of a good support from their hearers, must be supplied from hence that they be not in Contempt, but may be well provided for in those parts where the Governments are immediately dependant upon the Crown and Government of England.

After Mr. Keith came over, and had made a survey of the field before him, he, in conjunction with the few clergymen then in the northern part of the country (with the exception of the two or three in New England), made the following statement, designed for the Venerable Society. It contains no details of Mr. Keith's journeyings or labors, as set forth in his Journal; but is nevertheless valuable as contributing to a picture of the religion of the times, as viewed by the eyes of churchmen.

An Account of the State of the Church in North America, by Mr. George Keith and Others.

A Brief account of the State of the Church in the American parts, hereafter mentioned, and a scheme of such proper and expedient ways and methods as we humbly Conceive by the blessing of God, may be useful to the reducing the main body of the Dissenters of all sorts to ye Church of England, by way of Question and Answer.

In what circumstances the Church of England is, as by Law Established and the Schools?

Pensilvania.—There is no Church or School established by any Law in the Province, nevertheless in Philadelphia (the Chief Town in Pensilvania) there is one Church consisting of a large Congregation, having Mr. Evans for their Minister, and Mr. Thomas his Assistant, with three Congregations in the Country, viz. Chester, Radner (being a Welch Church), and Oxford, which are supplied only in the week days by the said Ministers.

West New Jersey.—There is no Church or School established by Law of the Province.

East New Jersey.—There are eight English Towns, and two Dutch, but neither Church or School established by any Law.

New York.—There are some Counties, five of which are inhabited by Dutch, and those of Dutch extraction, viz. Albany, Ulster, Dutchess, Orange, and King's County, in which the Church and Church of England Schools have not yet been settled, but the Presence of the present Governor of that Province, his Excellency the Lord Cornbury, has mightily influenced many of the people of the said Counties to desire that Church of England Ministers and Schoolmasters may be sent amongst them, particularly Albany representatives have desired his Lordship that an English Schoolmaster might be established in that county, and some of the Inhabitants of Ulster County passionately desire a Church of England Minister; Suffolk County is the only English County without a legal Establishment of a Church of England Minister; for in y[e] County of West Chester, Queen's County, Richmond, and New York County, the Church is Established by Law, this Province, though it hath a great number of Inhabitants, could never yet obtain a publick legally Established School.

New England.—There is no Church, nor Church of England School established by Law in all the Colonies Eastward of the Province of New York, viz. Connecticut, Rhode Island, Massachusetts Bay, Plymouth and New Hampshire, except at Boston, where there is one Church of England, consisting of a large Congregation, having two Ministers, Mr. Myles and Mr. Bridge, and one in Rhode Island consisting of a large Congregation and one Minister, viz. Mr. Lockier Lockyer], and another in Braintry which has no Minister.

How Ministers and Schoolmasters are maintained?

Philadelphia.—The two Ministers are maintained by the Voluntary subscriptions of the Congregation, and the constant munificence of his Excellency Col. Nicholson, Governor of Virginia.

Jerseys.—In the West and East New Jerseys, there is neither Minister nor maintenance.

New York.—A Provision is made by Law for six Ministers, viz: in the City and County of New York £100 per annum of the money of this province, for one Minister; In Queens County on Nassau Island £120 per annum for two Ministers to be equally divided betwixt them; £40 per annum for one Minister in the County of Richmond; in West Chester County a maintenance for two Ministers, viz. £50 for each, besides her Majesty allows £130 per annum for the maintenance of the Chaplain of the Forces. There is yet no provision for Schoolmasters made by Law, though by the zealous Recommendation of the Lord Cornbury to the general Assembly, a legal maintenance is undoubtedly expected, and till then the Church of England Schoolmaster in the County of New York as heretofore, will be supported by the Voluntary Contributions of those whose children are instructed by him; notwithstanding it is humbly conceived that an annual Pension from England for the Support and farther encouragement of some Ministers and Schoolmasters in poor Towns will be of great use and service to the Church.

Boston.—Mr. Myles is maintained by the Contribution of the Church and Mr. Bridge out of her Majesty's Treasury in England.

Rhode Island.—Mr. Lockier, the Minister, is maintained partly by the Contributions of the people, and partly by a Supply from England.

What Number of Churches, Schools and Ministers?

As for Pensilvania, Jerseys and New England this is answered already ut supra.

New York.—There are in this Province one Chapel and four Churches, viz. one Chapel in Fort William Henry, two Churches in Queens County, one in the County of West Chester, and one large Church in the City of New York, founded Anno Domini, 1695, and erected by the charitable Contributions of many well disposed persons, especially the generous donations of his Excellency Col. Nicholson, Governor of Virginia, and Col. Fletcher, late Governor of New York.

The Reverend Mr. Edmund Moll, is Chaplain to the Fort and Forces; Mr. Bartow, Rector of West Chester County; Mr. Vesey, Rector of New York; the Reverend Mr. Gordon, late Rector of Queens County, who to the grief of all good men is removed by Death.

No School house yet erected in this Province.

How the People are inclined to promote them?

Philadelphia.—The English Congregation is very forward to encourage and promote the Interest of the Church of England; as for the congregations of the County, being lately reduced from Quakerism, they are very averse from a Maintenance and therefore the Ministers of Philadelphia freely serve the Cures.

East and West Jersey.—There is a considerable number of People that were formerly Quakers, and other Dissenters in a good disposition to embrace Communion with the Church, but not so forward to contribute to the Maintenance of those who discharge these offices, wherewith God is served by his Church.

New York.—In all these Counties where the Church is established by the law of this Province, the People generally are in a readiness to embrace the Doctrines and Worship of the Church, and to Encourage Free Schools.

New England.—In Swansey, Naraganset, Seconet, Braintry, Salem, Ipswich, and Piscataway, there are several hundreds of People in those and other places of New England, desirous of Church of England Ministers among them, a considerable Number of which in Swansey and Seconet have already petitioned the Lord Bishop of London for two Ministers.

What Number of them are of the Church of England and in what Places?

In Philadelphia and the adjacent places by a modest Computation, there seems to be 7 or 800, the number being considerably increased since the arrival of the two present Ministers.

East and West Jerseys, ut supra in the 4th Question.

New York.—That large Church is now thronged, and the Congregation daily increasing, by an addition of Dutch and French, as well as English People, also in other Counties of this Province, the number of those who are earnestly desirous of a Church Minister is very considerable, though at present the exact number cannot be known.

New England, ut supra in the 1st Question.

What hopes there are to bring more over, and by what ways and means?

In Pensilvania, the West and East Jerseys, and the several Colonies of

New England, there are great hopes, were there a considerable number of pious, learned clerks, well versed in the controversies between the Church and the Brethren of the Separation, speedily sent over and supported by England and by maintenance, and as for the ways and means, we humbly conceive, that if the Queen, the Lord Chancellor, the Arch Bishops, Bishops, Collegiate Churches, and Universities, would be pleased to present as many pious and learned Ministers, as are needful, to livings, as they fall, of £200 per annum, at least, upon condition that they come to the aforesaid places, to preach the Gospel for such time as their Graces and Lordships shall soe arrange.

That if a competent portion of the Tyth may be reserved for the supply of the Cures, and the residue sent Yearly to supply the Missionaries; with submission, we believe that this would effectually contribute to the Proselyting, the main body of the Dissenting People, to their Ancient Mother, the Church; or if this Method be not so agreeable to the persons above mentioned, it is humbly suggested that until the fund to be raised by that Noble and Illustrious Society, for the Propagating of Christian Faith, in these Parts, be able to answer the charge of their great and pious undertaking, that their Lordships would be pleased to contrive how the profits of such Sine Cures, as are in the Queen's and their Lordship's gifts may be sequestred as they fall, for the supply of the Missionaries; and it is humbly prayed that a remarkable encouragement may be given to such as will undertake the study of the Indian languages in order to their Conversion; and that above all, a Suffragan Bishop may be sent over for the Confirming the Baptized, and giving orders to such as are willing and well qualified to receive them, there being a considerable number of actual preachers and others of New England education well disposed to serve in the Ministry.

New York.—If proper methods be speedily taken, we have reasonable hopes that the English Counties of that Province will be easily reconciled to the Church, as to ways and means, by sending a pious and learned Clergy among them as aforesaid: again that in the small Towns the Ministers have directions and Encouragement given them to officiate as Ministers and Schoolmasters, than which a more effectual way cannot be taken to establish the Church on the Sure and lasting foundations of Truth and Peace.

And as to the Dutch Counties and Towns in the Province it would be of admirable Service to send such Dutch Ministers to their Vacant Counties and Towns, especially forthwith one to Kings County, now destitute, ordained by the Bishop of London, with whom they would as readily comply as if they were Ministers of their own persuasion.

What opposition and Discouragement the Church of England meets with, from the Government, Society of people or private persons?

Pensilvania.—The chief opposition and discouragment the Church of England meets with, ariseth from persons disaffected being put into places and offices of trust in council, in Commission of the peace and Courts of Jurisdiction.

One other great discouragement which the Church labours under, is from the pretended Ministry of Quakers, who have threatened our Reverend and worthy Brother, Mr. Keith, at their Meeting places, which he has visited in

New England, Rhode Island, Long Island, and the two Jerseys, with the penalty of £20 for speaking in their Meetings, though without Interruption to their Speakers; and notwithstanding they have not qualified themselves according to the Act of Toleration. There is a great opposition also from all other Dissenters, as Presbyterians, Independants and Anabaptists, who daily increase in other Provinces, as well as Pensilvania, for want of an established Ministry of the Church in those Parts.

New York.—The Church of England under the late Administration of the Lord Bellamont and Captain Nanfan hath been grievously opposed and oppressed; but since the auspicious arrival of the Right Honorable the Lord Cornbury, has been delivered from the violence of the enemies, restored to her rights, greatly countenanced and encouraged, and lives under the just expectation of being more firmly established and enlarged. But many of the Dutch Dissenters and all the Quakers, though differing from one another amongst themselves, yet agree in opposing with great zeal and malice, whatever tends to the honour and interest of the Church.

New England.—Whilst the Council as well as the Assembly is in the choice of the people, and whilst the Assembly assumes a power to oblige the Members of the Church of England that maintain their own Minister, to contribute by a tax, in proportion much beyond others of the like Estate, to Support the Dissenting Ministry, there are but slender hopes to see the Church increase and flourish in that Colony.

How Quakers and others support their Meetings and Schools.

1. The Quakers support their Meetings and Schools by several ways and means, as first by their Established Weekly, Monthly, Quarterly, and yearly Meetings.

2. By the great and large collections of Money gathered, especially at their Monthly and Quarterly Meetings, which they put into a Common stock.

3. By their proselyting many poor People to their way, by their Charity.

4. By keeping their Trade within themselves and maintaining a strict Correspondence and Intelligence over all parts where they are.

5. By the many and sometimes great Legacies which the Quakers at their Death give to the Common Stock, they appointing persons to visit the sick, upon that Account, so that in Philadelphia they have £1000 given by Legacies in about two years last past, as appears by the Records of their Wills in Philadelphia.

6. By sending over great numbers of Missionaries yearly from England into these Parts and furnishing them well out of their National Stock, especially since Mr. Keith left them.

7. By their having George Foxe's Orders and Canons duly and orderly read in their Monthly and especially in their Quarterly Men and Women's Meetings; though they never read one chapter of the Holy Bible in the said meetings.

8. By spreading Books, printed both in England and here and dispersing them at cheap rates, which leavens their youth with prejudices against the Church and her Ministers.

9. By frequent Meetings of their Speakers to consider of ways and means to propagate their errors.

10. By their great hospitality to all friends, and others that come to their public Meetings, especially their Quarterly and Yearly Meetings.

11. By suffering none of themselves to marry but with those of their own profession.

12. By refusing to swear and fight, by which means many come over to them, to excuse themselves from being jurymen and serving in the Militia.

13. By building diverse large and fair Structures, for their Meeting houses, especially in Philadelphia, Burlington, and Rhode Island.

14. By keeping and publickly recording all Misfortunes and Accidents of Sudden Deaths that happen to their Adversaries which they call Judgments of God upon their Opposers, whether Priests, Impropriators, Magistrates, or others.

15. By keeping a true and exact Register of all their Births, Burials, and Marriages, and all Passages, Travels, and Sufferings of their travelling friends, especially by keeping a distinct and particular record of the Sufferings and Death of the friends of the Ministry with the Circumstances of the time and place of their decease.

16. By collecting into volumes the particular Treatises of the preaching Quakers of Account after their Deaths, after they have expunged some of their lying Prophecy's, and other Ridiculous and Scandalous Passages.

17. By their seeking out in what places in England and elsewhere what they can object of Scandals against either Ministers or People, professing Communion with the Church, reproaching the whole Church with them.

18. By their grossly misrepresenting the Doctrine of the Church of England and of all other Protestant Churches in all points of difference between them.

19. By their high pretences to the extraordinary gifts of the Spirit, the same in kind with those which the Apostles and Prophets had.

20. By their singularities in Common Speech, and refusing to give any marks of honour, or due respects to Magistrates and Superiors.

21. By setting up Meetings in all places where they can find access, though they have no resident Ministers to preach or pray in these said Meetings; hundreds of which sort are in England, and many in these American Parts.

22. By the People's great liberality to all their Itinerant Preachers, and putting their Ministers generally into a way of Trade, especially Merchandizing, and putting many poor Mechanics, Servants, and Women, that have no good way of living, pretending to the Ministry among them, into such ways of trade and business, whereby to live plentifully, by which means, many who had nothing are become rich.

23. By their great partiality in concealing the gross faults of their Ministers and People favouring them of their party, either in Arbitrations or Courts of Judicature, where they have the Government in their hands, or any share therein.

24. By their using all possible Endeavours to discourage, reproach, and scandalize all such Persons as leave their Communion for their errors and other unjust practices, and to ruin them if possible, and then to tell their hearers that the Judgment of God fell upon such who forsake the truth as they term it, by which they fright the people.

What ways and means are proper to put a stop to them?

By using some of the like ways and means above mentioned, such as are lawfull, proper and convenient; many of the above mentioned being very unlawfull which are used by them. By sending over such Books as are most proper and useful, not only for the detecting the Quakers errors, but also for informing the People in the Doctrine, way and Worship of the Church, especially all the Works of the Author of the "Snake in the Grass," particularly his five discourses printed together by Charles Brown, "the Invention of Man in the Worship of God," by Dr. King, Bishop of Londonderry, all the small treatises lately published against profane swearing and breach of the Sabbath. The abstract of the "London Cases," Dr. Beveridge's Sermon concerning the excellency and usefulness of the Common Prayer, "The unworthy communicant," "Comber upon the Common Prayer," "The Whole duty of Man," Mr. Brent, of Bristol, against lying, Common Prayer Books and books of homilies, and the articles of the Church of England, and Catechisms, the Exposition of the Church Catechism, by the Bishop of Bath and Wells. Lastly, Large and Common Prayer Books, for Churches; that the Executive part of the Government be put into the hands of persons well affected to the Church of England.

That Ministers of the Church of England in these American parts, as well as England, acquaint themselves well with the Quakers erroneous Doctrine and Principles, and that it be earnestly recommended to all such, where Quakers abound most, to preach against their sad Doctrines and principles, which are most erroneous, at least once every three months in their Parish Churches.

New York. Signed by us,

George Keith.

Evan Evans, Cler. Minister of Philadelphia.

Alexander Innes, Presbyter.

Edmond Mott, Chaplain of Her Majesty's Forces in New York.

John Talbot.

William Vesey, Rector of New York.

John Bartow.

Mr. Keith to Dr. Bray.

Philadelphia, 24th Feb. 1703–4.

"Dr. Bray—

"Reverend and Worthy Sir:

"My very humble and kind respects remembered to you, and all our friends with you; having this occasion I was glad to accept of it (as of all occasions that occur) to write unto you. I writ unto you from New York, in November last, together with our scheme of the State of the Church in these Northern parts of America, and therewith I sent a long letter to the Honourable Corporation for Propagating the Gospell in Foreign Parts, and a letter to my Lord of London, all which I enclosed in my letter to you, which I hope you have received. I have had no letter from you as yet, nor from any of your honourable Corporation, but one from my worthy friend, Mr. Chamberlayne,* wherein he signified to me that your Corporation had not met, betwixt his receiving my Letters and the time of his writing to me, so that he could not say any thing, what the Corporation would do, concerning allowing Mr. Talbot his charge in travelling with me, but he thought that they would be well satisfied that he was my companion, and would allow him what they thought was convenient. I have heard Mr. Talbot say that if they allow him £50 English money per annum, it will do, and indeed that is little enough, and would not near do, but that we are often upon free quarters, more especially among our friends. Mr. Talbot, I hear, has a good character given of him, to my Lord of Canterbury, and indeed he deserves it, he has been mightily serviceable and comfortable to me in all respects, as a Son to his Father, and is well beloved by all where we have travelled, who are well affected to the Church; and has been much desired by the People in several Places, to be their Minister (after he has finished his travels with me, which are like to be done, somewhat above a year hereafter) particularly at Chester, about 16 miles Southward from Philadelphia, by the river Delaware, where he has once preached, and hath brought over the same time there also, in the said Town of Chester, Mr. Yeates who lives there, and who has been the principal person, to cause build a Church, very decent and convenient of Brick, that will hold a thousand people, it is well glazed, but not as yet wainscotted nor plaistered, but it is fit for use, and we have preached in it twice: the 14th of this instant I preached in it, and there were above two hundred hearers, all generally well affected to the Church; but they greatly desire a Minister, and if the Corporation please to give an yearly supply of £50 per annum, the people there, and thereabouts, would contribute to make up the rest. This, Mr. Yeates desired me to write to you to lay before my Lord of London and the Honourable Corporation.

"Betwixt New York and Pensylvania we continued about a month, viz. from 14th of December to 11th of January travelling among the Friends, call'd formerly the Keithian Quakers especially for East Jersey, having been about a whole month travelling among them before that, which was in the month October; and by God's blessing our labour has had good success among them, so that generally very few excepted, all the Keithians in East Jersey are well affected to the Church, and we baptized twenty two persons

* He was Secretary of the Society.

in East Jersey, all either Keithians or Keithian children. I am forced to use this name of distinction to distinguish them from the other Quakers who are generally very stiff and averse from the Church, and all principles of true Christianity everywhere, and who decline all discourse or converse with us. Colonel Morris did very kindly entertain us at his house in East Jersey, and both he and his Lady went with us from meeting to meeting in divers places. At Amboy in East Jersey they have contributed about £200 towards building a Church and greatly desire a Minister. The Contributors are some Keithians and some other persons well affected to the Church. At Burlington also several persons (among whom some are Keithians) well affected to the Church have contributed about two hundred pounds towards building of a Church and they are to begin the Building this Spring. In all these new erectings of Churches in these Northern parts, Governor Nicholson has largely contributed, and is a mighty promoter and encourager of them by his Letters and Advice as well as his purse; as not only at Boston and Rhode Island, but at Burlington, in West Jersey, Chester, in Pensylvania, and here at Philadelphia. In all places where I have yet travelled, at Boston, Rhode Island, N. York and Philadelphia, the Ministers live very regularly and are in good esteem, and the Churches in good order, and the people generally devout, and well affected to the Word and the publick worship of God; at Concord, in Pensilvania, and thereabouts, especially at Thomas Powell's, formerly a Keithian, several people formerly Keithians, are well affected to the Church and entertained us kindly. Mr. Evans, Minister of Philadelphia, was with me and I preached at two severall places among them and they were well affected; also I had a publick dispute with one Killingsworth, an Anabaptist preacher at the house of Thomas Powell. This Killingsworth was sent for by some Anabaptists forty miles off to dispute with me. The dispute continued four hours, it has had good effect and it's hoped will have more; they belong to the new Church at Chester above mentioned. I have preached here at Philadelphia nine several times, and had great auditories, in some of them a thousand people were thought to be present, many besides the Church People, Quakers, Presbyterians and Anabaptists. But of late the Quakers have made an act in their meeting that none of them may come to Church, which has of late deterred them from coming. The ministers here are in very good esteem among the People and they have a brave vestry of good and wise men, and good concord, love and unanimity among them, so that the Church here is in a Flourishing Condition. And at Newcastle, 40 miles from Philadelphia, there is at present no minister, they had a Presbyterian minister called Willson, but he has been gone about half a year. Could a Minister of the Church of England be sent among them, it's thought they would gladly receive him, and it would be of mighty service for advancing the Church in this province, it being, as it were, the Frontier. Also in other parts below New Castle, they want a Minister.

"There is a mighty cry and desire, almost in all places where we have travelled, to have Ministers of the Church of England sent to them in these Northern parts of America; so that it may be said the Harvest is great but the labourers few, and some well affected to the Church have desired me to write to my Lord of London and to you that if a Minister be not sent with the first Conveniency, Presbyterian Ministers from N. England would swarm into those countries and prevent the increase of the Church. They have here a Presbyterian meeting and minister, one called Andrews; but they are not like to increase here. I have had severall meetings with the Keithian Quakers here at my lodgings, and friendly conferences with them and their Preachers, and last Sunday I preached at a Keithian meeting house, and was kindly invited to dinner after the meeting by a man and his wife of that meeting, and that evening I preached at the Church. Divers of them (God be praised for the success) are like to be gained to the Church who have heard us frequently at the Church and are well affected. Their chief speaker, John Hart, has vented a most absurd notion in his Discourses and vindicates it in his preaching, (viz.) That true Believers ought not to fear Hell and Damnation, so much as conditionally, and they ought to serve God only from love to him, without all regard to punishment or Scripture threatenings, so much as conditionally. I have in two severall meetings at my Lodgings, in the hearing of his followers, detected his errors, and last Sunday I preached a long sermon against it, in the Keithian Meeting, upon that Text, 1 Pet. 1–17, where I opened many other Texts of Scripture, to prove that a Conditioned fear is necessary to the best of Men: such as Heb. 4: 1; Rom. 14: 10, &c. Most of his hearers and followers are dissatisfied with the strange doctrine, and are like to forsake him. I have told them 'tis vile Antinomianism and the Root of Ranterism and Libertinism; and some of his female hearers are offended at him for his telling them, they need not fear to commit the sin of whoredom, being chaste women. He openly denied before many judicious persons to me at my lodgings last Monday, 22nd of this Instant, that publick punishment of death was inflicted upon a murtherer for a terror to others, if innocent, which I told him was contrary to Deut. 13: 10, 11.

"The six boxes you sent are all come safe; that to Boston, that to New York, that to the two Jerseys, and that to Pensylvania, are disposed of already according to your orders, and are very acceptable to the people. The great Bibles in folio I have given one of them to the Church in Philadelphia, at the Minister's request, another to the new Church at Chester above mentioned, another I think to give to the Church at Burlington, and another to that of Amboy, and the rest to other Churches when erected. There is a great need of Common Prayer Books in 8vo for the use of the people, many would gladly buy them and some might be given to the Poorer Sort. I wish 2 or 300 were sent over to these parts, direct them to Mr. Evans, the minister, if you send them; also the new Psalms, being only used here in this Church, the people want them greatly; if you would send over 100 of them at least, I believe the people would gladly buy them. They sing very well in the Church here, and the youth have learned to sing and delight much in it. I have disposed of many of your lectures in folio which are very acceptable to the people, and as you ordered, have desired them to read them to their families and neighbours on Sundays.

"Dear Sir! I long to have a letter from you to know of your welfare, and other good news you have to impart to me, and what hopes you can give us, of having good ministers sent over to these parts, which are so greatly wanted and desired; and if they come not timely, the whole country will be overrun with Presbyterians, Anabaptists, and Quakerism; the Quaker Missionaries do mightily swarm out of old England into these parts, and have proselited many; many in Long Island are Quakers or Quakerly affected.

"You see, Dear Sir, what a long letter I have writ to you, I question not your acceptance of it. It's but a summary of affairs here, but I keep a punctual Journal of all things worthy my notice in my Travells.

"I have written the more at length to you, hoping, Dear Sir, and desiring that you would be pleased to impart either the whole or what part of it you think requisite to my Lord of London, and my Lord of Worcester, and to your Honourable Corporation. We intend about two weeks hence to set forward to Maryland and Virginia. I have had a very kind letter from his Excellency, Governor Nicholson, inviting us to Virginia, but before we go hence, I purpose to have a Publick meeting in this place to detect the Quakers errors out of their own Books, after the method I used at Turner's Hall, in London. All course of Justice against Criminals is at a stop here, so that the Criminal Court can do nothing against murtherers; the Quakers throw the whole Burden of Jurymen upon the Churchmen, so that a great List of Churchmen have been summoned; such as have appeared (some formerly Keithians) men of good sense and repute have refused to swear, not that they think it unlawfull, but that there is no law in the Province, that enjoins swearing in any case, and severall persons have lain long here in Prison, some on suspected murther, and can have no trial, and are said to be in great want of Bread. Colonel Quarry I suppose will give my Lord of London or yourself, some more full information. This is one instance of many of the great Deficiency of Quaker Government. I send you herewith a small specimen of my printed Labors here away. My sermon I preached at Boston soon after my arrival, was sent to you soon after it was printed, but it hath not come to your Hands. I send you this one; the single sheet called a Refutation, &c., I lately printed at New York. Mr. Increase Mather has printed against the six rules in my Sermon, and I have my answer in the press at New York, in vindication of them; when it is done, I shall order some copies to be sent to you, all which I hope will be acceptable to you and the clergy.

"I remain your affectionate,
"Humble servant,
"George Keith."

Mr. Keith to the Secretary.—Extract.

"Philadelphia, 3d April, 1703.

"Worthy Sir:

"The main thing of importance I have at present to write to you here, is to tell you of the extreme desire that people have in severall parts where we have travelled to have Church of England Ministers sent to them particularly in East Jersey, at Amboy and in the Woods about where Colonel Morris lives, att Burlington, in West Jersey, also at Oyster Bay, in Long Island, and at Hampsted and in this province of Pensylvania, at Chester and at Frankford. At Chester, 20 miles from this, down the River, some well-affected have built a brave Church of Brick. Mr. Yates, who lives there, has been the principal promoter of it. Several hundreds come to Church there, when they hear of a Sermon to be preached, that is commonly supplied by the ministers there, once in two weeks, and the like at Franckford 7 or 8 miles from this upward the river.

"The 2 Ministers here (viz.) Mr. Evans and Mr. Thomas, have a very good character here, and to my knowledge are very laborious in the service of God and Exemplary in Life, the people of the Church generally zealous and well-affected, the most of them my former acquaintance and many of them my old friends, called Keithians, some are lately come to Church since my arrival here. This day I got from this place towards Virginia, having been in this province about ten weeks, and had much exercise with diverse opposite spirits; but all the Church people very loving to us and respectfull. If God please to bring us safe to Maryland and Virginia, you shall hear from us with the first opportunity. Thus, Dear Sir, I conclude, with my Hearty thanks to you for all your civilities and my sincere prayers to God for a blessing to you and yours, desiring your prayers for me.

"And remain your affectionate friend and servant,

"George Keith.

"P. S. I suppose long before this you have heard of the Decease of Worthy Mr. Gordon, who dyed at Jamaica, on Long Island, about six weeks after his arrival with us at Boston; his sickness was a violent fever that was then frequent at N. York, where it's thought he first had it.

"I hope his disease will be no discouragement to other Good men to come into these parts where the Harvest is so great and the Labourers so few.

"I thank God I have had generally good health of Body and great inward comfort, joy and peace of mind ever since my arrival, though I am weak in Body. My Companion also has had his health generally. In several Places in N. England, where we travelled, as I have formerly writ to the Honourable Society, there is a great desire for ministers of the Church of England to be sent to them, as at Narraganset, Swansey, Little Compton, alias Seconat. In all which places I have preached and was kindly received."

Mr. Keith to the Lord Bishop of London.

"Philadelphia, 26th February, 1702–3.

"My Lord:

"I think it not proper to write to your Lordship a long letter, to give your Lordship an account of the many circumstances relating to my travels and services, and success of them since I arrived into these northern parts of America, but rather in general to acquaint your Lordship with the state of the several particular Churches under your inspection and care, in these Countries where I have travelled; as at Boston in N. England, at Rhode Island, at New York, and here at Philadelphia; in all which places to my great satisfaction and joy, I did find great regularity and good order. The Ministers in very good repute among all, and the people devout in the publick Worship of God, and generally of good morals, so that if in all other Places the ministry and people were so pious, so moral, and so regular as I have found them, in those places where I have travelled, the Church of England would be in great esteem and greatly prosper. Here at Philadelphia, from a small beginning the Church is increased considerably, first by the pious endeavours and great diligence of Mr. Clayton, and since his decease by others, and especially by the pious endeavours and great diligence of both Mr. Evans, the Minister here, and of his Assistant, Mr. Thomas, of both whom, the adversaries of the Church give a good report, touching their sobriety and good conversation. The Congregation here has been considerably enlarged in number by those called Keithian Quakers, coming into the Church, whose good examples many others have followed both in town and country, and since my arrival in this Country there has been some increase in Divers places both of those formerly called Keithians and others who are well affected to the Church. In E. Jersey the Keithians are generally zealous for the Church and divers others whom they have an influence upon. Mr. Talbot, my Companion, and I have laboured among them, in preaching from place to place, and had much conference with them in private from House to House, for the space of two months, and we baptized two and twenty persons, young and old of those called Keithians. In W. Jersey also those formerly called Keithians are well affected and came from divers parts to visit me, and heard me, and showed me Love and Affection. I have been here not much above a month, and have preached nine times in the Church here, having had large auditories, sometimes about a thousand persons in the Church, but not all of the Church, many of them Presbyterians, some Anabaptists, and some Quakers, but the Quakers of late have made an Act that none of their way shall come, which has at present put a stop to their coming. I have also had much private discourse with some who yet remain Keithians, and use to meet together; of divers of them, I have good hope, they have frequently come to Church to hear me, and last Sunday I went and preached in their meeting, with which some of them were well pleased though others not.

"My Lord, there is an exceeding great desire in divers places that your Lordship would send over pious and able Ministers to them, both in Long Island, E. Jersey and W. Jersey, and also in divers places in this province of Pensylvania (as also in N. England, as I acquainted your Lordship in my former letter, November last.) The people well affected to the Church have gathered two hundred pounds towards building a Church at Burlington, in W. Jersey, they are to begin to build as they have told me this Spring; also at Amboy, in E. Jersey, they intend to do the like. Colonel Morris is a very good friend to the Church and a promoter of it, and was very kind and assistant to us, and is very regular in his family, and his Lady is a very pious and good Woman, his family is a little Church; he useth the Common Prayer in his family daily, and on Sundays his neighbours come to his house, as to a Church, and at times Mr. Junesse preacheth in his house. I suppose your Lordship remembereth Mr. Junesse, a good man, but a nonjuror.

"My Lord, if but 3 or 4 pious and able ministers were sent over to supply the present necessity in these provinces of E. and W. Jersey and Pensylvania, it would be of exceeding great service to promote and increase the Church. At Chester, in Pensylvania, 16 miles Southward from Philadelphia, by the River Delaware, some well affected persons have built a brave Church. Mr. Yates, who lives at Chester, has been the main promoter of it; they are to write to your Lordship earnestly to request your Lordship to send them an able and pious Minister. The Quakers are very many and rich, in and about that place, but some of good note of them called Keithians are well affected to the Church in that County who would certainly join with the Church, if they had a Minister. I have lately preached at Chester and had an auditory of above 200 persons, and also at the Houses of 2 Keithians, my former friends and acquaintances, who received me with much affection. I am forced to use this term of distinction to distinguish them called Keithians from the other sort of Quakers who generally are most refractory and pertinacious in their Errors, but yet there is hope of many of the Youth among them.

"There is here at Philadelphia a brave vestry of men, both pious and very discreet and in good unity and harmony one with another, and kind to their Ministers, and they have been very civil and Respectfull to us. We have lodged all the time of our stay here at Philadelphia, with an ancient Gentlewoman, a widow called Mistress Welch, formerly a Keithian but now a zealous Churchwoman and so is her daughter.

"My Lord, having thus far given you an account in general of things hereaway, I shall not enlarge upon this subject; what further shall occur in my Travels, I think to acquaint your Lordship from time to time. His Excellency Governor Nicholson is a very great patron and benefactor to all the New-Erected Churches in these Northern parts of America.

"I remain your Lordship's most humble
"And most obliged servant,
"George Keith."

Mr. Keith to the Secretary.

"Philadelphia, 4th September, 1703.

"Worthy Sir:

"These are to acquaint you that by God's help and favour I and my worthy associate Mr. Talbot, have finished our Travels in Maryland, Virginia and North Carolina, and are safely returned to this place. In all Countryes and places we met with very kind reception from persons of all conditions, high and low, having preached in all the several parts where we travelled both on Sundays and on Weekdays in their respective Churches, the Quakers only excepted, who not only in these parts of Maryland and Virginia, but in all other parts where we went to visit their meetings and have Friendly Discourse with them either at their meetings or at their houses, were generally very uncivil and rude to us, as in New England, at Piscataway, Rhode Island, and Long Island, E. and W. Jersey, declining generally all discourse with us, and returning nothing to our kindly offers to inform them, but reproaches and railings and gross reflections (not only upon us, but upon the Church of England and her clergy) used by some of them, whereof we have sufficient proof. In Virginia there are but few Quakers and very much asunder, and the time of their yearly meeting happened when we were on our travels returning from North Carolina, so that we had not timely notice to be there. The Quakers' yearly meeting in Maryland was over before we came into that Country. The Governors of the several Countries and Provinces, where we have travelled, and other inferior Magistrates and Justices of Peace, were very kind to us, and so were all the Ministers where we travelled; and kindly invited us to preach in their Churches, whenever we came, as accordingly we did. Virginia and Maryland are generally well provided with Ministers, and they are generally of good repute, but in some Places ministers are wholly wanting, as in Princess Ann's County, in Virginia, and at Anapolis, in Maryland; and in all North-Carolina there is not one minister since Mr. Brett is gone, of whom I need not to say anything, for I suppose you have heard fully of his bad character. In Maryland, Squire Finch, President of the Counsell there, and Sir Thomas Lawrence, Secretary, with divers Justices of Peace, and many other persons of good quality, showed so much kindness as to go with us to one of the Quakers' meetings, at a place called Herring-Creek, to countenance us; and not only so, but they invited us to go. But when we came, soon after I began to speak, the Quakers being there all silent; When I began, they did most universally and rudely interrupt me and would not suffer me to speak, notwithstanding that both the President, Squire Finch, and Sir Thomas Lawrence, the Secretary, did entreat them to give me a hearing and to have some friendly discourse with me, especially to vindicate the Church of England from the base reflections that one Thomas Story, a preaching Quaker from Philadelphia, had cast upon her and her Catechism in their last yearly meeting in Maryland, but by no means would the Quakers suffer me to speak nor regard the entreaty of those worthy Persons. They did mightily plead that their meetings were tolerated by the Act of Toleration, and that for my offering to speak in their meetings I had broke the Act of Parliament, and was lyable to the fine of Twenty pounds every time I offered to speak in their meetings. I told them I had not broke the Act of Parliament for I was qualified according to the Act to speak in their meetings, but they were not, and upon enquiry they will not be found comprehended in that Act, untill they fulfill the Conditions required of them therein, none of which they had done, so we were constrained to leave their meeting, not having any liberty to speak, nor would they give any except by violence; the magistrates then present had commanded some constables to turn them out of doors by violence who did interrupt me; but these worthy persons thought not fit so to do, knowing that they would call it persecution. Immediately after we came out of the Quakers' meeting, the President Squire Finch and Sir Thomas and the other Justices, and the whole Company above mentioned to the number of about sixty invited me to preach in a place near at hand, formerly a church but then used for a school, which I did. Mr. Hall minister of the parish there having read the prayers. And though we have had little success any where upon those called Foxonian Quakers, yet in all places where we travelled, I hope in God we have furnished the people with good and effectual antidotes to preserve them from the Infection of Quakerism by detecting their errors, both by preaching and spreading books among their vile errors. And by the blessing of God have been instrumentall to keep some from Quakerism who were in danger to be infected with it. But notwithstanding the averseness of those called Foxonian Quakers, everywhere generally (some few excepted) these formerly called Keithian Quakers both in E. and W. Jersey and Pensylvania and at New York did kindly receive us and most are come over to the Church with good zeal, so that in E. & W. Jersey and some other places above a hundred have been baptized by Mr. Talbot and me and Mr. Evans very lately; most of them Keithians formerly so called, and their children: and they greatly desire that good and able ministers may be sent among them, particularly at Burlington in W. Jersey, at Shrewsbury in E. Jersey, where Coll. Morris lives, and who has been very Instrumental to them, & very kind to us and hospitable; also at Chester in Pensylvania they greatly desire a minister, and at New Castle by the River Delaware. In Burlington, the people assisted by the county and some others, especially by the beneficence of Governour Nicholson, have built a church of Brick where I preached two weeks ago before Lord Cornbury, who was come thither to publish his Commission to be Governour of these two provinces of E. & W. Jersey now put into one. The Church was very full of People, and the next Sunday after that, I preached there again and had a considerable auditory. As also by the like beneficence of Governour Nicholson and other assistants, they have built a Church of Brick at Chester in Pensylvania, where both Mr. Talbot and I have preached several times; and so hath Mr. Evans and had large auditories, and the people zealously affected, and among them divers formerly called Keithians. The like beneficence that worthy Patriot Governour Nicholson hath given to the people at New Castle to build a church there, and to them at Amboy in E. Jersey, the like; and to many other Places (besides what he hath done very considerable) in Virginia & Maryland to the number at least of fourteen Churches, lately erected and designed to be erected, all by the Example and Encouragement he hath given them; to most of them Twenty-five pounds a piece, and to some more according as there was occasion: which hath raised a great esteem of him universally in these Northern parts of America, and earnest wishes that he may long continue in the station and dignity where he now stands, that he may be a further Instrument of good both to Church & State, as he hath already been. Besides my exercises in travelling and preaching in these American parts, I have had occasion of Writing and Printing several books for the service of God and his Church, and in vindication of the Truth against Quakers and some other Dissenters, particularly my first sermon at Boston in N. England, there printed, which I hope you have seen, and my vindication of it in answer to Mr. Increase Mather's exceptions, a copy of which I now send you: also a printed sheet against an absurd opinion of Mr. Samuel Willard, president of the College of Cambridge in N. England, which is that the sin of Adam and of all other men and Devils came to pass of necessity, by God's Decree, and his Determining their wills necessarily to Commit them. The which absurd opinion he hath endeavoured to defend in a late printed book of above four sheets, and which the Presbyterians cry up and esteem, but the Quakers dislike; I would to God that so they did their own errors. To which Book of the said Mr. Samuel Willard, I have now my answer ready to be printed. Also I have printed a book in answer to a most abusive book of one Caleb Qusey, a Quaker, against me, a copy of which I herewith send you: And there is now in the Press at New York a Book of mine against the vile Blasphemies contained in a printed Book of one William Davis, with whom I had some dispute here at Philadelphia some months agoe. I had your kind letter wherein you give me notice—that the Honorable Corporation hath allowed Mr. John Talbot to be my associate in my travels, and that they give £60 per annum to bear his charge, for which I humbly thank them: he hath been very comfortable to me and serviceable throughout, and is universally so well beloved that in every place where they want a Minister they have desired to have him, and especially at Burlington and in E. Jersey. He designs to stay in these American parts, and in my opinion I think the Corporation will hardly find any one fitter to send to be their missionary (and to give him the best post either on Long Island or E. or W. Jersey) than he is, being so well known & beloved both for his preaching and good Conversation, and civil and obliging behaviour. But I leave it wholly to the discretion of the Honorable Corporation where to fix him after his time is expired with me, which will be about eight months hence, when my two years which I design to travel in these American parts will be out; and, God willing, I design to come to England in the Fleet that is to sail from Virginia to London next Spring or Summer, if God please to spare my life and give me health and Preservation. In the meantime we think to be travelling through the several parts of these provinces of W. and E. Jersey and Long Island, and this of Pensylvania, where we have had much success and are likely still to have more, untill the next Spring that I prepare for my coming home to England. The late troubles by the Indians and French in New England who have killed several English People and carried away about one hundred Persons not far from Boston as we are informed by letters from Boston, do block up the way to N. England and do awaken many here away. My Lord Cornbury no doubt will endeavour to put the two Jerseys in a posture of defence as well as New York Province; but the Province of Pensylvania, for want of a Governor, and the great many Quakers who pretend they can't fight so much as in self-defence; lyes very naked and open at present both to French and Indians; however the three Quakers in E. Jersey, nominated to be of the Counsel there have taken the Attestation, and solemnly promised upon the Faith of a Christian (which I think they have not) to defend the Queen's majesty and her Government; this some other Quakers do dislike and construe to be a departing from their ancient Principle against fighting.

"Worthy Sir, I am afraid I have troubled you with too long a letter, at least it is too long to the Corporation, therefore please to give the heads of it to them or the worthy Committee appointed by them. As you advised me I keep a Journal of all observable occurrences which I hope to produce at my return. I remain,

"Your obliged and affectionate friend,

"George Keith."

[The reader will have made some acquaintance with Mr. Talbot from the preceding letters of Mr. Keith; but he will learn much more of his temper and disposition from the characteristic communications of Mr. Talbot himself, which, without further preface, we present.—PUB. COM:]

Mr. John Talbot to Mr. Richard Gillingham.

"New York, 24 November, 1702.

"MY DEAR FRIEND:

"I take all opportunities to let you know that I live, and shall be glad to hear as much of you. Friend Keith and I have been above 500 miles together visiting the churches in these parts of America, viz., New England, New Hampshire, N. Bristol, N. London, N. York, and the Jerseys as far as Philadelphia. We preached in all churches where we came, and in several Dissenters' meetings such as owned the Church of England to be their mother church, and were willing to communicate with her and to submit to her Bishops if they had opportunity; I have baptized severall persons, whom Mr. Keith has brought over from Quakerism, and indeed in all places where we come, we find a great ripeness and inclination amongst all sorts of people to embrace the Gospel. Even the Indians themselves have promised obedience to the Faith, as appears by a conference that my Lord Cornbury the Governor here has had with them at Albany: five of their sachems or kings told him they were glad to hear that the sun shined in England again since King William's Death; they did admire at first what was come to us, that we should have a squaw sachem, viz.: a woman-king, but they hoped she would be a good mother and send them some to teach them religion, and establish Traffick among them that they might be able to purchase a coat, and not go to church in Bear Skins, and so they send our Queen a present, ten Bear Skins to make her fine, and one for a muff to keep her warm; after many Presents and Compliments they signed the treaty and made the Covenant so sure that they said Thunder and Lightning should not break it on their part, if we did not do as the Lord Bellamont did, throw it into the sea. The papists have been zealous and diligent to send priests and Jesuits to convert these Indians to their superstitions; 'tis wonderfully acted, ventured and suffered upon that design; they have indeed become all things, and even turned Indians as it were to gain them, which I hope will provoke some of us to do our part for our holy faith and mother the Church of England. One of their Priests lived half a year in their wigwams (i. e. houses) without a shirt, and when he petitioned my Lord Bellamont for a couple, he was not only denyed but banished; whereas one of ours, in Discourse with my Lord of London, said, 'who did his Lordship think would come hither that had a dozen shirts.' If I had their language or wherewith to maintain an Interpreter, it should be the first thing I should do, to go amongst the thickest of 'em. Mr. Keith says if he were younger he would learn their language and then I'm sure he might convert them sooner than the Heathen called Quakers. Indeed he is the fittest man that ever came over for this province, he is a well study'd divine, a good philosopher and Preacher, but above all an excellent Disputant, especially against the Quakers, who use to challenge all mankind formerly. Now all the Friends (or enemies rather) are not able to answer one George

Keith; he knows the Depths of Satan within them and all the Doublings and Windings of the *Snake in the Grass*. In short he has become the best champion against all Dissenters, that the Church ever had, and he's sett up such a Light in their Dark places, that by God's blessing will not be putt out. The Clergy here have had a *sort* of Convocation at the Instance and Charge of his Excellency Col. Nicholson Governor of Virginia; we were but seven in all; and a week together, we sat considering of ways and means to propagate the Gospel, and to that End we have drawn up a scheme of the present state of the Church in these provinces which you shall see when I have time to transcribe it, and I shall desire you to send it afterwards to my good brother Kemble. We have great need of a Bishop here to visit all the churches to ordain some, to confirm others, and bless all. We pray for my good Lord of London, we cannot have better than he whilst he lives, therefore in the mean time we shall be very well content with a suffragan. Mr. Keith's mission will be out about a year hence; by that time I hope to get some tokens for my good friends and Benefactors. But as for myself I am so well satisfied with a prospect of doing good that I have no inclination to return for England; however be so kind as to let me know how you doe, which will be a comfort to me in the wilderness. You know all my friends, pray let them, especially my mother and my sister Hannah, know that I am well, God be praised, and shall be glad to hear so much of them. I cannot write many letters, much less one two or three times over as when I had nothing else to do. I pray God bless you and all my Friends, I desire the Benefit of their prayers, though I cannot have that of their good Company. I know you'll take all in good part that comes from

"Your old Friend,

"JOHN TALBOT.

"P. S.—I have many places offered me but I know not where I shall settle, in mean time you may direct your letters for me to be left with Mr. Bridge of Boston N. E, Mr. Vesey at N. York, Mr. Evans at Philadelphia and Mr. Wallace in Virginia."

Mr. Talbot to Mr. Gillingham.

"New Castle, 10th April, 1703.

"DEAR SIR:

"God be praised we are come thus far in health and safety in our way towards Virginia. We are to goe aboard a sloop on Monday morning and hope to be at James's Town next week. This is a pretty town on Delaware River, between Pensylvania and Maryland. There is no Church as yet, neither ever was an orthodox minister settled there; but one Mr. Wilson, a Presbyterian, that preaches to the People in the Court-House; he has left them this last winter, but finding it not for the better, he means to come again this summer, he has disobliged some people thereby which makes them the more favorable to the Church, which I hope by God's blessing to found here very speedily.

"The Place is very Pleasant, and agreeable as most in America, and would be very populous, but that there is no settled ministry nor Government, for what good does it do people to live in a Place void of Gospel and Law too; so that several people have moved and gone elsewhere to the Church, seeing the Church does not come to them.

"I have sent you a scheme of the present state of the Church in these parts as we have found in our travels; since it was drawn up I have gone with Mr. Keith and without him, about East and West Jersey Preaching and baptising several scores of men, women and children, encouraging them to build Churches by promising them in time ministers from England, and that the Honorable Society would take care to send none but sober, good men well qualified in all respects for the work of the ministry. I look upon it that the sending Mr. Keith in quality of a missionary, to travel for the good of the Churches, has been the best service that has been done yet for the Church of England in these parts of the world; for he is a general scholar, an able disputant and a perfectly honest man. He is in a word *Hereticorum malleus*, and so he had need; having to deal with some of the worst that ever troubled the Church or the World. Here is little or no Government, and people in many places take the liberty to say there be three Gods, or no God, and nothing is done to them. Certainly 'tis better to live where nothing is lawful than where all things are. Since I came to be more acquainted with the Quakers I have much worse opinion of them than ever I had. It appears by William Penn's book, that he is a greater Antichrist than Julian the apostate. He has said that Christ is a finite, impotent creature; and Faith in the History of Christ's outward manifestation is a deadly poyson these latter ages have been infected withal, to the destruction of holy Living. Who was defender of the Faith when the lewd Heretick was made Governor and Proprietor of a province? Certainly God gave this Land into the hands of the English, that they might Publish the Gospell and give knowledge of Salvation to these people; and I am sure the King gave this to William Penn, with Injunction expressly in his patent, that he should endeavour to convert the Indians to the Faith; but instead of that he labours to make Christians Heathens; and proclaims Liberty and Priviledge to all that believe in one God, and yet when they come here, they say there are three or none, and yet be borne out by the Quakers against the Christians. They pretend they ought not to fight, yet I have seen several commissions, under several of their Governor's hands to kill, &c. God bless Queen Anne, and defend her that she may defend the Faith; and her Faithful Councellours if they have any piety or policy I'm sure will take some course with these Heathens and Hereticks, for if they be let alone to take the sword (which they certainly will when they think they are strong enough) we shall perish with it, for not opposing them in due time. Notwithstanding the Toleration they are subject to all the penal laws, as you'll find if you read the Act, and were I in England, and had as much knowledge in Law as you, I would bring Statutes and Judgments against them. I have done so att New York where there is a good Governor, my Lord Cornbury.

"Last Lord's day I was at Burlington, the chief Town in West Jersey, where I have preached many times in a house hard by the Quakers' meeting: we shall have one too, I hope, when we return here again from Virginia, where we think to stay but two or three months; after sermon I went out with the rest of the people, and laid the corner stone of Saint Mary's Church. God grant it may rise to be the house of God, and the Gate of Heaven to them.

"It seems the Honorable Gentlemen of the Corporation have considered my Travels for the Service of the Church, and have given me a handsome allowance to bear my charges with Mr. Keith. Pray give them my hearty service and thanks to let them know that, by the grace of God, I shall make it my business to fulfil my mission. Pray remember my duty and Love to my Good Mother; I hope she is alive and well, let her not want £10 per annum, as long as I have £60 coming to me, which will be due the 12th of June next ensuing. It grieves me much to see so many People here without the benefit of serving God in the wilderness. I believe I have been solicited to tarry at twenty Places where they want much, and are able to maintain a minister, so that he should want nothing; they send to New England and call any sorry young man, purely for want of some good honest clergyman of the Church of England. Many go to the heathen meetings of the People called Quakers, because there are no houses of God in their provinces, till at last they come to be bewitched and forced out of their Faith and senses too. The country is a good *land* in all parts of it, bating the sudden change of Heat and Cold, which, if people be not careful, they are many times the worse for. The air is generally clear and pure. Nobody complains here of the spleen, unless he has also an evil conscience attending. I saw Mr. Burley, Mr. Scott's friend, at Philadelphia. I was at his house, he lives very well and entertained me very civilly, and was glad to hear of his old Friends. I am but poor at present, being robbed by a negro of all my money out of my Portmanteau; the young slut did not leave me one Token for myself, only I got the bag again. But blessed be God I never wanted meat nor drink, nor cloaths neither as yet; but if you don't send me some cloaths next shipping, instead of going as they do in White Hall, I shall go as the Indians do. I shall be content, let it be as it will. I might have had money enough here if I would have taken what People have offered me, but lest the Quakers should say truly, as they do falsely, that we come for money and preach for hire, I preach the Gospel as freely as the Apostles did to the first Churches.

"Virginia, 8th June.

"When I wrote this, I missed the opportunity to send it so I brought it hither with me so you must take it rough as it runs. We have been now at our journey's end in N. Carolina as far as we could goe, now we tack about and stand another way to Philadelphia again, thus George Keith's home and mine is *every where*. Governor Nicholson has been very kind and generous to me. I pray God prosper him long in his Government; he has some enemies as well as other men, but none of them can deny but he is a just magistrate in his place. I have sent the scheme of our Church affairs by one Mr. Beverly, an honest Gentleman of this Country, who is bound for England very speedily; you'll hear of him at Mr. Parry's, the Virginia Merchant. George Keith comes home next year; then if I can get anything worthy sending, I shall have a carefull hand to deliver it. There is one Mr. Keyes, my Lord of London's taylor; you may deal with him to send me a chest of cloathes, new or old, once a year. Direct them or anything else for me to be left with George Walker at Kecoughtan in Virginia. I am

"Semper Idem,

"J. T."

Mr. Talbot to Mr. Gillingham.

"Virginia, 3d May, 1703.

"Dear Friend:

"Now at last (God be praised) we are arrived at the Haven where we would be. Mr. Keith is got to his Daughter's house, and I am got amongst my old Friends and acquaintance in these parts, who are very glad to see me; especially those of the ministry, who came over along with me. Here has been great alterations in these ten years. Since I was here many of my old Friends are dead, but I have found some new in their stead; amongst which is the bearer, Mr. Robert Beverly, who has one of the best houses and plantations in this country, where I reckon myself as it were, at home, he has been so courteous and civil. But there is some dispute in Law concerning the Title, and he is come over to see about it; wherein I hope you will and can be serviceable to him, and I shall take it as done to myself. I have sent you several Letters, but have none yet from nobody. I hear the Honorable Gentlemen of the Society at Bow have ordered £60 per annum for travelling charges: £30 I have received upon Bill. I desire you to receive the other £30 to buy Books for a friend of mine here, who will repay me. I desire you to lay out £10 more in cloathes and shirts which I desire neighbour Leviton to buy for me, and send them in some ship to New York directed to me, to be left at Mr. Vesey's, minister there. I shall be glad to hear how all our Friends do, especially my good mother. Pray let me know where she is, and how she does, let her have *decem minas* upon my account as long as she lives. I have sent the present state of the Church, *apud Americanos* as far as we have gone; the first year from Dover, eighty miles eastward from Boston in New England, to Philadelphia in Pensylvania; since that scheme was finished, I have gone up and down in E. and W. Jersey preaching and baptizing and preparing the way for several Churches there. At Amboy they are going to build one, at Hopewell another, and at Shrewsbury, Coll. Morris is going to build one at his own cost and charge, and he will endow it as he says, which I don't doubt, for he is an honest Gentleman, and a member of the Honorable Society for Propagating the Gospel in Foreign parts. I was at Burlington last Lady day, and after prayers we went to the Ground where they were going to build a Church, and I laid the first stone, which I hope will be none other than the House of God and Gate of Heaven to the People. Coll. Nicholson, Governor here, was the chief founder of this as well as many more; and indeed he has been the benefactor to all the Churches on this land of North America. God bless this Church and let them prosper that love it. We called this Church St.

Mary's, it being upon her day. January last I was at the opening of a church at Chester; I preached the first sermon that ever was there, on Sunday the day before the Conversion of St. Paul, and after much debate what to call it, I named it St. Paul's. This is one of the best Churches in these American Parts, and a very pleasant place; but they have no minister as yet, but Mr. Evans of Philadelphia officiated there once in three weeks. The Governor of Virginia is building several more churches: Two at North Carolina, where we are going next week, and one at New Castle, where in all appearance we shall have a considerable Congregation of Christian People. The place is very well planted for trade both by sea and Land. It being allmost in the midway between Philadelphia and Maryland upon Delaware River; where, God willing, I intend to spend some labour and pains; though I can't find in my heart to settle in any place for my own, but to travel, as I told you, for the good of the Church in general. I should be glad to hear how you did about the Centurion, and how matters of account stand between us. Tis good to reckon some time if we never intend to pay, though I hope to be out of debt to the world. Yet I shall always count myself obliged to my friend. I have been with George Keith a year next June 12th, then my £60 becomes due. This has been a sickly year *apud Americanos*, but God be praised I have had good health all this time. And I believe I have done the Church more service since I came hither than I would in seven years in England. Perhaps when I have been here six or seven years, I may make a Trip home to see some Friends (for they won't come to me) but then it will be *Animo Revertendi*, for I have given myself up to the service of God and his Church *apud Americanos*; and I had rather dye in the service than desert it. Pray give my service and thanks to the Honorable Society for their Generous Allowance to bear my charges. I shall take care to fulfill my mission, and goe as far with it as any body that they shall send forth. We came hither in a sloop from Pensylvania, when we were out of Delaware River, a North west wind took us and carried us out to sea and lost us ten or twelve hours so as I was never lost in my life; 'tis true sometimes, as the sailor sayes, the last storm was the worst. The sea never got any thing before by my sickness, but then I was so sick that I had much adoe to keep my bowels within my body; we arrived safe at last, God be praised; but I shall be hardly catched on board so small a vessel again in a good while. We are going now by land to Pamplico in North Carolina, a place where there never was any minister but only one Dan. Brett, a scandalous Fellow, that has done more harm than good every where. He was the worst I think that ever came over.

"We want a great many good ministers here in America, especially in those parts mentioned in the scheme; but we had better have none at all than such scandalous beasts as some make themselves; not only the worst of ministers but of men. If you know none so good as to *come*, I hope you will find them that are willing to *send*. Some good books would do very well in the mean while. I am sure there is no want of them in England, they have enough and to spare. Indeed we have had many of Dr. Bray's books and I could wish we had more. But his way and method is not the best for this people that we have to do withal, Quakers and Quakers' friends; to most of them, nothing but controversy will serve their turn, 'tis a hard matter to persuade to the Baptismal Covenant, on which the Doctor has writ three or four Books to the folio, that they may be ever learning and yet never be able to come to the knowledge of the Creed, the Lord's Prayer, nor the Ten Commandments.

"Those that we have to deal with are a sharp and inquisitive people: they are not satisfied with one Doctor's opinion but must have something that is authentick if we hope to prevail with them.

"We should have some Common Prayer Books new or old, of all sorts and sizes with the thirty-nine articles, and some books of Homily's, to set up the worship and service of God till we have ministers; some of Dr. Comber's Books would be of right good use here to give those that ask a Reason of all things contained in our English Liturgies; which has still stood the Best Test of all adversaries that were not blind and deaf. Above all, Mr. Lesly, the Author of the 'Snake in the Grass,' has given Quakerism a deadly wound, I hope never to be healed: and his five Discourses about Baptism and Episcopacy have brought many to the Church. We want a 1000 of them to dispose of in the way that we goe. I use to take a wallet full of Books and carry them 100 miles about, and disperse them abroad, and give them to all that desired them; which in due time will be of good service to the Church; 'tis a comfort to the people in the Wilderness to see that some body takes care of them. There is a time to sow and a time to reap, which last I don't desire in this world. I might have money enough of the people in many places, but I would never take any of those that we goe to proselyte, especially amongst the Quakers; I resolved to work with my hands rather than they should say I was a hireling, and come for money, which they are very apt to do. The Governour of Virginia, my old Friend, has been very generous to us, and has taken care that nothing be wanting to us while we are in his Territories; if there were such another Governour in America, it would be much cheaper travelling for the missionaries. But alas! I am afraid we shall lose him before we get such another. There are a parcel of men in the world, that are given to change, and don't know when they are well themselves, nor can't let others alone that do. But more of this another time, I have writ enough to tire you and myself too: you must take it as it is. I have something else to do now than write letters twice over; rough as it runs I hope you'll take it in good part. With my Love and Service to all Friends, I desire your Prayers, and rest

"Your real Friend,

"And servant,

"J. T."

Mr. Talbot to the Secretary.—Extract.

"Philadelphia, 1st September, 1703.

"SIR:

"Mr. Keith and I have preached the Gospel to all sorts and conditions of men, we have baptized several scores of men, women and children, chiefly those of his old Friends (the rest are hardened just like the Jews who please not God and are contrary to all men), we have gathered several hundreds together for the Church of England, and what is more, to build houses for her service. There are four or five going forward now in this province and the next. That at Burlington is allmost finished. Mr. Keith preached the first sermon in it before my Lord Cornbury, whom the Queen has made Governour of Jersey to the satisfaction of all Christian people. Churches are going up amain where there were never any before. They are going to build three at N. Carolina to keep the people together, lest they should fall into Heathenism, Quakerism &c. &c., and three more in these lower counties about New Castle, besides that at Chester, Burlington and Amboy.

"And I must be so just to a member of your Society, his Excellency Francis Nicholson, Governour of Virginia, as to acknowledge him to be the Prime Benefactor and Founder, in chief of them all; so generous has he been to the church; so just to the State, so far from taking of bribes, that he will not receive a present from any, great or small. Therefore we have hopes that it will please God and the Queen to give him time to perfect the good works that he has begun; that he may see the Church prosper and prevail against all her enemies, which I dare say is all that he desires; being zealous for the honour of the Church of England which is the mother of us all. Upon her account it was that I was willing to travel with Mr. Keith, indeed I was loath he should go alone, now he was for us, who I'm sure would have had followers enough had he come against us. Besides, I had another end in it, that by his free Conversation and Learned Disputes both with his Friends and Enemies, I have Learnt better in a year to deal with the Quakers, then I could by several years' study in the schools. We want more of his narratives which would be of good use here where we often meet with the Quakers and their Books. More of his answers to Robert Barklay would come well to the clergy of Maryland and Virginia, &c. Barklay's book has done most mischief, therefore Mr. Keith's answer is more requisite and necessary. Mr. Keith has done great service to the Church where ever he has been, by Preaching and disputing, publicly and from house to house; he has confuted many (especially the Anabaptists); by Labor and Travel night and day, by writing and printing of books mostly at his own charge and costs and giving them out freely, which has been very expensive to him. By these means People are much awakened, and their Eyes opened to see the good old way, and they are very well pleased to find the Church at last take such care of her children. For it is a sad thing to consider the years that are past, how some that were born of the English, never heard of the name of Christ, how many others were baptized in his name and follow away to Heathenism, Quakerism, and Atheism for want of confirmation.

"It seems the strangest thing in the world and 'tis thought History can not parallel it, that any place has received the Word of God so many years, so many hundred Churches built, so many thousand proselytes made, and still remain altogether in the wilderness as sheep without a shepherd. The poor church of America is worse off in this respect than any of her adversaries.

"The Presbyterians here come a great way to lay hands one on another;

but after all I think they had as good stay at home, for the good they do. The Independents are called by their Sovereign Lord the People. The Anabaptists and Quakers pretend to the spirit. But the poor Church has no body upon the spot to comfort or confirm her children. No body to ordain severall that are willing to serve, were they authorized for the work of the ministry. Therefore they fall back again into the Herd of the Dissenters, rather than they will be at the Hazard and Charge to go as far as England for orders; so that we have seen severall Counties, Islands and Provinces, which have hardly an Orthodox minister amongst them, which might have been supplied had we been so happy as to see a Bishop or Suffragan *apud Americanos.*

"We count ourselves happy, and indeed so we are, under the protection and Fatherly Care of the Right Rev. Father in God, Henry Lord Bishop of London, and we are all satisfied that we can't have a greater Friend and Patron than himself. But alas! there is such a great Gulph fixt between us, that we can't pass to him nor he to us; but may he not send a Suffragan? I believe I am sure there are a great many learned and Good men in England, and I believe also did our Gracious Queen Anne but know the necessities of her many good subjects in these parts of the world, she would allow £1000 per annum, rather than so many souls should suffer; and then it would be a hard case if there should not be found one amongst so many pastors and Doctors (*de tot millibus, unus qui transiens, adjuvet nos*); meanwhile I don't doubt but some learned and good man would go further, and do the Church more service with £100 per annum than with a coach and six, 100 years hence.

"The Reverend author of the 'Snake in the Grass' has done great service here by his Excellent Book; no body that I know since the Apostles' dayes has managed controversie better against all Jews, Heathens and Heretics; many here have desired to see the author, however I hope we shall not want his works, especially against the Quakers, and the five discourses which have convinced many, and are much desiderated.

"Those boxes of books that were sent over last year, Mr. Keith has disposed of in their several Places as directed. I have carried of the small sort, in a wallet, some hundred miles, and distributed them to the people as I saw need. They have been long upon the search for truth in these parts, they see through the vanity and pretences of all Dissenters, and generally tend directly to the Church. Now is the time of harvest, we want a hundred hands for the work, meanwhile two or three, that are well chosen, will do more good there than all the rest; for we find by sad experience that people are better where they have none, than where they have an *ill* minister. Next unto God, our eyes are upon the Corporation for help in this heavy case. I dare say nothing has obtained more reputation to the Church and nation of England abroad than the honorable society for Reformation of manners and the Reverend and honorable corporation for Propagating the Gospel in Foreign Parts.

"The Quakers compass sea and land to make proselytes; they send out yearly a parcel of vagabond Fellows that ought to be taken up and put in Bedlam rather than suffered to go about raving and railing against the Laws and Orders of Christ and his Church; and for why? Their preaching is of cursing and Lyes, poysoning the souls of the people with damnable errors and heresies, and not content with this in their own Territories of Pensylvania, but they travel with mischief over all parts as far as they can goe, over Virginia and

Maryland, and again through Jersey and New York as far as New England; but there they stop, for they have prevented them by good Laws and due Execution; *Fas est ab hoste doceri.* Sir

"Your most humble and obedient servant,

"JOHN TALBOT."

Mr. Talbot to the Secretary.

"Philadelphia, 7th April, 1704.

"WORTHY SIR:

"Mr. Keith has fought the good fight, finished his race, bravely defended the Faith, done the Church of Christ true and laudable service, which I trust will be regarded here and rewarded hereafter. I may say he has done more for the Church than any, yea than all that have been before him. He came out worthy of his mission and of the Gospell of Christ. Taking nothing of the Heathen that he came to proselyte; besides his ordinary or rather extraordinary travels, his preaching excellent sermons upon all occasions, his disputes with all sorts of Heathens and Hereticks (who superabound in these parts;—Africa has not more monsters than America). He has written or printed ten or a dozen Books and Sermons, much at his own charge, and distributed them freely; which are all excellent in their kind, and have done good service all along shore. Now, since friends must part, I pray God, shew some token upon him for good, that he may arrive safe in England where he would be, that all his adversaries may see it, and be ashamed of their impious omens, &c. I have one prayer more to God for the sake of his Church in the deserts, viz.: That the Reverend and Honorable Corporation may find one amongst the thousands of the Reverend and Learned Clergy of England, worthy, honest, and willing to succeed, that the People of the Lord may not be scattered abroad in the wilderness like sheep without a Shephard.

"As for the affairs of the Church here, wee have said much formerly in Schemes and Letters, but have heard no great matter how or whether received; therefore I don't mean to be tedious at present; something I think I should say because you desired me to keep a Journall. To begin then where we began our Travells, at Boston New England. There is one Church, and there were two ministers, both sober and discreet men in the main, and I believe would have done good service at a distance; they were both our Friends, and I could wish they had been so to one another, or that those representations were true that are now gone to his Grace and to the Right Reverend Bishops of the Corporation, which say they parted good Friends; but to say the Truth as it is, there is such a variance that the Church can't flourish between them. Mr. Vesey does very well with his people at New York; Mr. Honyman is arrived but not yet settled, because he had been scandalized by an evil report which we have no reason to believe. I should not have forgott my honest brother Lockier of Rhode Island, who is very industrious when well. The Quakers themselves as far as I can hear, have no evil to say of that Priest. Nova Cesarea or New Jersey has been most unhappy; there is not, nor ever was, an orthodox minister settled amongst them. But there is one Mr. Alexander Innes a man of great Piety and Probity, who has by his Life and Doctrine preached the Gospell, and rightly and duly administered the Holy Sacraments. We hope he will find favour with the Noble Corporation because he is worthy, and has need of it; as the people have need of him and are not so able or willing as we could wish to support the ministry;—'tis pity those hands should be put to dig that are fitt to cultivate the vineyard. I come now to Philadelphia where there is now none but Mr. Evans a very sober, decent man, who has doubled his diligence since Mr. Thomas departed; he does the whole service of the Church now, and is more constant and frequent in preaching and performing divine service than any that I know upon the Continent; but the school is supplyed here by a Swede untill one can be sent from England, which I hope will not be long. Now there is a good salary paid, and it would be a very good school were there but a good master; 'tis hard that the Heathens should have schools in the town, and the Christians not one. The Church at Chester is almost finished, and one at New York is going to be reared, both by the care and industry of Mr. Jasper Yeates, and all by the generous bounty of Governour Nicholson. God send us such a Publick Spirited Minister in the Church here, as he is always and everywhere the best Friend and Patron of the Church, the Crown and Country that ever came over. I dare say this because I know it to be true, having had the honor to know his Excellency many years, though I know he has as many adversaries as the Church herself, and the more I dare say upon her account. . . . We received a box of books, by the hands of his Honor Governour Evans, written by the Reverend Author of the "Snake in the Grass;" we know not who sent them, but, being directed for Mr. Keith, we ventured to lend them abroad for the Publick good, and pray God to bless the Author and the Donors. There were the first and second defence of the Snake &c. but not the Snake itself; and four of his five discourses, but not that of Episcopacy, which are most desiderated here; we cannot purchase either of those books at any rate; we want 1000 Common Prayer Books; we can hardly get one in America, and when we do find one, it costs five times as much as it's worth in England. The Church wants to be published here, which can't be done without the Liturgy, and something to shew for what we say. Mr. Tate's and Mr. Brady's Psalms have obtained here, and would do so every where, if they had in them the Bishop of London-derry's book of the "Inventions of Men in the Worship of God" and Dr. Beveridge's sermons of the "Excellency of the Common Prayer," which have gone a great way here to save the Church. I can't tell what would do more except the Doctors should come themselves; however I hope they will send those books we mentioned with some others in the scheme, as Mr. Brent's of Bristol against Lying, which is not to be forgotten at this time and place. I'm sorry Mr. Barclay returned so soon from his post at Braintree in New England, the poor Christians are mightily opprest there by a sort of Hypocrites, who pretend to receive the Church, but indeed are her mortal enemies; their College also has gone a great way to poison this country with Damnable doctrines, which appears by the Learned books of the Rev. Mr. Keith to be worse than Heathenism or Atheism; we hope that care will be taken in this heavy case that some Grave and Wise Tutor and Philosopher will be sent to preside at the College of Cambridge in New England to teach them humanity in the first place, that in time they might be brought to Christian Principles and Practices; for at present they are not much better than the Quakers, and in the latter particular, much worse. If I had an Estate I could not have laid it out better than in the service of God, *apud Americanos* along with Mr. Keith, who is a true son of the Church of England, sound in faith and holy in Life, whom I love and reverence as my Father and Master, and shall be as Loath to part with him as if he were so indeed. Therefore I am the more obliged to the Reverend and Honorable Society for their generous allowance to me, that I might not be burdensome to him nor to others, but beneficial to all as far as we could goe. God be praised a Door is opened to the Gospel, and the true light shines to them in the Wilderness, but there are many adversaries; and now our Champion is gone, we must make a running fight out by God's blessing and his books. I shall do my best. I mean to gather up the arrows that he has shot so well at the mark, and throw them again where there is most need.

"Your most humble
"And obedient servant,
"JOHN TALBOT."

[The foregoing letters of Messrs. Keith and Talbot will have prepared the reader for the Journal of the former, to which allusion is made in the letters. This Journal was the *official* report of the Society's agent, and on its statements the Society acted in selecting the first missionary stations in what is now the United States.—PUB. COMMITTEE.]

A JOURNAL OF TRAVELS FROM NEW-HAMPSHIRE TO CARATUCK,

On the Continent of

NORTH-AMERICA.

BY
GEORGE KEITH, *A.M.*,
Late Missionary from the *Society for the Propagation of the Gospel in Foreign Parts;* and now Rector of *Edburton* in *Sussex.*

LONDON,
Printed by *Joseph Downing*, for *Brab. Aylmer* at the *Three-Pigeons*, over-against the *Royal-Exchange* in *Cornhill*, 1706.

TO THE

Most Reverend Father in GOD

THOMAS,

Lord Arch-Bishop of

CANTERBURY, &c.,

PRESIDENT;

And to the rest of the

MEMBERS

OF THE

Society for the Propagation of the Gospel in Foreign Parts;

This JOURNAL

Is most humbly Dedicated

By their late Missionary

George Keith.

A
JOURNAL
OF THE
Travels and Ministry
Of the Reverend
GEORGE KEITH, A.M.

THE Twenty eighth Day of *April* 1702, I sailed from *Cowes* in the *Isle* of *Wight*, in one of the Queens Ships, called the *Centurion*, whereof Captain *Herne* was Commander, who was very Civil to me, bound for *Boston* in *New-England;* and by the good Providence of God we arriv'd at *Boston* the Eleventh day of *June*, our whole time of Passage being Six Weeks and one Day. Colonel *Dudley* Governour of *New-England*, and Colonel *Povie* Deputy Governour, and Mr. *Morris*, with all whom we sailed in the same ship, were so generous and kind both to Mr. *Patrick Gordon* Missionary for *Long-Island*, and to me, that at their desire we did Eat at their Table all the Voyage on free cost.

At my Arrival the Reverend Mr. *Samuel Miles*, and the Reverend Mr. *Christopher Bridge*, both Ministers of the Church of *England* Congregation at *Boston*, did kindly receive me and the *two ministers* in company with me, and we lodg'd, and were kindly entertained in their Houses, during our abode at *Boston*.

June 14, 1702, being *Sunday*, at the request of the abovenamed Ministers of the Church of *England*, I Preached in the Queens Chappel at *Boston*, on *Eph*. 2. 20, 21, 22. where was a large Auditory, not only of Church People, but of many others.

Soon after, at the request of the Ministers and Vestry, and others of the Auditory, my Sermon was Printed at *Boston*. It contained in it, towards the conclusion, Six plain brief Rules (*Vide* Appendix), which I told my Auditory did well agree to the Holy Scriptures, and they being well observed and put in Practice, would bring all to the Church of *England* who dissented from her.

This did greatly Alarm the Independent Preachers at *Boston.* Whereupon Mr. *Increase Mather*, one of the chief of them, was set on Work to Print against my Sermon, as accordingly he did, and Published a small Treatise against the said six Rules, wherein he laboured to prove them all false and contrary to Scripture, but did not say any thing against the Body of my Sermon. And not long after, I Printed a Treatise in Vindication of these Six Rules, in answer to his, wherein I shewed the invalidity of his objections against them. This I had Printed at *New York*, the Printer at *Boston* not daring to Print it, lest he should give offence to the Independent Preachers there. After it was Printed, the printed Copies of it were sent to *Boston*, and dispersed both over *New-England* and the other parts of *North America.*

June 21, Sunday. I preached a second Sermon at the Queens Chappel, on *Rom.* 10. 6, 7, 8, 9.

June 28, Sunday. The Reverend Mr. *John Talbot*, who had been Chaplain in the *Centurion*, Preached there.

By the advice of my good Friends at *Boston*, and especially of Colonel *Joseph Dudley*, Governour of *Boston* Colony, I chose the abovenamed Mr. *John Talbot* to be my Assistant and Associate in my Missionary Travels and Services, he having freely and kindly offered himself, and whom I freely and kindly received, and with the first occasion I wrote to the Society, praying them, to allow of him to be my Fellow-Companion and Associate in Travels, &c., which they accordingly did, and indeed Divine Providence did well order it, for he proved a very loving and faithful Associate to me, and was very helpful to me in all respect, and was well approved and esteemed every where, both with respect to his Preaching and Living, in the several places where we Travelled.

July 1, Wednesday. I went from *Boston* to *Cambridge* in *New-England*, accompanied with my associate Mr. *Talbot*, and Mr. *Bridge* abovenamed, and I was present at the Commencement, which was that very day: and having heard Mr. *Samuel Willard*, President of the College, at the said Commencement maintain some Assertions that seemed to me very unsound, the next day I writ a Letter to him in *Latin*, shewing my great dislike of those his assertions, and after some days I sent it to him; after this, at the request of some there, I put it into *English*, and had it Printed at *New York*, and dispersed into many other places of *America*, as well as of *New England.*

The Assertions abovenamed of the said Mr. *Samuel Willard*, that seemed to me very unsound, were these: I. That the Fall of *Adam*, by virtue of God's Decree, was necessary. II. That every free act of the Reasonable Creature is determined by God, so that whatever the Reasonable Creature acteth freely, it acteth the same necessarily.

Not long after my Letter to him was Published and dispersed, he Printed a reply to it, in a small Treatise containing about four Sheets, where notwithstanding his many shufflings, and seeming to disown the charge, he very roundly and plainly not only asserts all that I had charged on him, but much more, as appears from his express Words, Page 50 of the said Reply, *Where* he saith, *Nor shall I part with my opinion?* viz. *that the Origine and Cause of the necessity of the first Sin is more to be derived from God, than from Man himself. Nay further*, (saith he) *that the whole cause of the futurity of it is owing to the divine Decree, though still the whole sin and blame of it is due to* Adam, *for that in the accomplishing of his Apostacy, he abused his own free Will, and Voluntarily transgressed the Command.*

After some time that his Reply to my Letter was Printed, I published in Print an answer to his Reply, my answer contains about six Sheets. My Endeavours in these matters, by the Blessing of God, had a good effect in quieting the Minds of many People in these parts, and bringing them over to the Church, in *East-Jersey*, especially at *Elizabeth* Town there. Such who desire to read both my Answer to Mr. *Samuel Willard*, and my letter, and also my Answer to Mr. *Increase Mather* in vindication of the six Rules above-mentioned, together with all the other Treatises I published in Print during my abode in *America*, from *June* 11*th* 1702, to *June* the 8*th* 1704, and some Printed Sermons within the said time, may find them at the most Reverend *Thomas* Lord Arch-Bishop of *Canterbury* his Library at St. *Martins*, all bound up together in one Volume, which I presented to the Society some small time after my arrival at *London.*

July 5, Sunday. I Preached again at the Queens Chappel in *Boston* upon *Rev.* 3. 20.

July 8, *July* 9, Thursday. I went from *Boston* to *Linn*, accompanied with Mr. *Talbot*, and the next day, being the Quakers Meeting day, we visited their Meeting there, having first called at a Quaker's House, who was of my former acquaintance. Mr. *Shepherd* the Minister of *Linn* did also accompany us, but the Quakers, though many of them had been formerly Members of his Church, were very abusive to him, as they were unto us. After some time of silence, I stood up and began to speak, but they did so interrupt with their Noise and Clamour against me, that I could not proceed, though I much entreated them to hear me: So I sat down and heard their Speakers one after another utter abundance of falsehoods and impertinencies and gross perversions of many Texts of the Holy Scripture. After their Speakers had done, they hasted to be gone: I desired them to stay, and I would shew them that they had spoke many falshoods, and perverted many places of Scripture, but they would not stay to hear. But many of the People staid, some of them Quakers, and others who were not Quakers but disaffected to the Quakers Principles. I asked one of their Preachers before he went away, seeing they Preached so much *the sufficiency of the Light within to Salvation,* (without any thing else) did the *Light* within teach him without Scripture, that our Blessed Saviour was born of a Virgin, and died for our Sins, &c. He replyed, If he said it did, I would not believe him, and therefore he would not answer me.

After their Speakers were gone, I went up into the Speakers Gallery, where they use to stand and Speak, and I did read unto the People that staid to hear me, Quakers and others, many Quotations out of *Edw. Burroughs's* Folio Book, detecting his vile Errors, who yet was one of their chief Authors, particularly in Page 150, 151. where he renders it *the Doctrine of Salvation that's only necessary to be Preached,* viz. *Christ within, and that he is a Deceiver that exhorts People for Salvation to any other thing than the Light within;* as appears by his several Queries in the Pages cited. And where he saith, Page 273. *that the Sufferings of the People of God in this Age* [*meaning the Quakers*] *are greater Sufferings, and more Unjust, than those of Christ and the Apostles; what was done to Christ, or to the Apostles, was chiefly done by a Law, and in great part by the due execution of a Law.* But all this a noted Quaker, whose name I spare to mention, (as I generally intend to spare the mentioning of their Names) did boldly defend. But another Quaker who stood by, confessed the last Passage in rendering the Quakers Sufferings greater and more unjust than the Sufferings of Christ, was not well worded, but to excuse it, said, *we must not make a Man an offender for a word.*

July 10. We came to *Hampton*, and were very kindly entertained there. *Hampton* is distant N. Eastward from *Boston* 50 Miles.

July 12, Sunday. Mr. *Talbot* Preached at *Hampton* in the forenoon, and I Preach'd there in the Afternoon on *Acts* 26. 18.

July 15, Wednesday. I Preached the Lecture there on the same Text.

July 16, Thursday. We went to the Quakers Meeting at *Hampton*, accompanied with Mr. *John Cotton* the Minister of the Parish, and Mr. *Cuslim* the Minister of *Salisbury* Parish, and very many Civil People of both these Parishes came, who were not Quakers, hoping to have heard some fair Dispute betwixt the Quakers and me. At the Quakers Meeting there we heard two Quaker Preachers. The first who spoke was a Ship Carpenter from *Situate*, who spoke about half an hour or more, but very Ignorantly, and most grossly perverting several Texts of Scripture, particularly *Job.* 17. 3. and *Rom.* 1. 19. which he brought to prove, that the ignorant People (to whom he directed his Discourse) as he accounted them, had a little Babe within them, lying in a Manger under the Earth, to which if they would hearken, that little Babe within them (*meaning by that little Babe, the Light within them*) would give them the knowledge of God, which was Life Eternal. He told them he could not read the Scripture, and hoped they would excuse him, if he did not so exactly quote the Words. After him the other Quaker Preacher, who came from *Shrewsberry* in East-*Jersey*, began and continued Preaching very long, above two Hours, and did mightily heat himself; he also most ignorantly spoke many things, and grossly perverted and misapplied many Texts of Scripture, to prove the sufficiency of the Light within to Salvation (*viz.* without Scripture or any thing else.) And as the Quakers ordinary way is in their Preaching every where, they have a set of Texts of Scripture which they commonly bring to prove *the sufficiency of the Light within to Salvation without any thing else*, but which they miserably pervert and misapply, such as *Job.* 1. 9. *Job.* 3. 19, 20. *Job.* 12. 36. *Job.* 16. 7, 8, 9, 10, 11. *Rom.* 10. 6, 7, 8. 2 *Cor.* 12. 9. *Titus* 2. 11, 12. Many of which Texts and others he did grossly pervert and misapply to prove his false Doctrine. And the like perversions of Scripture he used against Baptism, and the Lord's Supper, in the common road of other Quakers, as extant in their Printed Books. After he had done, having exceedingly tired and wearied all his Hearers who were not Quakers, I offered to speak, but immediately their Preachers went away in all hast after I began to speak, though I earnestly entreated them to stay; many also of the Quaker hearers went away with them, but some stayed, and all the people who were not Quakers, together with the two *New-England* Ministers abovementioned, did stay, and heard me about the space of an hour resume and refute the heads of the Quaker Preachers discourse, and rescue the Texts of Scripture which they had quoted from their gross perversions and misapplications, both as concerning the

Light within, and the *Holy Sacraments of Baptism and the Lord's Supper.* But the day being very hot, and the House not large enough to contain the Auditory, we kept the Meeting in an Orchard joining to the House, where we had some shade of Trees. Among the Quakers who stayed to hear me, one or two endeavoured to interrupt me in my Discourse; but a noted Quaker and Preacher of good repute belonging to their Meeting, did forbid them to make any interruption, telling them, I did not interrupt their Preachers, and therefore they should not interrupt me. I did also read to them many gross Antichristian expressions I had collected out of the Folio Book of *Edward Burroughs* (whom the Quakers have magnified with no less title than that of a Prophet, in their Title page of his Folio Book, published by them after his decease) and I told them if they were willing I would show them the Passages in the Book it self. To this the abovementioned Quaker Preacher replyed to me, I needed not to show them to him, for he believed the Quotations were truly made, and that there were great Errors in their Friend's Books. The same Quaker preacher did kindly invite us to his House, with whom I had much Discourse. He told me he approved very well of what he had heard me discourse, and that he did perceive my Doctrine about the necessity of Faith in *Jesus Christ*, in order to Salvation, was the same he had formerly heard me declare in their Meetings when I was among them about Twelve Years past. Some of his Neighbours told me, his manner of Preaching in the Quakers Meetings, was not to speak much, but what he spoke was generally no other than the express words of Scripture, without his putting any Commentary or gloss on them; he has the Character of a sober, honest, and very charitable Man among all his Neighbours, his Name is *Thomas Chase.* At this same Meeting of the Quakers at *Hampton*, one of the Quakers belonging to that Meeting did boldly affirm to me, before many Witnesses, that the Blood of Christ that was outwardly shed upon the Cross could do him no good, and he did extremely blame me, for owning to Mr. *John Cotton* the Minister of *Hampton* Parish, about Twelve Years past, that we were justified and sanctified by that Blood of Christ's Body that was outwardly shed on the Cross, and did earnestly contend that the Blood of Christ, whereby the faithful are said in Scripture to be justified and sanctified, was not any outward Blood of Christ, but the inward Blood of the Light within them, as they had learned from *George Fox*, and *George Whitehead*, and other Quaker Authors, in their Printed Books, whereof I have given a large and full Account, in several of my Printed Narratives at *London*, particularly the first, third, and fourth. I endeavoured to help the said Quaker's Understanding, by informing him, that by our being justified and sanctified by the Blood of Christ, that was outwardly shed, was not meant that it was by any material or outward application of that Blood to us, but by the Merit of our blessed Saviour's Passion and Death, in his being a most satisfactory and acceptable Sacrifice to God for our Sins, the which Sacrifice required that his Blood should be shed; for without the shedding of Blood, there could be no remission of Sins; and all Men who had remission of Sins by that Blood, it was by a true and lively Faith in that Blood; but all that I said or could say to him did not prevail, but he continued strong in his most unchristian assertion, still justifying it, and blaming me for my Christian Doctrine. This with all the other Passages I brought both from their Preachers words, then spoke by them, and quoted out of their Books, which the Quakers present did not contradict, did greatly satisfy the People there, who were not Quakers, that the Quakers chief Authors and Preachers were guilty of most unchristian Principles, repugnant to the Fundamentals of the Christian Faith; and that the inferior sort had received their gross Errors from their Leaders Words and Writings.

July 19, Sunday. Mr. *Talbot* Preached at *Salisbury* in the Forenoon, and I Preached there in the Afternoon, on *Philip.* 2. 13, where we had a great Auditory, and well affected, as also we had the like at *Hampton.* The occasion of our having so great an Auditory both at *Hampton* and at *Salisbury* was this, as some of them told us, that they had been inform'd concerning us, that *We being Ministers of the Church of England, we would Preach down-right Popery to our Hearers:* But (said they) we came the rather to hear you, to know whether we could hear any Popery Preached by you; but indeed, (said they which were the most Judicious, and most Ancient among them,) *Praised be God we heard no Popish Doctrine Preached by any of you, but good sound Protestant Doctrine, the same which we have heard our Ministers of* New-England *Preach to us, and which to our great comfort we have believed these Forty Years past, and we still continue to believe.* We replied, we were very glad to find that they were of the same Faith with the Church of *England,* in these great Fundamentals of the Christian Religion.

July 23, 1702. We came to the Quakers Meeting at *Dover* (by *Piscataway* River) distant from *Boston* North-Eastwards about Seventy Miles, where after some time of silence, we heard their Preacher, who was a Taylor, and lived in the Town of *Dover:* He did not speak long, but exhorted them to keep to the Foundation, and he quoted St. *Paul's* Words, Another Foundation can no Man lay, but that which is laid already, which is *Jesus Christ.* I heard him patiently till he had done; and after he had done, I perceiving, by the sequel of his discourse, that he meant nothing else by *Jesus Christ* being the Foundation, *but the light within them,* and as it is in all Men, according to their common Doctrine. I asked him what he meant by *Jesus Christ* being the Foundation, whether the Light within them only, or the Man *Christ Jesus,* who was, and is, both God and Man without them, and who is also in them as he is God, and is in all Men by his general Presence and Illumination, and is in all the Faithful by his special Grace and Illumination? But to this he would give no positive answer. But seemed greatly surprized, and as a Man astonished at my plain Question; for I found he had no other notion of *Jesus Christ* being the Foundation, but the Light within, which he called God, and said, God was *Adam's* Teacher the first, and will be the last; all which he applyed to the Light within, as it is in all Men, *Jews, Turks,* and *Infidels,* the same as in the Quakers by their plain confession. I asked him again, did the light within him, without the Scripture, teach him that *Jesus Christ* was Born of the Virgin *Mary?* He replyed by asking me, who taught *Joseph* that *Christ* was to be Born of her? I answered him, an Angel: But had an Angel taught him the same? He said the Holy Ghost had taught him. I again asked him, had the Holy Ghost Taught him that without the Scripture? To this he quite demurred, and was at a stand, until a Quaker that was next to him, whispered to him in the Ear, and bid him ask me, who taught *Nebuchadnezzar* that the fourth that was with the three Children in the fiery

Furnace was like the Son of God? I answered him, that case was Miraculous and extraordinary, which he could not pretend unto; nor do the Leaders among the Quakers pretend, that the *Light within them*, without Scripture, teacheth them anything of Christ as he was outwardly Born of a Virgin, or of his Death, Burial, and Resurrection, &c. for it is not needful (they say) to be taught them by the Light within them, and yet the Light within them doth sufficiently teach them all that is necessary to Salvation without any thing else; which plainly proves from their avowed Principle, that they do not think the Faith of Christ's Birth, Death, Burial, Resurrection, &c. necessary to their Salvation; but even this again is contradicted by some of them, who affirm it is necessary to them who have the Scriptures, to have that Faith, and to such not to have it, is a Damnable Sin. After this short Conference with him he went away, and some of the Quakers with him, but many stayed behind, both Men and Women, with whom we had much discourse, wherein they generally betrayed their horrid ignorance, and prejudice, against the very Fundamentals of Christianity. One of them did mightily contend against me, for the sufficiency of the Light within every Man to Salvation, without any thing else, and charged my denial of his Assertion to be Blasphemy; for (said he) the Light within is God, and God could do every thing, and can, and is sufficient to save us without any thing else. I replyed to him, there were several things God could not do. This again he charged to be Blasphemy, and bid me give him one Instance of any one thing he could not do. I told him, I could give him diverse Instances; as that he could not Lie, nor be the Author of any Sin, to which he assented. I told him again, as God could not Lie, so nor could he contradict his declared will and purpose plainly delivered to us in the holy Scripture, which was to save us by Jesus Christ, who died for us, 1 *Thess.* 5. 9. and therefore this being God's revealed Will to save us by Jesus Christ who died for us, to save us without Jesus Christ who died for us, would contradict God's revealed Will given us in the holy Scripture; this Answer did quite put him to silence. After I had thus said, one Mrs. *Knight*, a Quaker belonging to their Meeting, being present, (whose Name I mention to her Praise, and to make it known, that some among the Quakers are not such Infidels, as they more generally are, though all of them, even the best, are involved in great Errors) signified her good liking to my Answer, and said, she thought that I would give that Answer: she also did vindicate my Reputation against another Quaker-Woman there present, who said, they (*viz.* the Quakers) had no good opinion of me, when I was formerly among them in that Town, about Twelve Years past or more. I am sure, said Mrs. *Knight*, that is not true; for Friends then had a very good Esteem of him, and particularly so I had, and was glad that by my Husbands Invitation, he came and Lodg'd one Night at our House. And while we were discoursing about a sinless Perfection, whether it was attainable in this Life; another Quaker-Woman affirmed, that she was perfect to that degree, that she had not any Sin. What (said I) have ye no sin, neither actual nor original? Was ye not Born with original sin? nay, (said she) I was born of Holy Parents, and I knew never any thing but Purity and Holiness. But, said I, *David* came of holy Parents, and yet he said, *Psal.* 51. 5. *Behold I was shapen in Iniquity, and in Sin did my Mother conceive me.* Were your Parents more holy than *David's* Parents? To this she answered, what *David's* Parents were she knew not, whether holy or not, but she knew her Parents that they were holy. And this is the very Doctrine of *George Fox* and *Edward Burroughs*, in their Printed Books, that the Children of holy Parents are Born without all defilement of Sin. After this Mr. *Talbot* produced *George Fox's* Will in Print (which as it has received several Impressions at *London*, so it hath had one at least at *New-York* in *America*) and began to read in it, how *George Fox* left his Boots and Spurs, and Clyster-pipe, to *Thomas Lower;* by which Mr. *Talbot* did infer, that it seemed *George Fox* did leave them as holy Relicks. No, said she, *viz.* the above mentioned Woman who said she had no Sin, they have been silver Spurs, for she had seen silver Spurs, and the Clyster-Pipe was a Golden Pipe: To this I replyed, this made *George Fox* very vain and Proud, that his Spurs were silver Spurs; this was a great reflexion on *George Fox*, to say he wore silver Spurs; and that his Clyster-Pipe was a Golden Pipe, this was to render him very Prodigal indeed, who was but a poor Shoemaker Journyman (whose Master I knew) before he became the Ring-leader of the Quakers, that no less would serve him than silver-Spurs; and as for a Golden Clyster-Pipe, I never heard of any such thing before. We had also much reasoning with diverse of the Quakers in that Meeting, concerning the Sacraments, and particularly that of Baptism. The chief Person that did undertake to dispute with me against Baptism with Water, was a Quaker Justice of that Town, whose Name I spare, as I think fit generally to spare their names (except where I can say something to their commendation, and that is but very seldom) whereas I produced *Matth.* 28. 19. to prove that our Blessed Saviour had commanded the practice of Baptism to his Apostles, and to their Successors to administer it to all Proselytes to Christianity to the end of the World: To this he replyed, that Water was not mentioned, and that the Baptism that Christ there commanded, was not *outward Baptism* with Water, but *inward Baptism* with the Spirit. I asked him what *Teaching* was that, which Christ commanded there, *Matth.* 28. 19, 20. He said, it was inward Teaching; but in this another Quaker presently contradicted him, and said, it could not be inward Teaching that Christ commanded the Apostles; for none but God, and Christ, and the Holy Ghost, could Teach inwardly; but the Apostles being but Men, they could but Teach outwardly; I commended his answer, and from thence I inferred against them both, that as the Apostles could not Teach inwardly, so nor could they Baptize inwardly, the latter being as impossible to Men to do as the former; and therefore the Baptism that Christ commanded the Apostles to administer was outward Baptism with Water, and which accordingly they performed either by themselves, or by appointing others to do it by the Authority they had from Christ. This is but a hint of many things that passed in discourse betwixt us, having continued with them for many hours. After we came out of the Meeting, the Quaker-Woman who boasted so much of her sinless Perfection, did invite us to her House, and did kindly entertain us both with Victuals and Drink, and offered us a good Bed to lodge in, it being late. We thanked her for her Hospitality and proffer to lodge us, but we went into our Boat that waited for us, and went down the River that Night to the Town called *Strawberry-bank*, and lodged there at an Inn, or Public House of Entertainment.

Here it is worthy of notice, what some of the Neighbours of the Quakers of that Town did inform us concerning the Quakers there, *viz.* how that sometime after Quakerism had got entrance into that Town, and they had set up a Quaker Meeting there, the Quakers invited their Neighbours to come to their Meetings, where they should hear excellent Preachers, who should Preach to them freely without any Cost or Charge, not like their hireling Minister, who put them to great charge to maintain him: Upon this Publication, many or most of the Parish deserted the Minister, and frequented the Quakers Meetings. But not long after, the Contributions that the Quakers gathered in their Monthly and Quarterly Meetings for the Travelling Friends of the Ministry, were so frequent, and rose so high, that they far exceeded what they were to pay their Minister as the Law of the Country required; whereupon they generally concluded to desert the Quaker Meetings, and return to their Minister; for, said they, if this be the way of it, that the upholding the Quakers Ministers that come among us be so chargeable, far above what we pay to the Minister of the Parish, we will go back again to our own Minister Mr. *John Pike*, and accordingly so they did, and continue hearing their own Minister, who is of good Fame among the Neighbourhood, and whom we intended to have visited at his House, but it happened that he was gone abroad; however such as were more thoroughly leavened with Quakerism, keeped up their Meetings, and have Built a Meeting-House to themselves, where we did visit them, and discourse with them as abovementioned.

July 25, 1702. We Arrived at *Salem*, and had intended to have visited the Quakers at their Meeting there, the next Day, but we were informed that they had removed their Meeting for that Day from *Salem* to another Place, of which we could have no notice, though we made enquiry.

July 28. In our way from *Salem* to *Boston*, as we stayed some Hours at the Ferry by *Newberry*, I had much discourse with a sober Carpenter who was a Quaker, his Name was *William Clement.* He did readily confess to the Fundamentals of the Christian Faith, concerning our blessed Saviour; but had some dispute with me about Baptism, and by the Discourse I had there with him, seemed to be much convinced that it was his Duty to have his Children Baptized, as he had been himself, in Infancy, and had a Resolution to have it done.

August 1. We returned to *Boston.*

August 2, *Sunday.* I Preached again at the Queen's Chappel there on *Philip.* 2. 13.

August 3, 1702. I set out from *Boston* accompanied with the Reverend Mr. *Samuel Myles*, one of the Ministers of the Church of *England* Congregation there, and we arrived at *Newport* in *Rhod-Island* the next day, where we were kindly received. Mr. *Lockyer* the Church of *England* Minister there and diverse others of the Church came from *Newport* and met us at the Ferry, and conducted us to the Town, and place of our Lodging. Mr. *Talbot* stayed at *Boston* to officiate in the Church there for Mr. *Myles*, until his return.

August 6. I went to the Quakers Meeting at *New-port* on *Rhod-Island* accompanied with Mr. *Myles*, Mr. *Lockyer*, and many People belonging to the Church there, some of them being Justices of the Peace, to wit, Mr. *Carr*, and Mr. *Layton.*

After one of their Preachers had spoke a long time, and came to an end, having perverted many Texts of Scripture, to prove the sufficiency of the Light within, the inward Teacher, without any thing else, their common Subject; and though they do not so very frequently say, *without any thing else,* yet they always so mean it, and oft so express it, as they have very much of late both in their Discourses and Books. The two particular Texts of Scripture which he greatly perverted, to prove the Quakers false Notion of the sufficiency of the Light within all Men to Salvation, without any thing else, were *Job.* 16. 8. and *Titus* 2. 11. I began to speak, standing up in a Gallery opposite to the Gallery where their Teachers were placed, who were many; having intended in a friendly manner to inform them, how their Speaker had misunderstood and misinterpreted those, and other Texts of Scripture; and I much requested them to hear me a while without interruption, as I had heard their Preacher. But I was instantly interrupted by them very rudely, and they were very abusive to me with their ill-Language, calling me Apostate, &c. and they threatened me with being guilty of the breach of the Act of Tolleration, by which they said their Meetings were Authorized. I told them I had not broken the Act of Tolleration; for neither that Act, nor any Law of *England,* did forbid a Minister of the Church of *England* to speak in their Meetings, if he did not interrupt them, as I did not, nor did I intend so to do. And they who made the interruption were guilty of the breach of that Act, and not I; though upon good enquiry it will be found, the Quakers have not the benefit of that Act, for want of the Qualifications of their Preachers required by the Act.

Mr. *Myles* said I ought to be heard, I being a Missionary into these *American* parts, by the *Society for Propagating the Gospel in Foreign Parts,* sent on purpose to endeavour to reduce the Quakers from their Errors, the which Society hath a Patent from the Crown of *England,* and not to hear me, nor suffer me to speak, was a Contempt of Supream Authority. Some of the Quakers having said that Mr. *Myles* affirmed I was sent by the Queen: I told them I had no immediate Mission from the Queen, and I knew not that ever the Queen (whom God Bless and Preserve) had heard of me. But remotely and mediately my Mission was from the Queen, it being from the *Honourable Society,* who had a Patent from the Crown.

After this I applyed my self to their Governour, Col. *Cranston,* who was there present, and frequents their Meetings, but is no professed Quaker; and I said to him, May it please your Honour to command these Men not to interrupt me, but that I may have a Peaceable hearing among such here present who are desirous to hear me, as indeed many such were, not only of the Church People, but of Independents and Anabaptists, as well as diverse of the Quakers, especially the Younger sort of them. These modest words of mine to the Governour (who is chosen by the People, but is not their Governour by the Queen's immediate appointment) some Quakers have so wrested and falsified in Print, that they have affirmed I spoke to the Governour in a commanding way, to compel the Quakers to hear me, which were neither my Words nor Sense; for I only desired him, that by his Authority I might not be interrupted: And if I be interrupted, it behoved me to complain to the *Honourable Society,* that I could not have liberty to speak in their Meeting, and so, what in them lay, to frustrate the end of my

Mission. For where could I have opportunity to inform them, but in their Meetings? Should I go to their Houses, they would not let me come into them. The Governour, at this, went away, and Civilly said to me, he thought I had done better, to have stayed till they had done. I told him, then they would be gone, as they had served me at *Lynn*, at *Hampton*, and at *Dover*. After the Governour was gone, one of their Speakers, who was the Deputy Governour, and had been formerly their chief Governour, took out of his Pocket a Printed abusive Paper full of Lies, having no Name to it, and began to read it in the Meeting, on purpose to drown my Voice, that I might not be heard. The Title of it was, *One Wonder more:* or *George Keith the eighth Wonder of the World*, Printed at *London* several Years before. Mr. *Myles* said it was an Infamous Libel, without a Name to it, and it was a shame for such a man as he, being Lieutenant Governour in the Place, to read such an Infamous Libel against any Man, on purpose vilely to defame him.

After he had done, another Quaker Preacher, who had been formerly their Governour, began to Preach; he told the Auditory he had read the Scriptures in three Languages, but neither in *Latin*, *Greek*, nor *Hebrew:* but first Literally, secondly Carnally, thirdly Spiritually. He said the Grace [the Light within all Men] was all-sufficient, which he brought as a Proof for its being sufficient to Salvation, without Scripture, or Christ's Blood shed, without us, or any thing else. He also said, it was to as little purpose to Preach to natural Men, or for natural Men to read the Scriptures, as to Four-Footed Beasts; whereby he not only condemned the Practice of the Apostles, who Preached to natural Men, as Christ commanded them; but also he condemned the Practice of the Quaker Preachers, who both Preach, and write Books to natural Men, whom they call the World in order to Convert them to Quakerism; all this, and many other gross falshoods and nonsensical Words he there uttered. And yet all this the Quakers swallow down, as the Infallible dictates of the Light within them, as they pretend; for as *George Whitehead* hath affirmed in his little Book, called, *The Voice of Wisdom, such Ministers who want Infallibility, and speak not from the Infallible Spirit, are no Ministers of Christ.* And *George Fox*, in his *great Mystery*, calls them, *Thieves, Witches, Conjurers, who speak or write, and not from the Infallible Spirit;* surely by this Quaker-test, their greatest Authors and Leaders are no other, whose Discources and Books are full of notorious falsehoods, and contradictions to the holy Scriptures.

At last the first Speaker made a long rambling Prayer, full of Tautoligies, and vain Repetitions, and presumptuous Boastings, as their manner is, after they have vented forth abundance of falshoods in their Preachings, running down the Scriptures and Sacraments, and the Resurrection of the Body after Death, and other great Doctrines of the Christian Religion, they commonly conclude with their Prayers, Blessing God for his glorious presence among them, and his mighty power that has been with them, to assist, refresh, and comfort them, to which the Quaker hearers do frequently echo to them with several sorts of Hummings and Sounds, whereby to Seal to the Truth not only of the Words, but of the mighty Power and Life that has attended their Speakers. But while they utter such falshoods and contradictions to holy Scriptures, as also such uncharitable Speeches against all other Communions and ways of Worship, and Ministry, but their own; it is impossible that they can be acted by any divine Life or Power to do this: And yet some Power more than ordinary doth frequently Act them, in their Speakings, and commonly works most strongly among them, when they are vehemently running down the necessity of the Scriptures, or the Sacraments, and Preaching up the sufficiency of the Light within them to Salvation, without any thing else, as I have oft observed. The strong impression their Speakings in their Meetings frequently have (or used to have more formerly than of late) upon their Hearers; manifestly to be observed by the visible effects of it upon many of them, causing them, some to shed Tears in plenty, some to shake and Quake, some to utter deep Groans, others to Sing; sufficiently prove that some Power, more than ordinary, doth at times Act them, and this Power doth at times Act and Operate among them, and in them, in a total silence of Words, (as well as when they utter words) in their Assemblies, of which they glory not a little. The most tolerable Construction that can be made of this Power, what it is, or whence it proceeds, seeing it can be no Divine Power, is, that it is some strong natural Enthusiasm, raised by heighth of fancy, and exalted imagination, such as Mr. *Causabon* has described in his Treatise of *Enthusiasm.* But then it must needs be granted, that when they are Acted so furiously and outragiously, to contradict the plainest Doctrines of Christianity, and defame and reproach Christ's sacred Institutions, that Satan acts together with this Power of *Strong Fancy* and *Imagination,* and makes use of it, as its Organ and Instrument, or Conduit of Conveyance. For it's hardly to be conceived, how a meer natural or Animal Power, without the influence of some Diabolical Spirit, can act Men with such zeal and industry to Preach and Propagate most destructive Errors to Mens Perdition. Seeing, according to Holy Scripture, the Devil is the Father of Lies; and all Damnable Doctrines, are the Doctrines of Devils; of which they have a great many, as their Words and Books plainly shew. Immediately after their Prayers, all their Preachers went away, and many of the Quaker Hearers, but many of them also stayed, especially the Younger sort, both Men and Women; and generally all the People who were not Quakers, both those of the Church, and those called Independents and Anabaptists stayed. I told their Preachers, as they were making hast to be gone, it was a shame to them to go away, and leave so many of their Sheep exposed to the *Wolf,* as they have affirmed me to be, but I thank God I am none; but by their own Argument, by their so flying and running away, do not they prove themselves not to be true Shepherds, but Hirelings?

I had now full liberty without any interruption to speak, perceiving the Auditory generally desirous to hear me. I recollected and resumed most of the heads of their discourse, such as I could remember, and the Texts of Scripture, which they had grossly perverted and misapplied, and refuted their Perversions and Falshoods; and thus I continued some considerable time speaking in their Meeting-House, having a considerable large Auditory, all very attentive. Before I had made an end, diverse of the Quaker Preachers returned, and stood quietly and heard me, but said nothing, neither made they any offer to dispute any matter with me. I was informed by some credible Persons, that the occasion of their Preachers returning to the Meeting, while I was speaking, was, that some Quaker Zelot-Women went to their Preachers, and told them, it would greatly reflect on them, to absent themselves while I was speaking in their Meeting-House, and might expose the Weak Friends to be deceived by me. However after their return, they said nothing, but suffered me to proceed in speaking as long as I thought fit; and thus our Meeting ended Peaceably.

The Quakers had Built a new Meeting-House at *Newport*, large enough to hold Five Hundred Persons, or more, with fair and large Galleries, and Forms or Benches below. But one thing very singular I observed, that on the Top of the Turret of their Meeting-House, they have a perfect *Iron Cross*, two large Iron Bars crossing one the other at right Angles, a more perfect Cross I never saw any where on any Church. I mention this the rather, because *George Fox*, in some of his Printed Pamphlets, makes a great outcry and noise against the *Steeple Houses* in *England*, as he calls them, for having Crosses on the Tops of them, and that it is Popery; what can the Quakers say to this? Are their Brethren of *Rhod-Island* guilty of Popery, for having the Cross on the top of their Meeting-House, which I suppose remains there to this day?

August 9, 1702. Sunday. I Preached at *Newport* on *Rhod-Island*, my Text was *Job.* 1. 9. and I had a very numerous Auditory, not only of the People of the Town, but of many that came from other parts of the *Island* with a desire to hear me. I told my Auditory after I had concluded my Sermon, that I was to have a publick Meeting the 14th Instant at the Colony House in *Newport*, to detect the Quakers Errors out of the Printed Books of their chief Authors, and that I had obtained leave of the chief Governour Collonel *Cranston* to keep the Meeting in that House; and that I was to give notice to the Quaker Preachers to meet me there about the first Hour after Noon, if they thought fit to defend their Principles and Authors.

August 10. I sent a written Paper to the Quaker Preachers there, to meet me at the Place and Time abovementioned, to which they sent me their Answer soon after, that they would meet me, so that things should be carried fairly, and each Party should have liberty to speak an Hour without interruption, and two Moderators should be chosen, each on a side, to keep good order; to which I consented, though I told them, an hour at once was too long, yet I would yield to their Proposition, rather than that the Meeting should fail.

August 14. We Met about the first Hour after Noon, the time appointed: They allowed me to begin my Charge against them, and the Hour Glass was turned to measure the time. I brought with me *George Fox's* Book, called the *Great Mystery*, and diverse other Quaker Books, *viz. Richard Claridge* his Book, called, *Lux Evangelica Attestata*, and Mr. *Pen's* Book, called, *Primitive Christianity.* I spent my first Hour mostly in reading to them, and to the Auditory, which were some Hundreds of People, both of the Town and Country, many Quotations out of *George Fox's* great Mystery, full of most dreadful Errors and Heresies, and detecting the gross absurdity of them, contradicting the Holy Scriptures; and in the conclusion, before my hour was quite spent, I told them, I was to expect from them a particular answer to each Quotation I had read to them, and I proffered to them, that if they questioned my true Reading, they might Read them, laying the Book open before them. And for better Method's sake, I offered to Read again the quotations to them singly one by one, and let them give their Answer to each single quotation, whether they owned them to be according to their Principles, yes, or no, seeing *George Fox* was the first and most Authentic Author among them, whom the Quakers at *London* have in Print called, the *Apostle of this Age.* But instead of any such performance by them, to the great disappointment of all the Auditory who were not Quakers, nor Quakerly affected, such as the far greatest part of the Auditory was not, they gave not the least Answer directly, or indirectly, to any one of the quotations I had read to them, nor gave they any reason of excuse why they declined to give any Answer to them. But as they had projected it before hand, one of chief Note among their Speakers, *viz.* the Deputy Governour abovementioned, did read to the Auditory, the Printed sheet, called, the *Christianity of the People called Quakers*, &c. and after that was fully read, he read one or two other scurrilous Libels, having no Name to them, that some Quakers had Printed against me, about the Year 1700, when I joined to the Church of *England*, one of which was that abovementioned, called, *One Wonder more: or George Keith the eighth Wonder of the World.* Having thus spent their Hour, all their Speakers rose up to be gone, pretending the Agreement was but for two Hours in all, which I denied; and the Moderator chosen by them, to whom I appealed, gave it against them, that the time was not limited to two Hours in all, but to one Hour to one side at a time.

So I began my second Hour, and I first shewed how unfair and unreasonable they were, to give no Answer to my Charges I had given out of *George Fox*, and other approved Authors, with whom they pretend to be one in Doctrine, and that they are not varied in a tittle from their first Principles; but *as God is the same, and the Truth is the same, so his People* (the Quakers) *are the same;* so one of their approved Authors has lately Printed in his Book at *London;* after this I proceeded to reply to what was fit to be said, to those Printed Libels, their chief Speaker had read against me. And first, as to the Printed sheet, called, *The Christianity of the People called Quakers*, asserted (as they say) by *George Keith;* which is a deceitful contrivance of the Quakers, as if I had composed that sheet in form and manner as it is there Printed, which is altogether false. The sheet, I grant, contains some quotations, collected by the Quakers out of my former Books many Years ago, when I was among them; all which, so far as they were contrary to sound Doctrine contained in the holy Scripture, I had in Print retracted several Years ago; and therefore they did not now affect me. Though none of those quotations, however erroneous, contradict the Foundation of the Christian Faith, concerning our Blessed Saviour Jesus Christ, his Person, and twofold Nature, and Offices of Prophet, Priest, and King, and the necessity of Faith in him, as he outwardly came in the Flesh, died for our Sins, and rose again, &c. in order to Mens Salvation. Whereas the System of Quakerism, set forth in *George Fox's* great Mystery, and other Quaker Authors, is a point blank contradiction to this Faith.

Next, As to their Printed Libel, called, *One Wonder more*, &c. having no Name to it of any Person or People, I was not obliged to take notice of it; and it contained several notorious falshoods, as that I had said, in the Book called, *Help in time of Need*, that I had taken the *Scots* League and Covenant, and that Libeller positively charges me with having taken it, both which are utterly false; for I being Born in the Year 1638, I was not capable of taking it, when it was given, *viz.* about the Year 1643, by reason of my *non-age*, and it was never given in a National way since, in *Scotland*, that I know of: Again, that Libeller falsely accuseth me that I had said, I was not changed in my Perswasion in any thing since I had left the Quakers, from what I had, when among them. For, on the contrary, I have owned in Print that I was changed in my Perswasion and Judgment in several things, and had Printed a Book of Retractation of many Errors I had been in, whilst I was among them. But, I thank God, I never had the worst of their Errors, nor any (that I can remember) that contradicted the necessity of Faith in Christ Jesus, who is both God and Man, in order to Mens Salvation, to which the Quakers Fundamental Principle, *that the Light within them is sufficient to Salvation without any thing else*, is a perfect contradiction. This vile Antichristian notion that sets up Deism, and overturns the Christian Faith, I never had, and I challenge my greatest Adversaries to prove it against me. Let the Quakers Retract and Renounce their Errors, as I have done mine, to God's Praise, who has so enabled me, and I shall no more charge them therewith. And whereas they had upbraided me with my changing, I told them many Quakers had made as great changes as I had, and particularly *Richard Claridge*, now a great Author among them, who was first an Episcopal Preacher, then an Anabaptist Preacher, and now a Quaker Preacher.

After I had thus replyed to their malicious Libels Read against me, I proceeded to read diverse other Quotations out of *Richard Claridge's Lux Evangelica*, and Mr. *Pen's Primitive Christianity*, and so continued detecting the gross absurdity of their assertions, till my second Hour was almost spent; and I renewed my demand to them, to give their Answer to what I had further both read and said in my second Hour.

But nothing did they say, to any one thing I had said; but after a long time of silence, they began to Preach, one after another, after their common way, intermixing therewith false accusations against me, that I did pervert their Friends Words, and charged them falsely, but did not give one Instance to prove I had done so. And after they had continued their second Hour, Preaching and Railing against me, they went away.

Before the People that were not Quakers went away, I told them, I purposed to have another publick Meeting in the same place the 17th Instant, to begin about Eight a Clock in the forenoon, to detect the Quakers great Errors, particularly in their rejecting the Divine Institutions of Baptism and the Lord's Supper; and of this I gave notice to the Quaker Preachers, desiring them to come and defend themselves if they could, they should have a fair hearing; but not one of them came. However many People of the Town came, both Church People and Dissenters, who (with great attention and satisfaction) heard me prove the Divine Institution of both Baptism and the Lord's Supper, and refute the Quakers Idle and absurd evasions and glosses, whereby they use to pervert the plain Texts of Scripture upon those heads, as they do upon all others controverted by them.

And here I think fit to give a List, or Catalogue, of the chief and most scandalous quotations I did read to the Quakers and Auditory present, at the abovesaid Meeting at *Newport* on *Rhod-Island*, out of *George Fox* his Great Mystery, *Richard Claridge* his *Lux Evang. attest.* and Mr. *Pen's* Primitive Christianity.

The Quotations out of *George Fox's* Great Mystery, &c.

I. Pag. 246. Christ, God and Man, Flesh and Spirit, is in the Quakers.

II. Pag. 149. Whole Christ, God and Man, is in Men.

III. Pag. 211. Christ is not absent from his Church, as touching his Flesh.

IV. Pag. 322. The Flesh of Christ is in them, because they Eat it.

V. Pag. 322. The Flesh of Christ came down from above.

VI. Pag. 250. And the Devil was in thee, and thou saith, thou art saved by Christ without thee, and so hast recorded thy self to be a Reprobate.

VII. Pag. 246. He Quotes *Isai.* 9. 6. to prove, that God the Father took upon him Man's Nature.

VIII. Page 9. He will not allow, that Christ is to come to Judgment without us, at the end of the World; but saith, Christ is come to *Judgment* and he blames his Opponent, for having any such expectation;—*who are come to Christ the Light, the Life, they need not go forth*, viz. to look for a Christ without them.

IX. Page 350. The Scriptures are not the means, nor the Rule of Faith. The means of Salvation is not ordinary, nor outward.

X. Pag. 302. The Spirit is the Rule, saith Christ.

XI. Page 229. He blames the Ministers of *New-Castle*, and saith, they are not fit to be Ministers who know not the State of Souls from Eternity to Eternity.

XII. Page 281, and 318. He pleads for a Perfection in fulness, above any degree, before the death of the Body; and saith, he witnessed it. And pag. 282, 197. He pleads for a Perfection, as God is Perfect, in *equality* and not in *quality* only. Like to this is what he saith to his Opponent.

Pag. 67. Again: Thou makest a great pudder, that any one should witness he is *equal* with God. And in his Answer he proves his equality with God against his Opponent, from the *Westminster* Catechism.

Pag. 127. He giveth the same Proof that he *is equal with God*, from the Assemblies Catechism made at *Westminster;* his Opponent being some Presbyterian or Independent, who owned that Catechism: But that Catechism doth not say, that *George Fox*, or any meer Man, was equal with God; but that the Son, and the Holy Ghost, are equal with God the Father; which is orthodox Doctrine. But the Mystery of *George Fox's* Argument did conflict in this, that he was the Son, and consequently he was equal with God. The dispute betwixt him and his Opponent, was not, whether the Son, *viz.* the second Person of the Holy Trinity, was equal with God the Father, for his Opponent owned that.

XIII. Pag. 73. None can know Christ by the Scriptures.

Pag. 168. Them that never heard the Scripture outwardly, the Light that every Man hath that cometh into the World, being turned to it, with that they will see Christ, with that they will know Scripture, with that they will be led out of all delusions, come into Covenant with God, with which they will come to Worship God in the Spirit, and serve him.

Pag. 47. The Light in Men sufficient to Salvation, without the help of any other means or discovery.

XIV. The Quakers are the only Ministers of Christ, since the Apostles days.

The Quotations I did then read out of a Book of *Richard Claridge*, called *Lux Evangelica attestata.*

I. Pag. 17, 18, 19. He saith God doth afford to all Men, even in the ordinary way of his Providence, such a manifestation of his Light or Spirit, as is sufficient to lead and Guide the *Faithful* into all truth necessary to Salvation, without Scripture. Note, by *Faithful*, he means *Faithful to the Light within* them, who have not the Scripture.

II. Pag. 49. Faith in Christ, as outwardly, (he saith) is no essential part of the Christian Religion.

III. Pag. 26. He denies that Christ's Body is the same in Substance he had on Earth.

IV. Pag. 90. He justifies that Assertion of Mr. *Pen*, in his Preface to Mr. *Barclaye's* Folio Book, pag. 36. Oh Friends! great is the Mystery of Godliness, God manifest in the Flesh; —— and if that be a Mystery, how much more is the Work of Regeneration a Mystery, that is wholly inward and Spiritual. And to confirm it, the said *R. C.* calls Christ within the Mystery of that Mystery, *viz.* of Christ without.

The Quotations I did then read out of Mr. *Pen's Primitive Christianity.*

I. Pag. 30. Concerning the *Light within* all Men, he saith: If it reveal God, (which he affirms from *Rom.* 2. *ver.* 7, to 17. in pag. 73, 74.) to be sure it manifests Christ.

II. Page 50, to 55. The Heathens have the same Light in them, that true Christians have.

III. Pag. 78. All Religion is but one in the many modes and shapes of it: if Men be obedient to the Light within. Note, this takes away all real and substantial distinction betwixt Deism, and Christianity, and betwixt natural and revealed Religion.

August 16, Sunday. I Preached in the Church at *Newport* on *Rhod-Island*, on *Acts* 26. 18. having Preached on the same Text, the *Wednesday* foregoing, in the same plaae.

August 24. Being the Tenth Day after the Conference I had with the Quakers at *Newport* on *Rhod-Island*, a Quaker Preacher Woman, living at *Newport*, who has been a Speaker in the Quakers Meeting upwards of Forty Years, writ a long Letter to me, which I have by me, where, after diverse severe Charges against me, in meer generals, she blames me for saying to the Quaker Preachers at *Portsmouth*, which is at the other end of the *Island*, where I went to visit them, at their Meeting there *August* the 13*th*, that they did not Preach Christ enough, as he was outwardly Crucified and lifted up on the Tree of the Cross; and whereas I had said unto them, that they should direct their Hearers, to look by Faith to Christ, as he was Crucified, and lifted up on the Tree of the Cross, in order to be spiritually healed, as the *Israelites* in the Wilderness were directed by *Moses* to look to the *Brasen Serpent*, to be healed Bodily, after they were bit by Serpents there, for which I had quoted *Job.* 3. 14. This most ignorant Woman Preacher, in her said Letter to me, denies that the lifting up of Christ in *Job.* 3. 14, is to be meant of his lifting up on the Tree of the Cross, or that People should be directed to him for healing, as he was there lifted up.

To overthrow my assertion she gives diverse Reasons.

I. That lifting up, *Job.* 3. 14. is the same with that whereof he said, I, when I am lifted up, will draw all Men after me: but that was not his lifting up on the Cross.

II. The Enemies of God, did lift him upon the Tree, &c.

III. He is not now upon the Tree, nor did he long stay there.

IV. It would be a great fallacy, and known Error, for any to Preach to People, that they should look for him upon the Tree, seeing he is not there, but risen.

Some time after I received her Letter, I writ an answer to her, and laboured therein to convince her of her gross ignorance, as well as of perverting both my Words and Sense, as if what I had said to the Quaker Preachers at *Portsmouth*, where she was present, that they were to Preach to People, to direct them to look to Christ for healing, as he was lifted up on the Tree, did purport, that they were to go on Foot to *Jerusalem*, to look to him with their Bodily Eyes, than which there could be no greater perversion of Words. And if this be not a wilful perversion in her, she is most extreamly ignorant, to think that there can be no looking to Christ, as he suffered on the Tree of the Cross, but by the bodily sight, seeing it is very common in Scripture, to express Faith in God and in Christ by looking to him.

And her pretended Argument from *Job.* 11. 32. is most evidently against her, for that his lifting up, *Job.* 12. 32. is to be understood, his lifting up on the Tree, whereon he was Crucified, is clear from V. 33. *This he said, signifying what manner of Death he should Die.* She was so mightily pleased with her Letter to me, that lest it should miscarry, some Months after I received it in *Pensilvania*, she sent me a duplicate of it, as if it had been some Jewel.

This Letter of hers is a fresh Instance, beside many more, to prove that the Quakers have no real devout regard to Christ, as he suffered Death for our Sins, and rose again without us, &c. in order to our Salvation, as the necessary object of Faith. They do commonly say, they believe all that is written of Christ, his Birth of the Virgin, his Life, Miracles, Death, Burial, Resurrection, Ascension, &c. But the fallacy lies here, that all this Faith (they say) is but Historical, and not the saving Faith; they believe it as they believe any other History, but they think it not necessary to Salvation, and that because it is necessary, it is to be Preached; nay, *George Whitehead* a great Author among them, hath said in his Book, called, *Light and Life, That to confide in Christ without us, is contrary to* Deut. 30, *and* Rom. 10. And the like he saith in *Truth defending.* And as plainly as any of them, Mr. *Pen* hath declared himself, *Quakerism a new nickname,* &c. pag. 6. *Faith* (saith he) in *the History of Christ's outward manifestation is a deadly Poison these latter Ages have been inflicted with to the destruction of godly living.*

August 23, Sunday. I Preached at *Naraganset,* (that lyes on the Continent, but is not far from *Rhod-Island*) at the House of Mr. *Opdyke's* where I had a considerable Auditory, my Text was *Titus* 2. 11. The People there are very desirous, that a Church of *England* Minister be sent to them.

August 27. I Preached at *Little Compton,* alias *Seaconot,* that lyes on the Continent also, not far from the *Island,* at the House of *Henry Head,* where I had a large Auditory; my Text was *Jer.* 31. 33. They are there also very desirous, that a Minister be sent to them. Mr. *Lockyer* went a long with me, and read the Prayers at both Places.

August 30, 1702. Sunday. Being accompanied with Mr. *Lockyer*, we crossed the Ferry at *Portsmouth* in the Morning, in order to be at *Swansey*, on the Continent, to Preach there, as accordingly I did; Mr. *Lockyer* read the Prayers; there was a large Auditory. My Text was 1 *Thess*. 1. 5. They greatly desire a Minister to be sent unto them.

As we were crossing the Ferry at *Portsmouth* on *Rhod-Island*, by the good Providence of God we escaped a great danger; we had essayed to cross the Ferry the Day before, but the Wind was so strong, it was not safe to try it, hoping the next day would be more Calm; but the Wind little abated the next day, so that both Wind, and Sea, were very boisterous; when we were about half over the Ferry (that is of a considerable breadth) our Mast and Sail were beat down by the Wind, the Mast at its fall, touched gently my shoulder, and did me no harm; we had no ability to get up our Sail again, there being but one Negroe Man to manage the Boat, and we were in all three Passengers, and having three Horses in the Boat. So for some time we remained there much tossed by the Waves of the Sea, and were in danger to be driven out to the Sea and overwhelmed. After some time a Boat came off from Land to help us, and to Tow us to Land. But the Rope they gave us broke, and the Rope we gave them did also break, and so we were left helpless. But a Quaker of my former acquaintance, whose Name is *John Burden*, who had also a Ferry-Boat, came with all Speed in his Boat to relieve us, and Towed us to Land, having several able Men with him in the Boat, to manage her. After we landed, I offered Money to his Men, but he would not permit them to receive any. I thanked him very kindly for his help in our great Danger, and said to him, *John*, ye have been a means under God to save our natural Life, suffer me to be a means under God to save your Soul, by good information to bring you out of your dangerous Errors. He replyed, *George, save thy own Soul, I have no need of thy help*; then, said I, I will pray for your Conversion; he replyed, the Prayers of the Wicked are an abomination; so uncharitable was he in his opinion concerning me, (as they generally are, concerning all who differ from them) though Charitable in this action.

The next Day, we crossed the Ferry in his Boat: After our landing he entertained us civilly at his House, with whom I had much Discourse, and I laboured much to inform him, how that the Quakers Principle, *that the Light within every Man was sufficient to Salvation without any thing else*, did plainly overthrow the Christian Faith, and set up meer *Deism* or *Heathenism* in the room of Christianity. But I could not prevail to convince him. He had a great many of the Quakers Printed Books lying in a Window in his House, which I looked upon, and asked him that he would sell them to me, for they would be useful to me in that Country; but he earnestly refused, and said, I should not have them, though I should give double Money for them: Why, said I? Because (said he) thou wilt do Mischief with them; he meant, that I would expose the Quakers Principles, and make them known, what they are, out of their own Books; which the Quakers are loath should be known, and therefore when Quotations are produced out of their Books, though ever so fairly Quoted, they use confidently to deny, there are any such in their Books, when the Books are not present to lay before them.

September 6, 1702. Sunday. I Preached again at *Newport* on *Rhod*-

Island, on *Job.* 12. 36. Mr. *Talbot* also Preached there several times, and commonly wherever we Travelled, the one of us Preached in the Fore-noon on the *Sundays*, and the other in the After-noon, except when the days were short, that there was no Sermon usual in the Afternoon ; and sometimes, for the greater Service in diverse places, one Preached in one part, and one in another, at the same time.

The time that we remained at *Newport*, on *Rhod-Island*, Mr. *Carr*, and Mr. *Laiton*, Inhabitants on the *Island*, both of them of the Church of *England*, and of good repute among their Neighbours, shewed us several Commissions in writing, given to them, by Quaker Governours, with their Hands and Seals affixed, Commissionating them to be Military Officers, to fight against the *Indians*, and *French*, in the times of the several Wars the *English* had with them ; to Kill and destroy their Enemies. The Quaker Governours Names, who gave these Commissions to several, to be Military Officers in the Quaker Government, whose Commissions in the Original Signed and Sealed by them, we saw, and read, are, 1. *William Coddington.* 2. *Walter Clark.* 3. *John Eston.* 4. *Henry Bull*, all Preachers but the first ; *Walter Clark*, and *John Eston*, were alive when we were there, and I suppose still are alive, the other two were dead ; true Copies of which Commissions, are now in the Custody of a Person of Quality in *England*, and can be produced if occasion require it. This I thought fit to make known, that it may evidently appear, how contrary the Quakers Practice, where they have the Government, is, to their professed Principle, that it is unlawful to them, to fight with a Carnal Weapon, so much as in their own defence. The like Commission I have seen in the Original, given by some Quaker Magistrates at *Philadelphia*, in *Pensilvania*, about fifteen Years ago, giving three Persons, there Commissions to be Captains, to go with their Companies to recover a Sloop by force of Arms, that some Privateers had stolen out of the Harbour.

That it is the Quakers professed Principle that they cannot Fight, or Kill, in their own defence, is evident from seueral Declarations of their Leaders and Authors in Print, but especially from Mr. *Pen's Key*, which has been oft reprinted. In Pag. 34, 35. he saith, They (i. e. the Quakers) cannot Kill or slay their own kind ; for Proof of which he quotes 2 *Cor.* 10. 3, 5. *The Weapons of our Warfare are not Carnal, &c.* This again was contradicted by the Quakers Practice in *Pensilvania*, who by his Authority or Allowance put several Persons to Death judicially, for suspected Murthers. (to several of which they had no Evidence made either by Witness, or by their Confession, whom they caused to be put to death.) And as to that Text Mr. *Pen* has quoted in his *Key*, 2 *Cor.* 10. 3, 5. for a Reason why the Quakers cannot use a Carnal Weapon. *Query*, Is not a Gallows, or Gibbet, on which the Quaker Judges in *Pensilvania* (some of which were Preached also) caused some to be hanged for suspected Murther, a Carnal Weapon as really as a Sword, Gun, or Spear ?

The like Contradiction, the Quakers are guilty of, in their late common Practice, of their Solemn calling God to Witness about worldly matters, contrary to their Professed Principle, published in Print by Mr. *Pen*, and several other Quakers, in their Treatise of Oaths. In that Book Mr. *Pen* saith, *To attest the Name of God in any Terrestrial Matter, is a breach of Christ's Command, Matt.* 5. 34, 37.

Again, in Mr. *Pen's Key*, which hath had several impressions (Pag. 36. of one impression) he saith, *The Quakers can go no further than Yea, and Nay,* [*viz.* in their declarations in Civil Judicatures, &c.] This Mr. *Pen* knoweth is contradicted, (if not by himself) by the frequent practice of Quakers, both in *England* and *America*, who, beyond their Yea, and Nay, solemnly call God to Witness in their affirmations before Magistrates, which, in the judgment of the most judicious, is the substance of an Oath, and without all controversie is more than Yea, and Nay. And this the prevailing Party of the Quakers in *England* have not only practised, but with no small endeavour have Petitioned to be granted unto them, by Act of Parliament, and which they have obtained. It is true, there is a small Party of Quakers opposite to this Practice, who think it is a going off from their Ancient Testimony of Yea, and Nay. But the other Party has carried it against them. And yet they would have it believed, they are all in perfect Unity of Principles, whereas they are much divided, as in their Principles about Swearing and Fighting, so in diverse others. A Quaker of good Note among them, has not only declared for Baptism, as being an Institution of Christ, but has actually received it, but not by any Minister of the Church of *England*, (as I am informed) which I wish he had done, if he was not formerly Baptized. I am also informed, that he has declared his mind concerning the Lord's Supper, that it is of Divine Institution. I hope God in due time will further enlighten him to see, how grosly the Quakers have erred in other things, as much as in their throwing away those Two Divine Institutions, and calling them, worldly Rudiments and beggarly Elements, which Mr. *Pen* said, in Print, *The Quakers have been led to reject by the same Spirit by which Paul* (*and the Apostles*) *were led to reject Circumcision ;* yet I have not heard that the Quakers have cast him out of their Communion, for his taking up, what both he, and they, had so long thrown away. I hope he is not of his Brethrens Opinion, that *the Light within him, and within all Men, is sufficient to Salvation, without any thing else ;* for if he were, I cannot see, what need he could think he had, either of Baptism, or the Lord's Supper, or of the Scriptures, or of Christ without him, and his precious Blood, and Sacrifice upon the Cross for our Sins, and his continual Intercession for us in Heaven with the Father ; all which are something else, than the Light within him.

I happened in *America*, while I was there Travelling, to see a Book lately Printed, called *New-England* Judged, having a Printed Appendix to it, by *John Whiting* Quaker, who has set up of late for a great Author among them, and who is extreamly ignorant as well as confident, to utter Falshoods and abusive Slanders. In his said Appendix, he utters a notorious Falshood upon me, as if at *Philadelphia*, about the Year 1692, I had fained my self a Prisoner, and to make this Fiction to be believed, I had gone to the Porch of the Prison, the Prison door being shut against me, and from the Porch of the Prison, had writ and dated a Paper of complaint against the Quakers for my imprisonment ; and to make his Reader take the greater notice of it, he has caused the following Words to be printed on the Margin in great Black Letters ; *Note, George Keith's-Mock Imprisonment.* Now to prove the notorious falshood of this, I need go no further than a Book of one of his Brethren, *viz. Samuel Jennings*, Printed at *London* 1694, called by him, *The State of the Case, &c.* wherein, though he has uttered many falshoods, concerning the State of the Case, about our differences in Principles of Religion, in the Years 1691, and 1692, whereof I had largely detected him in my Printed Reply to his Book; yet he saith true, in what he did Report in his Book, concerning two Persons, whom the Quakers had put in Prison, the one for Printing a sheet of mine, I called an *Appeal*, &c. and the other for selling one or two of them when Printed; the Name of the Printer is *William Bradford*, the Name of the other is *John Mackcomb*. Now concerning them the said Quaker, *Samuel Jennings*, Reports, that *they signed a Paper from the Prison, when they signed it in the Entry common to the Prison, and the next House.* Thus he gives the true matter of Fact, and tells truly who Signed that Paper in the Entry or Porch, which were those two abovenamed persons, but mentions not me, as being concerned in Signing that Paper, either in the Entry or Porch, or any where else. And to be sure if I had been one of the Persons, who had Signed that Paper, he would have told the World of it, as thereby thinking to have some great matter against me. For he chargeth it upon these two abovenamed Persons, *William Bradford*, and *John Mackcomb*, that it was deceit in them *to Sign a Paper from the Prison, when they were not in the Prison*, but in the Porch or Entry of it, as he saith. In my Answer to him, I have shewed it was no deceit, nor had any thing blame-worthy; the Case was this. They were Prisoners by a Warrant from some Quaker Justices, for the Fact abovementioned, and had been detained in Prison for some time, and were ordered to be kept in Prison until the next Court, unless they gave security by Bonds to Answer at the next Court. After some time the Jaylor by favour let them go home, but still they were Prisoners, not being released by any Judicatory; and the Quaker Justices delaying to bring them to a Tryal, they went to the Prison to Write, and Sign their Petition from the Prison, to have their Tryal at the next Sessions; but it happened that the Jaylor was gone abroad, and had the Key to the Prison with him, so that they could not get in. Now I see no deceit or insincerity in this, more than in the common Practice of many Quakers, who have printed Records of their suffering Imprisonment (for not paying Tithes) some Years, and yet they oft had liberty to go home, by favour of the Jaylors, to my certain Knowledge. But whether *William Bradford* and *John Mackcomb*, were guilty of deceit or not, is not material to the present Case of *John Whiting* his Vile Slander, as if I had been the Person, or one of the Persons, who had Writ that Paper from the Porch or Entry of the Prison. This is sufficient Proof, that what *John Whiting* has thus Printed against me, was not from the infallible Spirit, and that he is therefore by *George Fox's* Sentence, a Deceiver.

September 10, 1702. We came from *Newport* on *Rhod-Island* and crossed the Ferry over to *Naraganset*, and lodged that Night at Mr. *Balfures* House, who Entertained us very kindly and hospitably, and next day we Travelled about 25 Miles, and lodg'd at Mr. *Sextons*, an Inn-keeper; and next day we safely arrived at *New-London* in *Connecticot* Colony, and Government, which stands by a Navigable River.

Septemb. 13, Sunday. Mr. *Talbot* Preached there in the Forenoon, and I Preached there in the Afternoon, we being desired so to do by the Minister, Mr. *Gurdon Saltenstall*, who civilly Entertained us at his House, and expressed his good affection to the Church of *England*, as did also the

Minister at *Hampton*, and the Minister at *Salisbury* abovementioned, and diverse others *New-England* Ministers did the like. My Text was *Rom.* 8. 9. The Auditory was large, and well affected. Col. *Winthrop*, Governour of the Colony, after Forenoon Sermon, invited us to Dinner at his House, and kindly Entertained us, both then, and the next day.

Sept. 15, 1702. We hired a sloop to carry us from *New-London* to *Long-Island* over the Sound, being about Six Leagues Broad, and that day we safely arrived at a Place on *Long-Island*, called, *Oyster-Ponds*, about Noon, after that we came on Horseback that Day 24 Miles, and lodged at Mr. *Howel's* an Inn-keeper, the next Day we Travelled 45 Miles, to *Seatalket*, and lodged at Mr. *Gibs*, Innkeeper; the next Day, being the 17th Instant, we Travelled 32 Miles, all upon *Long-Island*, and arrived at *Oysterbay*, where we were kindly received, and hospitally entertained by Mr. *Edward White* at his House, on free cost, for several Days, where we staid to rest and refresh us. He was a Justice of Peace, and had been formerly a Quaker, and his Wife had been a Quaker also, and was not quite come off from the Quakers.

Septemb. 20, Sunday. At the Request of Mr. *Edward White*, and some other Neighbours in the Town, having used the Church Prayers before Sermon, I Preached on *Titus* 2. 11, 12. And that Day Mr. *Talbot* Baptized a Child, at the request of the Child's Mother, her Husband being from home.

Septemb. 24, 1705. I went to the Quakers Meeting at *Flushing* on *Long-Island*, accompanied with Mr. *Talbot* and the Reverend Mr. *Vesey*, the Church of *England* Minister at *New-York*, and diverse other Persons belonging to *Jamaica* (a *Town on Long-Island*,) well affected to the Church of *England*. After some time of silence, I began to speak, standing up in the Gallery, where their Speakers use to stand when they speak; but I was so much interrupted by the Clamour and Noise, that several of the Quakers made, forbidding me to speak, that I could not proceed. After this, one of their Speakers began to Speak, and continued Speaking about an Hour, the whole was a ramble of nonsense and perversion of Scripture, with gross reflections both on the Church, and the Government there. Several times speaking of Christ, he said, *while Christ was in that Prepared Body*, which is a common Phrase among them; whereby they plainly intimate, they do not believe he is now in that Body, or that he has any thing of that Body, which he had on Earth. Nor do they own that Christ has any Body but his Church, or such a Body as he had from all Eternity, and is every where; all which hath been sufficiently proved out of the Printed Books of their most noted Authors. He said, they (*viz.* the Quakers) believed in that very Christ that died at *Jerusalem;* and a little after he said, that, that Christ, was the Seed that was oppressed by Sin in Men.' He Preached against all Creeds, and accused all their Adversaries that they kicked against the Spirit. This was a reflexion upon the Church of *England*, because she doth not hold, that Men have those extraordinary Gifts of the Spirit, to Preach, and Pray, as the Quaker Preachers pretend to have; but as they have it not, it is evident they have an extraordinary impudence to father all their ignorant and nonsensical Expressions, and perversions of Scripture, (which they commonly utter in their Meetings) upon the Holy Ghost, which is a most dreadful Sin. He said, Vice was set up, which was a reflexion upon the Government there, because some were lately made Justices of the Peace on *Long-Island*, that were not greatly affected to Quakerism. After he had done, he went away out of the Meeting in all hast, fearing (I suppose) he should be questioned about the things he had said. I stood up again to speak in their Meeting, but they made a new interruption, and threatened me with being guilty of the breach of the Act of Toleration, and that by my so doing, I had put my self Twenty Pounds in the Queen's Debt; I told them, I had not broke the Act of Toleration, for I made no interruption, but was silent all the while their Preacher was speaking; but they had broke the Act of Toleration, by interrupting me, when I began to Speak; they told me, I had no right to Speak in their Meetings. I answered, I had better right to Speak in these Meeting-Houses, than any of their Speakers had; at this they seemed greatly to Wonder; and asked how I could make that appear, for the House and Ground was theirs, which they had bought with their Mony, and to which I had contributed nothing: And one of them was so hot, that he commanded me to go out of the House, for it was his House, and for me to stay in his House, against his Will, was contrary to Law, and he could Prosecute me. I Answered him, it was not his Property; all who have a Mind to come into that House at Meeting time, may come, it being appointed for a Religious Meeting-House, where all have a common Right; and according to the Act of Toleration, ye are bound to keep your Doors open where ye Meet; and if ye shut them against me, or any, we may prosecute you by Law. But, said they, How has thou a better right to speak in our Meeting-House than we? I told them, in a double respect: First, that Meeting-House was appointed for the service of Truth, (which is their own manner of Phrase,) and that what was Truth, should be spoken in it, and not falshood and error; and therefore, while I speak Truth in it, and your Speakers speak not Truth, but falshood and errors, I have a better right than they. Secondly, None of your Speakers have any right to Speak in your Meeting-Houses, because ye have not your Meeting-Houses Licensed, as the Act of Toleration expressly requires; nor have any of your Preachers qualified themselves as that Act express, *viz.* to Sign to Thirty-four of the Articles of Religion of the Church of *England;* this they have not done, nor can do, because the Quakers Principles are contrary to most of them, or rather indeed to them all, whereas I am qualified, as the Act requires. They accused me, that I came not in Love to Preach to them, but was hired by the Bishops to come, and that the Love of Money brought me to *America*, and not Love to their Souls. I told them it was a false accusation.

I owned it, that God had raised up Friends to assist me with Money, in such a chargeable Undertaking; but this was no more than what the Quakers at *London* did, who largely supply the Travelling Friends who come over from *England* into *America*, with Money out of their National Stock, beside what they gather up in the several Meetings in *America*, which they visit. They replyed, they never knew any Mony given to any Travelling Friends, by their Meeting. And they asked me, if I had any Mony from them, while I was a Travelling Friend among them? Yes, said I, I have had from this very Meeting. They asked of whom, and when? I told them, of an honest Woman, yet living not far distant; they replyed, Art not thou a Treacherous Man to tell this? Why, said I, to tell the Truth, in answer to your Question.

It is a thing well enough known to themselves, that they have frequent Collections, at their Monthly, and Quarterly Meetings, one chief use whereof is, to furnish the Travelling Friends with Mony.

One of the Quakers at that Meeting in *Flushing*, that made the interruption, did openly accuse me in the Meeting, that I had defrauded the Poor of 50 Pounds of Mony, which *Miles Forster* had delivered to me to give the Quakers at *London*, for the use of their Poor, being part of what Colonel *West* had left to them by Legacy in his Will, (whereof *Miles Forster* was the sole Executor.) The which Scandalous accusation, the Quakers of *Long Island* had industriously spread over the Country against me; and the same was objected against me, by a Quaker at *Burlington* in *West-Jersey*, in the hearing of many present. But as I then declared, and I now declare, I had no Mony delivered to me by *Miles Forster*, to give to the Quakers at *London*, whether Poor or Rich. At my coming from *America*, in the Year 1693, the said *Miles Forster* gave me a Bill of 40 Pounds *English* Mony to be paid me at *London*, to my own proper use, (he being indebted to me, in some part of the like Sum.) But the Mony of this Bill, was no part of the Poors Mony, but was *Miles Forster's* own Mony, which he drew by Bill, upon a Person at *London*, that did owe him a far greater Sum; the which Bill was duly paid to me. When he gave me that Bill, he told me what was the occasion and cause, that moved him to do it, which was this, That to his certain knowledge, Col. *West*, out of the special respect and love he had to me, by his reading my Books, about the time the difference betwixt the Quakers of *Pensilvania*, and me, about matters of Religion began, had designed to give me some considerable Benefaction; and in order to that, when he lay sick at *Miles Forster's* House at *New-York*, he desired *Myles Forster* to Write to me to come to him. I was then living with my Family at *Philadelphia*, distant about an Hundred Miles from *New-York*. After I received this Message, I made all the hast I could to go to *New-York* unto him. But it so happened, that Col. *West* was Dead and Buried before I arrived. To answer the intent of Col. *West*, *Myles* told me, he gave me that Bill, to be paid to me at *London*, as some gratification to me, for the respect Col. *West* had to me, and also for the labour, and charge, I was at in my Journey, to come unto him. But none of the Money of that Bill, was any part of what Col. *West* left in his Will to the Poor of the Quakers at *London*, but was *Mgles Forster's* own Money, which was owing to him at *London* by the Person on whom he drew that Bill. If *Myles Forster* paid himself again that Money he gave me to my own proper use, out of that part of Col. *West's* Estate, that was left in Legacy to the Poor of the Quakers at *London*, *Myles Forster* was to be accountable to the Quakers, if they have any right to it, for his so doing, and not I; for it was simply *Miles Forster's* benefaction to me, though he gave it to me on Col. *West's* Account; Col. *West* having left to him, not only a considerable Legacy, as being his Executor, but had also left to him in his Will, full Power to dispose of what Money was left to the Poor of the Quakers at *London*, to what Quakers, or what sort of Quakers he thought fit; for no Names of Quakers, nor sort of Quakers were mentioned in the Will, nor no Name of any Meeting of Quakers mentioned therein, (there being at that time two sorts of Quakers at *London* opposite to one another) and *Miles Forster* informed me, that much, if not most of what was left by Col. *West* in his

Will to the Poor of the Quakers at *London*, was depending on a Condition expressed in the Will, that was not performed, and by somewhat that happened could not, nor even can be performed; and consequently the far greatest part thereof, which was much more than the contents of that Bill which he gave to me, did wholly belong by right to him, being the Executor. But the Quakers and *Miles Forster*, are to debate the case betwixt them. The Quakers Lawyers at *New-York*, have sufficiently informed them, that they can have no Claim or Action against me, for what I received of *Miles Forster*. And *Miles Forster's* Lawyers, have declared their Mind in the Case, that the Quakers can have no right to sue him, for what he gave to me, whether he gave it out of the Money left in Col. *West's* Will to the Poor, or otherwise. Because, by the Will, he had Power to give to me what part of it he pleased, as well as to any other. And when I was lately with *Miles Forster*, at *Amboy* in *East-Jerssy*, where he now lives; he told me some *London* Quakers had sent their Letter of *Attorney* to some Quakers of *New-York* Province, to demand of him the Poors Money, that was left to their Poor of *London*, by the Will of Col. *West*, and that they of *New-York* and he had some Meeting about it; and that he asked them, By what Right these Quakers at *London* did demand that Money, more than any other Quakers there, seeing their Names were not in the Will, nor the Names of any other, either of Persons, or Meetings. But to this they could give no satisfactory Answer, and so the Matter remains in suspence betwixt them.

September 27, 1702. Sunday. I preached at *Hampsted* on *Long-Island* in the Afternoon, where was such a Multitude of People, that the Church could not hold them, so that many stood without at the Doors and Windows to hear; who were generally well affected, and greatly desired that a Church of *England* Minister should be settled among them; which has been done, for the Reverend Mr. *John Thomas* is now their Minister. My Text was, *Luke* 10. 42.

September 28. We arrived at the Ferry by *New-York*.

September 30, Wednesday. At the Request of Mr. *Vesey*, the Minister at *New-York*, I preached at the Weekly Fast, which was appointed by the Government, by reason of the great Mortality that was then at *New-York*, where above *Five Hundred* died in the Space of a few Weeks; and that very Week, about *Seventy* died. My Text was, *Jam.* 5. 13.

October 1. From the Ferry by *New-York*, we came to *Reedhook* on *Long-Island*, where we waited for a fair Passage, and next Day we got over to *Staten-Island*, and from *Staten-Island* to *Amboy* in *East-Jersey*.

October 3, Sunday. I preached at *Amboy* in *East-Jersey;* the Auditory was small: My Text was *Tit.* 2. 11, 12. But such as were there, were well affected; some of them, of my former Acquaintance, and others who had been formerly *Quakers* but were come over to the Church, particularly *Miles Forster*, and *John Barclay* (Brother to *Robert Barclay*, who published the Apology for the Quakers) the Place has very few Inhabitants. We were several Days kindly entertained by *Miles Forster* at his House there.

October 10, 1702. Sunday. We went to the Meeting of the Quakers at *Toponemes*, in Freehold in *East-Jersey*, who used to keep a separate Meeting from the other Quakers, for their gross Errors; and joined with me and my Friends in the Separation, about the Year 1692; and it happened to be their

Yearly Meeting, where diverse came from *West-Jersey* and *Pensilvania:* One of their Preachers pray'd and preached before I began. After he had done, I used some of the Church Collects I had by heart, in Prayer; and after that, I preached on *Heb.* 5. 9. There was a considerable Auditory of diverse sorts; some of the Church, and some Presbyterians, besides the Quakers; they heard me without any Interruption, and the Meeting ended peaceably. Their two Speakers lodged in the same House with me that Evening, at the House of *Thomas Boels*, formerly a Quaker, but is now of the Church. I had some free Discourse with them about several weighty things: I told them, so far as they used their Gifts to instruct the Ignorant, and reclaim them from the vile Errors of Quakerism, they were to be commended; but that they had taken upon them to Administer Baptism and the Lord's Supper to any, they were greatly to be blamed, having no due external Call, or Ordination, so to do.

October 11, Monday. We met again the next Day, and had the like Auditory: Their other Speaker aray'd and preached, and after that, I pray'd, using the same Collects as the Day before, and preached on 1 *Thes.* 5. 19. without any Interruption, and the Meeting peaceably ended. I could blame nothing in the Matter of their second Speaker, nor in the former, except where he said in his Discourse, *That they who were in Christ, need not fear Hell.* I endeavoured to clear the Matter in my Discourse, by distinguishing betwixt an Absolute Fear of Hell, such as the Wicked ought to have, and a Conditional Fear, which Good Men, even such who are in Christ, ought to have; and about this he and I had some private Discourse also betwixt us, but he was dissatisfied, and would not own, *That any who were in Christ ought to have any Fear of Hell*, so much as Conditional.

October 17, Sunday, I preached at *Midleton* in *East-Jersey*, where, before Sermon, Mr. *Talbot* read the Church Prayers, and I preached on *Mat.* 28. 19, 20. One main part of my Sermon being to prove Infant-Baptism to be included in the Apostles Commissions, as well as that of Adult Persons, there being several of the Auditory who were Anabaptists, who heard me civilly, without any Interruption; but most of the Auditory were Church People, or well affected to the Church.

October 24, Sunday, 1702. I preached at *Shrewsbury* in *East-Jersey* at a House near the Quakers Meeting-house, and it happened that it was the Time of the Quakers Yearly Meeting at *Shrewsbury:* My Text was 2 *Pet.* 2. 1, 2. The Church Prayers being read before Sermon, we had a great Congregation, generally well affected to the Church, and diverse of them were of the Church, and that Day I sent some Lines in Writing to the Quakers at their Yearly Meeting; which Mr. *Talbot* did read to them in their Meeting, wherein I desired them to give me a Meeting with them some Day of that Week, before their Meetings were concluded; in which Meeting, I offered to detect great Errors in their Authors Books, and they should have full Liberty to answer what they had to say in their Vindication. But they altogether refused my Proposition; and several Papers pass'd betwixt us: In some of their Papers, they used gross Reflections on the Church of *England*, as much as on me. We continued our Meetings three days, as the Quakers did theirs. And the second Day of our Meeting at the same House, where we had formerly met, I detected the Quakers Errors out of their printed Books, particularly out of the Folio Book of *Edw. Burroughs* Works, collected and published by the Quakers after his Death, and did read the Quotations to the Auditory, laying the Pages open before such as were willing to read them, for their better Satisfaction, as some did read them.

Some of the Quotations were such as follow.

Page 126. (i. e. the Ministers) *Prophecy and Preaching would soon be ended, if they had not the Scripture to preach their Imaginations upon.*

Pag. 273. *Quakers Sufferings greater and more unjust than the Sufferings of Christ and the Apostles.*

Pag. 19. *He denies a written Word.—No other Word* (saith he) *do I own but Christ.*

Pag. 402. *He will revoke if any can prove, that the Scriptures call themselves the Word.*

Pag. 484. *The Spirit of God, the only standing Rule to walk by, not the Scriptures.*

Pag. 292. *The Flesh of Christ's Body Infinite.*

Pag. 515. *God and the Spirit, not Persons, but Infinite Beings.*

Pag. 698. *They* (i. e. the Quakers) *are One with the Father in Nature.*

Pag. 413. *All that Christians practise is become Idolatry.*

Pag. 27. *That which sinned could not be saved, &c.*

October 26, 1702. Tuesday. I preached again at *Shrewsbury* on *Mat.* 7. 13. In all these Meetings at *Shrewsbury, Midletown,* and *Toponemes,* or where ever else, on *Nethersinks,* Mr. *Lewis Moris,* and diverse others of best Note in that Country, frequented the Congregations and Places where we preached, and did kindly entertain us at their Houses, where we lodged as we travelled too and again; particularly Mr. *Moris,* Mr. *Innes,* Mr. *Johnston,* Mr. *Boels,* and Mr. *Read;* Mr. *Innes* being in Priest's Orders, has oft preached among them, and by Preaching, and Conferences frequently with Quakers and other sorts of People, as also by his pious Conversation, has done much Good among them, and been very instrumental to draw them off from their Errors, and bring them over to the Church.

October 29, 1702. We arrived at *Burlington* in *West-Jersey.*

November 1, Sunday. We preached in the Town-House at *Burlington,* (the Church not being then built) and we had a great Auditory of diverse sorts, some of the Church, and some of the late Converts from Quakerism. Mr. *Talbot* preached before Noon, and I in the Afternoon. My Text was, *John* 17. 3. Col. *Hamilton,* then Governour of *West-Jersey,* was present both Forenoon and Afternoon, and at his Invitation we dined with him.

November 3. At *Burlington* I detected the Quakers Errors out of their great Authors, *George Fox* his great Mystery, and *Edward Burroughs* Folio Book, and others, having given the Quakers Preachers Notice two Days before, to come and defend their Principles and Authors; but none of them would appear in the Cause.

November 5. We arrived at *Philadelphia,* and were kindly received by the two Ministers there, and the Church People, and especially by the late Converts from Quakerism, who were become zealous Members of the Church.

November 8, Sunday. I preached in the Church of *Philadelphia,* at the Minister's Request, on 2 *Pet.* 3, 15, 16. in the Afternoon. Mr. *Talbot* preached there in the Forenoon. And again I preached another Sermon, on the same, that Evening, after six a Clock, (it being usual once a Month to preach an Evening-Sermon in that Town.) We had a very great Auditory, so that the Church could not contain them, but many stayed without and heard.

That Week a Meeting of the Clergy being appointed to meet together at *New-York* by general Consent, we accordingly did meet, being Seven in number; at our Meeting we drew up an Account of the State of the Church in these *American* Parts of *Pensilvania, West* and *East-Jersey*, and *New-York* Province; a Copy whereof we sent to the Honourable Society at *London, for the Propagation of the Gospel in Foreign Parts.* Colonel *Nicolson*, Governour of *Virginia*, to encourage us to meet, was so generous to bear our Charges, (I mean of all of us that lived not at *New-York*) beside his other great and generous Benefactions to the Building and Adorning many Churches lately built in these Parts, whereof a particular Account has been given to the Honourable Society.

November 15, 1702. I preached at *New-York* on *Revel.* 3. 20. being Sacrament-Day.

November 22, Sunday. I preached again at *New-York*, on *Rom.* 6. 17, 18. in the Forenoon, and Mr. *Talbot* in the Afternoon. My Lord *Cornbury*, Governour of *New-York* and the *Jerseys*, was very kind to us, and at his Invitation, we did eat at his Table both *Sundays* and other Times.

November 26, Thursday. I Preached at *Hampsted* on *Long-Island*, on *Acts* 26. 18.

November 29, 1702. I Preached again at *Hampsted*, on *Heb.* 8. 10, 11, 12.

Sunday, *December* 3, 1702. I visited again the Quakers Meeting at *Flushing* on *Long-Island*, having obtained a Letter from my Lord *Cornbury*, to Two Justices of Peace to go along with me, to see that the Quakers should not interrupt me, as they had formerly done: But notwithstanding the Two Justices that came along with me, to signifie my Lord *Cornbury's* Mind, by his Letter to them, which was read to them in their Meeting by Mr. *Talbot*, they used the like interruption as formerly, and took no notice of my Lord *Cornbury's* Letter, more than if it had been from any private Person. They renewed their former accusation against me, that I had broke the Act of Toleration; I replyed, I had not broke it, for I did not interrupt any of them; they answered, I interrupted their silent Worship; I said, I knew no Clause in *that Act*, that forbid the interruption of their silent Worship. I brought the Printed Act of Toleration with me to their Meeting, and Mr. *Talbot* did Read several Passages out of it to them, to shew that they had neither qualified their Meeting-Houses, nor their Preachers, as the Act required. But notwithstanding they objected the Act of Toleration against me; when I objected it against them, they said, that Act did not extend to *America*; Behold their Partiality! We stayed and heard three of their Speakers one after another, though it was very grievous to us to hear so much nonsense, and perversion of Scripture, uttered by them; and all this upon pretence of being moved by the Spirit of God. Their chief Speaker, who is a most ignorant Person, said, *Balak had sent Balaam to Curse the People of God:* His Sense and perverse Application of that historical Passage of Scripture, is easie to understand without a Commentary. After they had done, they generally went away, Speakers and others; bnt many, who were not Quakers, stayed, and heard me resume and detect the gross Perversions and Misapplications of the Scriptures, which they had made. And after this, I detected out of a Book of *George Whitehead*, called, *The Divinity of Christ*, his vile Error concerning Christ, both with respect to his Godhead and Manhood, and I did read the Passages out of his Book in the Hearing of the Auditory. In his said Book, he blames his Opponent, *Thomas Vincent*, for affirming, that the Son proceeded from the Father by an eternal Act of Generation, and chargeth it with Confusion and Nonsense. Also in the same Book he brings many Places of Scripture, all which he grossly perverts, to prove that Christ suffered as God. And in the Appendix to his Book, he blames his Opponent, *Th. Danson*, for saying, *Christ, as Man, had a created Soul and Body;* and from his so saying doth infer, by way of Query, Doth not this render him a Fourth Person? And *George Fox* in his Preface to that Book, most ignorantly and perversely argues against the Three Persons in the Godhead, inferring, by way of Quæry, (their common way of Disputing) Doth not this render them Four Persons? Just as *John Whiting*, a late Author among them, in his Book called, *Judas and the Chief Priests*, doth ridicule that Passage in the Litany of the Church of *England*, *O Holy, Blessed and Glorious Trinity, Three Persons and One God;* inferring, that from this there should be Four Persons; for that Three and One are Four: Whereas in the Act of Toleration, there is an express Clause that excludes all such from the Benefit of the Act, *That either in their Speaking or Writing, deny the Holy Trinity, as taught and professed in the Church of* England: And yet these very Persons that thus revile and ridicule the Doctrine of the *Holy Trinity as taught in the Church of* England, are mighty Pleaders for their Liberty by the Act of Toleration; as if not only their Meetings and Preachings were Tolerated, but Authorized by the Act.

December 6, 1702. I Preached at *Oysterbay* in the Town-House, on *Rom.* 10. 7, 8, 9. And we were kindly entertained at the House of Mr. *Edward White* abovementioned.

December 13. I preached at *Staten-Island* in the Town-House, on *Titus* 2. 11, 12.

December 20, 1702. I preached at Dr. *Johnston's*, at *Nethersinks*, on *Rev.* 22. 14.

December 25, Friday, being Christmas day. I preached at the House of Mr. *Morris*, on *Luke* 2. 10, 11. And after Sermon, diverse of the Auditory received with us the Holy Sacrament; both Mr. *Morris* and his Wife, and diverse others. Mr. *Talbot* did administer it.

Decemb. 27, Sunday, 1702. I preached in *Shrewsbury* Town, near the Quakers Meeting-House, at a Planter's House, and had a considerable Auditory of Church People lately converted from Quakerism, with diverse others of the Church of best Note in that Part of the Country. My Text was *Heb.* 8. 10, 11.

January 1, Friday. I preached at the House of Mr. *Thomas Boels* at *Freehold* in *East-Jersey:* My Text was *Isaiah* 59. 20, 21. Before Sermon, after the Church Prayers, I baptized all his Children; two Sons and three Daughters. He was formerly a Quaker, but is now come over to the Church; also a Son of *Samuel Dennis*, a late Convert from Quakerism.

January 3, Sunday, 1702. I preached again at his House, on the same

Text, and before Sermon Mr. *Talbot* baptized two Persons belonging to the Family of *John Read*, formerly a Quaker, but was lately come over to the Church with all his Children; one Son and two Daughters. His two Daughters were baptized by Mr. *Talbot*, *October* 24, 1702. As also the same Day were baptized *William Leads* and his Sister *Mary Leads*, late Converts from Quakerism to the Church: And some Days before, at the House of *John Read*, Mr. *Talbot* baptized the Wife of *Alexander Neaper* and his three Children. He had been a Quaker, but was come over to the Church.

January 4, 1702. I came to the House of *Robert Ray* in *Freehold* in *East-Jersey*, accompanied with *Thomas Boels*, and lodged at his House that Night. At his and his Wife's Desire, I baptized all his Children; some Boys and some Girles, in number Five: they both had been Quakers, but he was not then come throughly off from Quakerism.

January 10, Sunday. I preached at *Burlington* at the House of Mr. *Revel*, on *Mat.* 6. 33. And I baptized a Man's Child who was a Churchman, where I had a large Auditory.

January 11. We came to *Philadelphia*, and lodged at the House of Mrs. *Welch* all the Time we happened to be at *Philadelphia*, until we went from *Pensilvania* to *Virginia* and *North-Carolina*, in the Months of *April* and *May*, 1702. She had been a Quaker for many Years, and of good Repute. About the Years 1691 and 1692, it pleased God, by my Means, through the Illumination of the Holy Spirit, to give her and her Daughter (who was educated in Quakerism) to see their Errors and forsake them; and also many others in that Place about that time; who afterwards gradually came off from Quakerism, and at last came clearly off, and joined to the Church, whereof they are become zealous Members. She entertained us both at her House, (*viz.* Mr. *Talbot* and me) all the time, abovementioned, and also after our Return, so long as we stayed there, *gratis.*

January 17, Sunday. I preached at *Philadelphia*, on *John* 3. 5. in the Forenoon, and Mr. *Talbot* preached in the Afternoon. I preached again on the same Text, an Evening Sermon, that begun after the sixth Hour at Night.

January 24, Sunday, 1702. I preached at *Philadelphia* on *Mat.* 5. 17. both in the Forenoon and Afternoon; Mr. *Evans* the Minister of *Philadelphia* having that Day been at *Chester* in *Pensilvania*, to accompany Mr. *Talbot*, who was to preach there the first Sermon in the Church after it was built.

January 31, Sunday. I preached at *Philadelphia*, on *Mat.* 5. 17. being my third Sermon on that Text; and the same Day at the sixth Hour at Night, I preached there on 1 *Cor.* 11. 28.

February 7, Sunday, 1702. I preached at *Chester* in *Pensilvania*, in the New Church, on *Mat.* 16. 18.

February 9, Tuesday. I preached a second Sermon on the same Text at *Concord* in *Pensilvania*, at the House of *John Hanon*.

February 11. I preached a third Sermon on that Text at the House of *Thomas Powel* in *Chester* County; both these Men, *John Hanon* and his Wife, and *Thomas Powel* and his Wife, had been Quakers, but are become zealous Members of the Church, with diverse others their Neighbours.

February 12, 1702. I had a Dispute with Mr. *Killingsworth* an Anabaptist Preacher, at the House of *Thomas Powel*, before a great Auditory. The Subjects of our Dispute were, First, About Set Forms of Prayer. Secondly, About the manner of Baptizing, whether by Dipping or Sprinkling? Thirdly, Whether Infants of Believers are proper Subjects of Baptism? Fourthly, Concerning Ordination. It had a good Effect upon several present; and I hope upon himself; for by a Letter I received sometime ago from Mr. *Talbot*, this Mr. *Killingsworth* is become well affected to the Church, and has proferred Ground to build a Church upon, and Wood to build it, upon his Land where he lives, at *Salem* in *West Jersey*.

In the first Week of *February*, 1702, I had a Meeting with the Separate Quakers and their Preachers, who left the Quakers Meetings for their gross Errors, and joined with me about the Year 1691. They met at my Lodging in *Philadelphia*, at my Request; and the next Week thereafter, we had another Meeting at the same place. I told them, that the Reason why I desired to have a friendly Meeting and Conference with them, was, that I might answer their Objections against their Conformity to the Church of *England*, and particularly their Objections against Infants Baptism: Also I had some Discourse with one of their Preachers, to convince him of his *Antinomian* Notion, and the great Error and Hurt of it, *viz. That they who are in Christ, ought not to fear Hell in any respect, not so much as Conditionally.* He was very earnest and warm in the Defence of it, and pressed it very much, that that matter should be first discoursed upon, thinking to have some Advantage against me in that Point; but the Success proved the contrary, so that his maintaining of it, offended diverse of his Hearers, that soon after they left him, and came over to the Church. I asked him, If they who were in Christ, could possibly fall from that good State. He said, they might possibly fall from it. I replyed, then there is the more Cause of Fear; as they who are in a Castle, yet they have just occasion of Fear, conditionally, lest if they should go out their watchful Enemies should destroy them; and Fear is very useful to them to keep them within. And as God Almighty had indued all living Creatures with a natural Fear, that is of great use to them to preserve their natural Life; so he had indued all his Children with a spiritual Fear, that is as useful and as necessary to them to preserve their spiritual Life. And as Hope is necessary to keep Men from Despair, so Fear is necessary to keep them from Presumption. I mentioned also several Texts of Scripture to him, and desired him to consider them, *viz. Job* 31. 24. 1 *Cor.* 9. 27. *Heb.* 4. 1. *Rom.* 8. 31. But he continued resolute in his erroneous Opinion. Next we proceeded to discourse about other matters, as, What were their Objections against their Conforming to the Church, and against Infants Baptism? I laboured very much, in Love, to satisfie them about all those matters; but I found they were resolute to keep up their Separate Meeting, though it be dwindled away and diminished to a very small Number from what it was at the Beginning, after the Separation, about 1692, and which continued several Years, until a Church of *England* Congregation was set up at *Philadelphia;* soon after which, most of that Party, both in Town and Countrey, and also in *West* and *East-Jersey*, and some in *New-York*, came over with good Zeal, and according to good Knowledge, to the Church, praised be God for it.

February 14, Sunday. I preached at *Philadelphia*, on *Acts* 26. 22, 23. at the Evening Lecture, after Six at Night.

February 21, Sunday, 1702. I preached at *Burlington* in *West-Jersey*, on *Rom.* 10. 7, 8, 9. and *Feb.* 22. I baptized the Wife of Mr. *Rob. Wheeler* and his three Children, and five others: in all 9 Persons. He and his Wife had been Quakers, but are come over to the Church. He did most kindly and hospitally entertain us at his House, *gratis*, the several times that we travelled to and fro in those Parts: And the like kind and free Entertainment he gives to all Ministers of the Church that travel that way.

February 28, Sunday. I preached at *Philadelphia* on *Mat.* 5. 17.

March 4. I had a publick Meeting at *Philadelphia*, at the House that formerly belonged to *Zacharia Whitbane*, to detect the Quakers Errors, by plain Quotations out of their approved Authors, particularly Mr. *Pen's Sandy Foundation;* having before given intimation to the chief Preachers of the Quakers at *Philadelphia*, to defend their Principles and Authors, if they could; but none of them would appear in the Cause. One *William Southsby*, who is a sort of Preacher among them, told the Auditory, he was not come to dispute, but to complain against me, that I had said, he denied the Resurrection; and he came to clear himself, and desired leave to read a short Paper, wherein he gave Account of his Faith of the Resurrection. After he had read his Paper, which contained some Words he had Transcribed out of 1 *Cor.* 15. and some other Texts of Scripture; I asked him, *Did he believe the Resurrection of that Body of his standing before us?* He said, *He would not Answer to that ensnaring Question.* By this it plainly appeared to the Auditory that were not Quakers, that he did not really believe the Resurrection of the Body, even when he seemed to confess it, after the manner of all Hereticks, who profess to give their Faith in Scripture Words, but quite contrary to the true and real sense of the Scripture, as *Arius*, *Sabellius*, *Nestorius*, *Eutyches*, *Pelagius*, *&c.*

March 7, 1702, Sunday. I Preached at *Philadelphia*, on *Philip.* 2. 13.

March 10, 1702. I had a publick dispute at *Philadelphia*, with one *William Davis*, who had been formerly a Quaker; but some time after he left them, he set up for a new Sect-Master, to draw Disciples after him, and Published a Book full of Blasphemous Notions, as that there are three Gods; and that none of these three Gods are any where but in Heaven; and that Christ as God, suffered upon the Cross; with diverse other gross Blasphemies; a particular Account of which, I have given in Print, Bound up with other Printed Tracts, which I did present to the Honourable Society.

March 14, Sunday. I Preached at *Philadelphia* a second Sermon on *Phil.* 2. 12, 13.

March 21, Sunday. I Preached at *Philadelphia*, on 2 *Cor.* 12. 9.

March 28, Sunday. I Preached at *Philadelphia* a second Sermon on 2 *Cor.* 12. 9.

April 4, Sunday. I Preached at *Chester* in *Pensilvania* on *Titus* 2, 11, 12.

April 8, Thursday. I Preached at *New-Castle*, on 1 *Thess.* 5. 19.

April 11, Sunday, 1703. I Preached at *New-Castle*, on *Jude* 20. Mr. *Talbot* Preached there in the Afternoon, and Baptized three Children of Mr. *James Claypool* (who had been formerly a Quaker) and another Child of a Churchman. And at our return to *New-Castle* from *Virginia*, I Baptized the said Mr. *James Claypool*, he was much afflicted with a *Palsie.*

April 18, 1703. I Preached at *York Town*, by *York River*, on *Acts* 20, 21.

April 20, 1703. We arrived at *Williamsburgh* in *Virginia*, (having come by Water in a Sloop, from *New-Castle* to *York River*,) and were very kindly received there, and entertained by Col. *Nicholson*, then Governour of *Virginia*.

April 21, Wednesday. I Preached in *Williamsburgh* Church, before the Convocation of the Clergy then Assembled, on 1 *Job*. 1. 7.

April 25, Sunday. I Preached at *James-Town* on 1 *Job*. 1. 3. at the request of the Reverend Mr. *Blair* Minister there, and Commissary, who very kindly and Hospitally Entertained us at his House.

May 2, Sunday, 1703. I Preached at *Kicketan* Church by *James River*, on 2 *Cor*. 3. 18.

May 4, Tuesday. I Preached there the Thanksgiving Sermon, on *Psal*. 18. 48, 49. the Minister, the Reverend Mr. *Wallis*, being then in *England*.

May 9, Sunday. I Preached at a Chappel in *Elizabeth* County in *Virginia*, on *Psal*. 1. 1. 2, 3.

May 10. We took our Journey from thence to *North-Carolina*.

May 16, Whitsunday, 1703. I Preached at the House of Capt. *Sanders* in *Corretuk* in *North-Carolina*, on *Rom*. 1. 16.

We designed to have Travelled further into *North-Carolina*, but there was no Passage from that Place by Land convenient to Travel, by reason of Swamps, and Marishes; and we had no way to go by Water but in a Canow over a great Bay, many Miles over which we essayed to do, but the Wind continuing several Days contrary, we returned to *Virginia*.

May 23, Sunday, 1703. I Preached at the Church in Princess *Anns* County in *Virginia*, on *Heb*. 12. 1. and I Baptized Eight Children there. Mr. *Talbot* Preached the same Day at a Chappel belonging to the same County, and Baptized Ten Children.

The whole County is but one Parish, and is about Fifty Miles in length; the People are well affected, but they had no Minister, and greatly desire to have one; and as they informed us, the Minister's Salary being paid in Tobacco, (as it is generally all over *Virginia* and *Maryland*) the Tobacco of that County was so low, that it could not maintain him.

May 30, Sunday, 1703. The Reverend Mr. *Blair* Commissary, Preached at *Kicketan*, where I was an Hearer, having no occasion that Day to Preach any where in that County.

June 6, Sunday. Mr. *Talbot* Preached at *Kicketan*, we stayed there about Ten Days, at my Daughters House at *Kicketan* by *Jamas River*; she is fully come off from the Quakers, and is a zealous Member of the Church of *England*, and brings up her Children (so many of them as are capable through Age,) in the Christian Religion, Praised be God for it.

June 13, Sunday. I Preached at the Church of *Abington*, on the *North-side* of *York-River*, the Reverend Mr. *Smith* is Minister there, and did Read the Church Prayers. My Text was, 1 *Thess*. 5. 19. I lodged at Major *Burrell's* House, and was kindly Entertained. Mr. *Talbot* Preached at *Williamsburgh*.

June 20, Sunday. I Preached at *Hampton* Church in *Virginia*, on *Jam*. 1. 22.

June 27, Sunday. Mr. *Talbot* Preached at *York-Town* by *York-River*, where I was present with him; we were kindly Entertained there at the Collector's House several Days, waiting for Passage up *Maryland-bay*.

June 28, 1703. We sailed in a Sloop from *York-Town*, up *Maryland-bay* to *West-River;* the Master of the Sloop was a Quaker, whose Name is *Thomas Sparrow.* After our Landing, he kindly Entertained us at his House that Night, and refused to take any thing either for our Passage or Entertainment at his House. And as to our Provision on Board the Sloop, the Governour of *Virginia* sent us in Plenty. I had much Discourse and Reasoning with the said *Thomas Sparrow*, both aboard the Sloop, and at his House, especially about Baptism and the Lord's Supper, but he used the same evasions to the Texts of Scripture I brought for them, as the Quakers commonly use.

July 1, 1703. We came to *Annapolis* in *Maryland*, where we were kindly received and Entertained by Esquire *Finch*, then President of *Maryland*, and Sir *Thomas Lawrence* the Secretary there.

July 4, Sunday. I Preached at *Annapolis*, on 1 *Thess.* 1. 5. and had a large Auditory well affected; my Sermon at the request of a worthy Person who heard it, was Printed at *Annapolis*, mostly at his Charge; and Copies of it sent by him, to many parts of the Country. It is Bound up with other Printed Sermons and Tracts, in the Book abovementioned, which I Presented to the Honourable Society, soon after my arrival into *England*.

July 7, 1703. At the desire of some Persons of best Note in that part of *Maryland*, I went to the Quakers Meeting at *Herring-Creek* in *Maryland*, to have some friendly Conference with them. The aforesaid Esquire *Finch*, Sir *Thomas Lawrence*, and several Justices of the Peace, and many Persons of goed Note, came along with me to the Quakers Meeting there, and also the Reverend Mr. *Hall*, the Minister of the Parish, and diverse other Ministers of the neighbouring Parishes. While the Quakers were all silent; after some time, I stood up to speak among them, intending a brief Discourse on *Job.* 7. 38, 39. I had spoke but a very few Sentences, when they interrupted me very rudely; and notwithstanding the kind and gentle Entreaty of Esquire *Finch* and some others there present of their kind Neighbours, praying them to hear me, by no means would the Quakers suffer me to proceed in my Discourse. They told the Auditory, I was none of them, and they had disowned me. I asked them for what? But they would give no Reason for their so doing. One of them stood up, and accused Mr. *Hall* the Minister of the Parish, and also the Sheriff, of Theft; And being inquired what the Theft was, whereof he accused them. He answered, that the Sheriff had given some Tobacco of his, to the said —— *Hall*, which was none of his. The Case was this. The Sheriff having a quantity of Tobacco belonging to this Quaker in his Custody, as is usual in that Country. The Sheriff, in Kindness and good Neighbourhood to the said Quaker, rather than to distrein upon him, according to the Law, paid to Mr. *Hall* so much out of the Quakers Tobacco, as was due to Mr. *Hall* by the said Quaker, by an Act of the general Assembly, and confirmed by the Queen. And when some present said to him, his calling it Theft, reflected on the general Assembly, he still persisted in it, that it was Theft. I did again offer to Speak, but they did interrupt me again, and abused me with reviling Speeches in meer Generals, as the manner generally of the Quakers is, to all who Endeavour to reform them from their Errors, and especially to any who with a good Conscience upon Divine Conviction, have forsaken their Erroneous ways, to whom they are most outragious, as the *Jews* were to St. *Paul*, after his Conversion to Christianity. The aforesaid Persons, my worthy Friends, who came with me to the Quakers Meeting, finding that the Quakers would give me no hearing in their Meeting, desired me to Preach to them my Sermon which I had begun upon, (but was interrupted by the Quakers) at a Chappel very near to the Quakers Meeting, where they would gladly hear me before they went away, on that Subject, to which I readily agreed. Mr. *Hall* the Minister of the Parish did begin with the Church Prayers, and after the Prayers, I Preached my Sermon to them, in the said Chappel, (where was a great Auditory of both Men and Women) the same in Matter, as near as I could, which I had designed to deliver in the Quakers Meeting; for I made no use of Notes at that time, knowing that if I had used Notes, the Quakers would have made the greater exceptions, and have said, I was only a Minister of the Letter, as their manner is to object against them, who make use of Notes; and I doubted not but that God would assist me, to deliver what was proper and Edifying, though I had no Notes at that Time. Though I oft made use of Notes in my Sermons which I Preached, and continue to do, and I do well approve of it.

The Matter which I mainly insisted upon, in my Discourse on that Text, *Job.* 7. 38, 39. was, that though we had no Warrant from this, or any other place of Holy Scripture, to expect those Miraculous and extraordinary Inspirations of the Spirit given to the Apostles, which enabled them to Preach without Study, and to Speak with Tongues they had not learned by Industry, yet we had sufficient ground from many Texts of Holy Scripture, to believe, that God continues to give to all the Faithful, such plentiful Inspirations, Influences, and Assistances of his Holy Spirit, as are necessary to their Sanctification, and to their continual Growth and Progress therein, and to enable them to serve him acceptably, and comfortably, in all Duties of Holiness and Righteousness, and especially to assist them in their Prayers and Thanksgivings to Almighty God, in the due Use of the Means of Grace; and to assist the Ministers of his Word, in their Preaching and Praying, and in all other Parts of their Ministerial Calling.

And I shewed, that the Ministers and People of the Church of *England*, had a better Belief, Trust, and Hope of the inward Assistances of the Holy Spirit, than the Quakers had, notwithstanding the Quakers proud and presumptuous Affirmations and Pretensions to the Spirit above others. For (said I) the Quakers, and the Quaker Preachers, have such a Distrust of the Spirit's Assistance to pray, or give Thanks vocally, that they think, or pretend they oft have it not: and for that Reason given by them, they oft neither pray in their Families, nor at their Meals. And for want of the Spirits Motion and Assistance, as they pretend and profess, so as to enable them, either to Preach or Pray in audible Words, they used to have many silent Meetings, where one Word is not uttered among them from first to last; and in many Places they have them still. And it is certain, that generally in the Quakers Families, there is no vocal Prayer used at all, and rarely, even in their Preachers Families. But none of them use constant Prayer in their Families, either twice or once a Day, that ever I heard of, and some not once in a Year, in the Family, whatever they do in their Publick Meetings for Ostentation. The Reason of this Omission, which they think not to be any

Sin, is, that the Spirit doth not move or assist them. But what Spirit is that, but a Spirit of Ostentation and Vain-Glory, that moves them so frequently to pray in their Publick Meetings, and so rarely, not once in a Year, in their Families? Now whence doth this proceed, that they pray so seldom in their Families and in some of their Meetings, but either from their great Distrust, (as is said) or from a political Contrivance of their first Authors, the more to make their Proselytes believe, they waited for some extraordinary Inspiration and Impulse: For they had wont to say, *That they who could pray or preach at set Times, have not the true Gift of Prayer or Preaching.* And yet it is sufficiently known, that many of them are arrived at that Confidence, to preach and pray in their way of Rhapsody, at any time, in their Meetings; and they have their ordinary Set-times, especially at *London*, when to begin and when to end; so that if any of their Preachers happen to transgress the ordinary time, they oft get some Reprimand. Such of them who had not arrived at this Confidence and Conceit of their Ability, to preach or pray at any time, except when the Spirit moves them, I compared them to a Mill that stands by a small Brook, or Run of Water, that has oft so little Water as cannot make the Wheels of the Mill to go, till there come afresh, they know not when.

Whereas the Faithful of the Church of *England*, both Ministers and People, and in all true Christian Churches, have no such Distrust of the Assistance of the blessed Spirit of God, but believe that blessed Spirit will never be wanting to them, to give them his Assistance in some Measure and Degree, more or less, according to his good Pleasure; sufficient to enable them to perform all requisite Duties unto God acceptably.

Another thing I insisted upon from the Words of the Text, was, That these inward Aids and Assistances of the Holy Spirit given to the Faithful, were only promised to them who believed sincerely in Jesus Christ, both God and Man, who is now in Heaven without us, our blessed Mediator and Intercessor with the Father; and who believe that he is to come in his Glorified Body, the same in Substance he had on Earth, (in which he suffered Death for our Sins) to be the Judge both of the Quick and Dead, at his Coming and Appearing visibly without us, as really as he visibly ascended into Heaven, in the Sight of his Disciples. And that therefore the Quakers who generally have not this Belief in Jesus Christ, as above declared, (as hath been fully and evidently proved, and can still be proved out of the printed Books of their noted Authors.) But instead of the true Christian Faith in Jesus Christ (according as the Holy Scripture hath set him forth) have set up a Belief only in the Light within them, as the said Light is in all Men. These, I say, can lay no Claim to any such Assistances of the Holy Spirit, as are only promised to sincere Believers in Jesus Christ, according to the Words of the Text, *Joh.* 7. 38, 39. *He that believes in me, out of his Belly shall flow Rivers of living Water. But this spake he of the Spirit, which they that believe on him should receive,* (to wit, that very Man which they both saw with their outward Eyes, and heard with their outward Ears) who, as he was visible as Man, yet was invisible as he was God: And that it is said in the following Words, *The Holy Ghost was not yet given, because that Jesus was not yet glorified:* that is, He was not given, until after His Ascension, either in that Plenty and Variety of miraculous Gifts, or in that Plenty and large

Measure of the ordinary Gifts and Graces of the Spirit, as were afterwards to be given to the Faithful after his Ascension.

July 10, Saturday. I preached at *Herring-Creek* Church, at the Request of Mr. *Hall* the Minister, on the two Sacraments, my Text was, 1 *Cor.* 12, 13.

July 11, Sunday. I preached at Mr. *Colback's* Church in the next Parish a second Sermon on *Joh.* 7. 38, 39.

July 14. I crossed *Maryland-Bay* over to the Eastern Shore, accompanied with Mr. *Hall* abovementioned, from *Annapolis* to *Kent-Island:* We had a fair and easie Passage, in the Space of three Hours. Mr. *Talbot* had gone up the Western Shore to preach at several Places on that side, and after some time to come to me.

July 15. We travelled from *Kent-Island* to the House of the Reverend Mr. *Lilingstone*, where we were kindly entertained some Days.

July 18, Sunday. I preached at Mr. *Lilingston's* Church in *Talbot County*, on *Eph.* 2. 10, and had a great Auditory, and well affected.

July 21, Wednesday. I preached at Mr. *Bourdly's* Church, on *Rom.* 10. 7, 8, 9. and had a great Auditory, and were kindly entertained at his House.

July 25, Sunday. I preached at the Church of *Shrewsbury* in *Maryland*, on 1 *Cor.* 3. 11, 12. where was a large Auditory out of diverse Parishes: But that Parish of *Shrewsbury* had no Minister, nor have had for some considerable Time past. We were kindly entertained by Mr. *Blays* at his House in that Parish, some Days. On *Sunday* in the Evening, I had some Discourse with a Quaker who came from *London* and sold Goods to the Planters, for Tobabco. I found him so extream ignorant, that I could not perswade him, that our Blessed Saviour, as he was *Man*, had a created Soul. I asked him, If he himself had a created Soul? This also he denied. I mentioned that place of Scripture to him, *The Soul that Sinneth shall die:* And could a Soul sin, that was not created? If the Soul of Man be not created, it must be God, and God could not Sin. But no Reasons can prevail with them, however so plain, who are given up to strong Delusion, as indeed they too generally are. This Discourse I had with him in the Hearing of another Quaker, who came with him, at the House of Mr. *Blay*, who was present.

July 28. I crossed *Sasafrax-River*, (Mr. *Hall* having gone home) and came that Day to the Reverend Mr. *Sewils*, Minister of *Cecil-County* in *Maryland*, where Mr. *Talbot* came to me. Mr. *Sewil* kindly entertained us at his House, and accompanied us to the Mannor, by *Bohemia* River, where we lodged, and were kindly entertained by the Master of the House, who was a *German.*

July 29. We came from thence to *New-Castle*, by *Delaware-River*, and were kindly entertained at the House of Mr. *Robert French*, some Days.

August 1, 1703, Sunday. I preached at *New-Castle*, on *Heb.* 5. 9. and had a large Auditory of *English*, and some *Dutch:* They have had a Church lately built, and the Reverend Mr. *Rosse*, a Missionary from the Honourable Society, has been sent to them, which they greatly desired.

August 2. I came to *Upland*, alias *Chester*, by *Delaware-River*, Mr. *Talbot* having gone before to preach there, *August* 1.

August 3, Tuesday. I preached in the Church at *Chester*, a second Sermon on *Titus* 2. 11, 12, 13, 14. and had a considerable Auditory: we were kindly entertained at the House of Mr. *Jasper Teates* there.

August 4. We came from *Chester* to *Philadelphia*, where we were kindly received and entertained by our Friends, and especially by Mistress *Welch*, at whose House we again lodged as formerly.

August 8. Mr. *Talbot* preached in the Forenoon at *Philadelphia*, and I preached there in the Afternoon, on 2 *Cor.* 12. 9.

August 15, Sunday. I Preached at *Philadelphia* on 1 *Job.* 5. 3.

August 22, Sunday. I preached at the New Church at *Burlington*, on 2 *Sam.* 23. 3, 4. My Lord *Cornbury* was present and many Gentlemen who accompanied him, both from *New-York*, and the two *Jerseys*, having had his Commission to be Governour of *West* and *East-Jersey*, Read at the Town-House there, some Days before. It was the first Sermon that was Preached in that Church.

August 29, Sunday. I preached again at the Church in *Burlington*, on *Jam.* 1. 22.

Sept. 5, Sunday. I preached at *Philadelphia*, on *Acts* 2. 41, 42. being Sacrament Day.

Sept. 12, Sunday. I preached at the Church in *Burlington*, a Second Sermon, on *Jam.* 1. 22. Mr. *Talbot* preached that Day at *Chester* in *Pensilvania*.

Sept. 15. I preached at *Will. Hewlins* in *West-Jersey*, on *Tit.* 2. 11.

Sept. 19, Sunday. I preached at *Philadelphia* in the Afternoon, on *Mat.* 16. 6.

Sept. 21, Tuesday. I preached at *Philadelphia*, on *Jude* 3. This week being the time of the Quakers yearly Meeting at *Philadelphia*, the Minister of *Philadelphia*, the Reverend Mr. *Evans*, with the consent of the Vestry, having agreed together with us, to have both Prayers and Sermons at the Church in *Philadelphia*, all the Days that the Quakers had their Meetings in that Week, which use to continue three Days; there happens commonly in that Week to be a great concourse of People at *Philadelphia*, not only Quakers, but also of many others, as at some great Fair.

Sept. 21, Tuesday. Mr. *Talbot* went to the Quakers Meeting at *Philadelphia*, that met at the New Meeting-House, called, the *Banck-Meeting*, about 9 of the Clock in the Forenoon, and began to read a Paper to them which I had Writ, containing some Observations on the Attestation, taken and Signed by some of the most noted Quakers in *West-Jersey*, in order to their being made Members of the Council in the Province of *West* and *East-Jersey*. The Quakers were so rude, that they pushed him on the Breast, and drove him by violence from the threshold of the Door, where he stood; yet he continued Reading, till he had finished it; but by the Tumult that the Quakers raised he was little heard. After which, I went in to their Meeting-House, and stood up on a Bench to Read it in their hearing within doors, but I had scarce read three Lines, till a Quaker, whose Name I spare, pulled it out of my Hand with great violence, and some of them overturned the Bench I stood upon, but I had no hurt, Praised be God; for as I was falling, some that were not Quakers supported me with their shoulders till my Feet gently touched the Ground; another Person that was no Quaker, pulling the said

Paper out of the Quakers hand, it was torn in two pieces betwixt them; but by the order of a Justice of Peace, who was no Quaker, the Quaker returned to me that torn piece of the Paper which he had kept. Of this Rude and Disorderly Carriage of the Quakers at the said Place, the said Day, diverse Persons of good Credit gave an Affidavit before a Justice of Peace at *Philadelphia.* I need not here recite the Contents of my Observations on these Quakers Attestation, for the like Observations have been made by another hand, and published in Print lately, in these *American* parts, and perhaps may be Reprinted at *London* ere long.

Sept. 26, Sunday. I preached in *Burlington* Church, a third Sermon, on *Jam.* 1. 22. in the Forenoon, and Mr. *Talbot* in the Afternoon.

October 3, Sunday. I preached in *Burlington* Church, on *Heb.* 8. 10, 11, 12. both Forenoon, and Afternoon, and read the Prayers before Sermon.

October 10, Sunday, 1703. I preached at *Toponemes* in *Freehold* in *East-Jersey*, on *Acts* 2. 41, 42. and had a considerable Auditory, diverse of them late Converts from Quakerism to the Church. Mr. *Innesse* abovementioned did read the Prayers. Mr. *Talbot* staid to preach in several places in *Pensilvania*, and *West-Jersey*, for some time.

October 17, Sunday. I preached at *Shrewsbury* near the Quakers Meeting there, on *Psal.* 103. 17, 18.

October 24, Sunday. I preached again there, on *Heb.* 8. 10, 11. And Mr. *Innesse* Baptized two Men and a Child.

October 31, Sunday. I preached at *Amboy* in *East-Jersey*, on *Titus* 2. 11, 12, 13, 14.

November 3. I preached at *And. Craig's* in the *Township* of *Elizabeth Town*, on 2 *Pet.* 1. 5. and Baptized his Four Children.

November 4. I Baptized the Children of *Andrew Hemton*, eight in Number; He and his Wife are come over from Quakerism to the Church. And *November* 3, I Baptized Seven Children of a Widow Woman there.

November 7, Sunday. I preached at *New-York*, on *Acts* 2. 42. and that Sermon was soon after Printed at *New-York*, at the desire of some who heard it, and did contribute to the Charge of its Printing.

November 14, Sunday. I preached at *Jamaica* on *Long-Island*, on *Heb.* 8. 9, 10.

November 17, Wednesday. I preached at *Oysterbay* on *Long-Island*, on *Jude* 20, 21. And *Novemb.* 19. there I Baptized Mrs. *White*, Wife to Mr. *Edward White*, and all his Children, *viz.* three Sons and five Daughters. He and his Wife were formerly Quakers, but are come over to the Church. And the same Day I Baptized Mrs. *Jones*, Wife to Captain *Jones* of that *Township.*

November 20, Saturday. At *Oysterbay*, I Baptized *John Townsend*, a Justice of Peace, and his three Children. And Mr. *Nathaniel Cole*, and his Wife, and his three Children. There had scarce been any Profession of the Christian Religion among the People of that Town; they had scarce any Notion of Religion but Quakerism: The Quakers had formerly a Meeting there, but many of them who lived in that Town, became Followers of *Thomas Chase* (not the *Thomas Chase* of *Hampton* in *New-England* abovementioned) and were called, *Chase's* Crew, who set up a new sort of Quakerism, and among other Vile Principles, they condemned Marriage, and said, it was of the Devil, perverting that Text of Scripture, *The Children of the Resurrection neither Marry, nor are given in Marriage;* and they said they were the Children of the Resurrection; and indeed, as the Author of the *Snake in the Grass* has well observed; This Mad sort of Quakers, called *Chase's Crew*, did but consequentially practice, what the followers of *George Fox* held very generally in Principle, *viz.* that they were come already to the Resurrection, and had their vile Bodies already changed; so *George Fox* has expressly Taught in Print, in a Printed Treatise of his about the Supper, where he will have the Lord's Supper now to be only inward.

November 21, Sunday. I preached at *Hampsted* Church on *Long-Island*, on 1 *Pet.* 2. 9. and Lodged that Night at *Isaac Smith's* House, Four Miles distant from the Church, and there I Baptized a Young-Woman of his Family, and a Boy, and a Girl of his Relations, and a Neighbours Child, a Boy. This *Isaac Smith* had been formerly a Quaker, and was scarce then fully come off, but came and heard me Preach, and was well affected, and did kindly Entertain me.

November 28, Sunday. I preached at *New-York* on 1 *Cor.* 12. 13. and that Sermon also was Printed at *New-York*, at the desire of some who heard it, and contributed to the Charge of Printing it; and by the Blessing of God, both these printed Sermons have been serviceable to many in these *American* Parts, and to some also in *England*, to reclaim them from their erroneous Opinions about the two Sacraments, Baptism and the Lord's-Supper.

December 5, Sunday, 1703. I preached at *New-York*, on *John* 12. 35, 36.

December 12, Sunday. I preached at *Amboy*, at my Lord *Cornbury's* Lodging, where he was present, and many with him. My Text was *John* 12. 35, 36.

December 19, Sunday. I preached at the House of Col. *Tounfly* in *Elizabeth-Town*, both Forenoon and Afternoon, on 1 *Pet.* 2. 9. Many of that Town having been formerly a sort of Independents, are become well affected to the Church of *England*, and desire to have a Minister of the Church of *England* sent to them: There I baptized a Child of Mr. *Shakmaple.*

December 25, Christmas-day. I preached at *Amboy* in *East-Jersey*, on 1 *Tim.* 3. 16.

December 26, Sunday. Mr. *Talbot* preached there on *Psal.* 125. and baptized a Young Man, called *John Brown*, who had a Quaker Education, and a Young Woman.

December 21, 1703. I preached at Capt. *Bishops* by *Ravai-River* in *East-Jersey*, on *Jude* 20. and baptized a Child of *Robert Wright.*

December 29, Wednesday. I preached at the Independents Meeting-House in *Woodbridge*, at the Desire of Mr. *Shepherd*, and some others there, on 1 *Tim.* 3. 16. After Sermon Mr. *Shepherd* kindly entertained us at his House.

December 30, Thursday. I preached at *Piscataway* in *East-Jersey*, on *Rom.* 10. 6, 7, 8, 9.

January 2, Sunday. I preached at *Amboy* on *Heb.* 8. 10, 11.

January 9, Sunday. I preached at the House of Dr. *Johnston* on *Nethersinks*, on *Psal.* 119. V. 113. and had a considerable Auditory.

January 16, Sunday. I preached at Mr. *Morris* House at the *Falls* of *Shrewsbury* in *East-Jersey*, on 2 *Cor*. 5. 17.

January 23, Sunday. I preached again at Mr. *Morris* House on 2 *Pet*. 1. 5.

January 30, Sunday. I preached at the House of Mr. *Thomas Boels* in *Freehold* in *East-Jersey*, on 1 *Cor*. 15. 58.

February 6, Sunday. I preached at the House of Mr. *John Read* in *Freehold* in *East-Jersey*, on *Psal*. 119. 96.

February 13, Sunday. I preached at *Burlington* Church in *West-Jersey*, on 1 *Cor*. 15. 58.

February 20, Sunday. I preached at *Philadelphia* both Forenoon and Afternoon, on *Psal*. 119. 96, 97.

February 27, Sunday, 1704. I preached at *Trinity-Chappel* at *Franckfort* (alias *Oxford*) in *Pensilvania*, on 1 *John* 2. 24. As I returned from *Franckfort* to *Philadelphia*, that very Day, about the 4*th* Hour in the Afternoon, being *Sunday*, both I and those in company with me, observed that a Corn-Mill belonging to some Quakers was Grinding, which they told me, is very common there.

March 5, Sunday, 1704. I preached at *Philadelphia*, on *Luke* 2. 29, 30, 31, 32, in the Afternoon.

March 12, Sunday. I preached at *Philadelphia* on 1 *Tim*. 2. 1, 2.

March 16, Thursday. I preached at *Trinity-Chappel* at *Franckfort*, on 1 *Tim*. 2. 1, 2.

March 19, Sunday. I preached at *Philadelphia* a second Sermon on 1 *Tim*. 2. 2, 3, 4.

March 26, Sunday, 1704. I preached both Forenoon and Afternoon, at *Burlington* Church, on 1 *Cor*. 15. 58. two other Sermons, being my last I preached there.

April 2, Sunday, 1704. I preached at *Philadelphia* on *John* 4. 24. being my last Sermon I preached there.

After my Return from *East-Jersey* to *Philadelphia*, about the middle of *February* 1703. for the Space of Six Weeks, I remained mostly at *Philadelphia*, and was very kindly and hospitally entertained by Mr. *Joshua Carpenter*, at his House, where I lodged all that time, until I began my Journey from *Philadelphia* towards *Virginia*, to take Passage for my Return to *England*. Mrs. *Welch*, with whom I lodged formerly, having been Sick and Weak all that time; but some time after it pleased God to restore her to Health.

During the most part of Winter, in the Year 1703. Mr. *Talbot*, by my free Consent, did travel in diverse other Parts in *Pensilvania*, *West* and *East-Jersey*, Preaching and Baptizing many in those Parts where I was not with him. For the greater Service of God and his Church, we did oft travel separately, (being still one in Heart and Affection) and I had very good Friends that travelled with me in his Absence, to accompany me from place to place, in all those places where I travelled.

April 9, Sunday. I preached at *Chester* Church in *Pensilvania*, on *John* 4. 24. being my last Sermon there.

April 12, Wednesday. I preached at *Newcastle*, on *Jude* 20.

April 16, Easter-Sunday. Mr. *Talbot* preached at Mr. *Bourdly's* Church in *Maryland*, where I had preached before *July* 21, 1703.

April 23, Sunday. I preached at *Annapolis* in *Maryland*, Col. *Seamour* Governour of *Maryland*, being present, who very kindly entertained us at his House both then and at other times, during our Abode there, as we waited for Passage down *Maryland-Bay* to *James-River* in *Virginia*.

Mr. *Talbot* accompanied me from *Philadelphia* to *Annapolis* in *Maryland*, where with true Love and Affection, we did take our Farewell of one another, and he returned to serve God and his Church, as formerly, especially in *Pensilvania*, *West* and *East-Jersey*, where he was like to have the greatest Service and Success: And some time ago, the Right Reverend *Henry*, Lord Bishop of *London*, has writ to him to fix at *Burlington*, to be Minister of the Church there, where is now a large Congregation; and where, not long ago, there was little else but Quakerism or Heathenism.

April 26, 1704. I sailed down *Maryland-Bay* to *Virginia*, in Captain *Pulman's* Ship, who very kindly entertained me and Mr. *John Barclay*, my good Friend with me: He, in true Love and Affection, travelled with me from his dwelling House at *Amboy* in *East-Jersey*, to *James-River* in *Virginia*, and he staid with me until he saw me aboard the Ship, *June* 8. where we took our Farewell.

May 2, 1704. We arrived at *Kicketan* by *James-River*, and staid some Days at the House of my Son in Law there.

May 7, Sunday. I preached at *Williamsburgh* Church in *Virginia*, on 1 *Tim*. 2. 3, 4. Col. *Nicolson*, then Governour of *Virginia*, being present, who kindly entertained us.

May 14, Sunday. I heard Mr. *Grace* preach in *Kicketan* Church, on *Luke* 23. 43.

May 21, Sunday, 1704. I preached at *Kicketan* on *Acts* 20. 21.

May 28, Sunday. I preached in the Queen's Ship, called, *Dread-Nought*, Capt. *Evans* Commodore to the *Virginia* Fleet bound for *England*.

June 4, Whitsunday. I preached again in the Commodore-Ship, on *Job*. 16. 7.

June 8. I came aboard the Commodore, and was kindly and generously entertained by Capt. *Evans* at his Table, all the Voyage, *gratis*, and I lodged (near to him) in the great Cabin.

August 6, 1704. We arrived safe at the *Downs*, praised be God our Preserver.

August 6. Having taken my Leave of Captain *Evans* at the *Downs*, I came aboard a Merchant-Ship, whose Commander was Captain *James Thomas*, and sailed in his Ship until we arrived into the *Thames*, about ten miles from *London*, being kindly entertained by him: And that Evening, being the 14*th* of *August*, I came to my Family in *London*, safe and well, notwithstanding of the false Prophecy of some of the Quakers, *That I should never see* England *any more, after my Departure out of it*, in *April*, 1702. The abovementioned Captain *James Thomas*, my good Friend, some Years ago came off from Quakerism (wherein he was educated) and his Wife also, and are come over to the Church. He was baptized above three Years ago, by the Reverend Mr. *Stubs*, in St. *Alphage* Church by *Zion-College*, whereof he is Minister; to whose Baptism I was one of the Witnesses.

Thus I have given an entire Journal of my two Years Missionary Travel and Service, on the Continent of *North-America*, betwixt *Piscataway-River* in *New-England*, and *Coretuck* in *North Carolina;* of extent in Length about Eight hundred Miles; within which Bounds are Ten distinct Colonies and Governments, all under the Crown of *England*, viz. *Piscataway*, *Boston*, *Rhod-Island*, *Connecticut*, *New-York*, *East* and *West-Jersey*, *Pensilvania*, *Maryland*, *Virginia*, and *North-Carolina*.

I travelled twice over most of those Governments and Colonies, and I preached oft in many of them, particularly in *Pensilvania*, *West* and *East-Jersey*, and *New-York* Provinces, where we continued longest, and found the greatest Occasion for our Service.

As concerning the Success of me, and my Fellow-Labourer Mr. *John Talbot's* Ministry, in the Places where we travelled, I shall not say much; yet it is necessary that something be said, to the Glory of God alone, to whom it belongs, and to the Encouragement of others, who may hereafter be imployed in the like Service.

In all the places where we travelled and preached, we found the People generally well affected to the Doctrine that we preached among them, and they did generally join with us decently in the Liturgy, and Publick Prayers, and Administration of the Holy Sacraments, after the Usage of the Church of *England*, as we had Occasion to use them.

And where Ministers were wanting, (as there were wanting in many Places) the People earnestly desired us to present their Request to the *Honourable Society*, to send Ministers unto them, which accordingly I have done: and in answer to their Request, the Society has sent to such Places as seemed most to want, a considerable Number of Missionaries.

Beside the general Success we had, (praised be God for it) both in our Preaching, and much and frequent Conference with People of diverse Perswasions, many of which had been wholly Strangers to the Way of the Church of *England;* who, after they had observed it in the Public Prayers, and reading the Lessons out of the Holy Scriptures of the Old and New Testament, and the Manner of the Administration of Baptism, and the Lord's Supper, were greatly affected with it, and some of which declared their great Satisfaction and the Esteem they had of the Solemn and edifying manner of our Worship and Administration, far above whatever they could observe in other Ways of Worship known to them.

To many, our Ministry was as the sowing the Seed and Planting, who, probably, never so much as heard one orthodox Sermon preached to them, before we came and preached among them, who received the Word with Joy; and of whom we have good Hope, that they will be as the good Ground, *That bringeth forth Fruit, some Thirty, some Sixty, and some an Hundred Fold.* And to many others it was a Watering to what had been formerly Sown and Planted among them; some of the good Fruit whereof we did observe, to the Glory of God, and our great Comfort, while we were with them, even such Fruits of true Piety and good Lives, and sober and righteous Living, as prove the Trees to be good from which they did proceed.

Many or most of those who had born the Name of *Separatist Quakers* (for their leaving the Meetings of the Quakers, because of their Opposition to the great Fundamentals of the Christian Faith, and had embraced the Doctrine they heard preached by me, concerning the Way of Salvation by Faith in Jesus Christ, both God and Man, as he outwardly came in the Flesh, died for our Sins, and rose again, &c. about the Years 1691 and 1692, and had set up distinct Meetings), we found had joined with the Church of *England* Congregation at *Philadelphia*, before our Arrival, when we came among them: they received us with great Joy and Satisfaction to hear us preach what tended to their farther Confirmation in the Christian Faith, and in Communion with the Church of *England*. And they expressed the great Benefit they had received by my several Epistles I wrote to them from *London*, about the Years 1698 and 1699, to answer the Scruples and Objections some of them had made to me in some of their Letters, against joining with the Church of *England*, which they told me, gave them great Satisfaction, by the Blessing of God, to join with the Church, and with which they joined soon after. And the like Service my Epistles did to others of their Friends, in *East* and *West-Jersey*, and other Parts of that Country, to whom they had imparted them, at my Desire.

The Reverend Mr. *Evan Evans*, the Minister of the Church of *England* Congregation at *Philadelphia*, informed me, that (beside the considerable Number of Converts to the Church from Quakerism, that the former Minister, the Reverend Mr. *Claiton* had baptized) by his Account, since he was Minister there, he had baptized of Men, Women, and Children, in *Pensilvania* and *West-Jersey*, of *English* and *Welsh*, about Five hundred; many, or most of them, having been Quakers, and the Children of Quakers, and Quakerly affected; and beside these, many who had left Quakerism, and had joined to the Church, had been baptized in Infancy, not having been born of Quaker Parents.

Since our Arrival into those *American* Parts, by the Blessing of God upon our Labours among them, in *Pensilvania*, *West* and *East-Jersey*, and *New-York* Province, there have been, by modest Computation, at least two hundred Persons baptized of Quakers, and their Children, and Servants, and of such who were Quakerly affected, by Mr. *Talbot*, and Mr. *Evans*, and by me, and some by the Reverend Mr. *Vesey*, Minister of *New-York*, in that Town. And beside these, many who had been baptized in Infancy, have come off from Quakerism and joined to the Church in these Countries, since we travelled and preached among them, and had much Conference with diverse of them in private from House to House. Diverse also of Dissenters formerly disaffected to the Church, who were not Quakers, are become well affected to the Church, and her Publick way of Worship, and Administration of the holy Sacraments, as well as to the Truth of Her Doctrine, since our Labouring among them, both in *East* and *West-Jersey*, and else where; so that, God be Praised, almost in all these Countries where we Travelled and Laboured, in some of which there was little to be observed but Quakerism, or Heathenism, which are much one (and if we may believe some of the Quakers great Authors, they are altogether one, *viz.* the Religion of the Quakers, and of such Heathens, who were obedient to the Light within them, but without all Faith, and Knowledge of Christ, as he came in the Flesh). I say, in all these Countries almost, by the Blessing of God on our Labours, there are good Materials prepared for the Building of Churches, of living Stones, as soon as, by the good Providence of God, Ministers shall be sent among them, who have the discretion and due qualifications requisite to Build with them. The Truth of which some of the late Missionaries have found, to their great Comfort, who, as soon as they Arrived into these Parts, unto which they were sent, did find a People prepared to receive them ; so that what others had Sown before them, they have Reaped, and I hope will more abundantly Reap.

In *Pensilvania*, where there was but one Church of *England* Congregation settled, to wit, at *Philadelphia* (and even that but of few Years standing) at our Arrival there; there are now, Blessed be God, Five Church of *England* Congregations supplied with Ministers, and who have convenient Churches, where the People assemble constantly every Lord's Day to the Prayers and Sermons, and where the Holy Sacraments are duly Administered, according to the Church of *England*. The places in *Pensilvania*, where these Churches are set up, are, the first, *Philadelphia*, the second *Chester* or *Upland*, the third *Franckfort* alias *Oxford*, the fourth *New-Castle*, the fifth *Apoquimene*.

At *Philadelphia*, they have Prayers in the Church, not only on the Lord's Days, and other holy Days, but all *Wednesdays* and *Fridays* weekly, and the Sacrament of the Lord's Supper administered Monthly, and the Number of the Communicants considerable. The Church is commonly well filled with People every Lord's Day, and when they are fully assembled, both of the Town and Country that belong to that Congregation, they may well be reckoned, by modest Computation, to amount to Five Hundred Persons of Hearers. But sometimes there are many more; and generally the Converts from Quakerism, are good Examples, both for frequenting the Church Prayers, and frequent partaking of the Lord's-Supper, with zeal and devotion, and also of sober and virtuous Living in their daily conversation, to the frustrating the lying Prophecies and Expectations of the Quaker Preachers especially, who used to Prophecy, that whoever left the Profession of Quakers, after that should be good for nothing, but as unsavoury Salt, to be trod under foot of Men. But to God's Praise be it said, they may be generally compared with the best Quakers for their Morals, and far to exceed many of them in that respect; and which greatly casts the Ballance, *that the Morals* of those converted from Quakerism, both in *England* and *America*, or any where else, are Built on the Foundation of the Prophets and Apostles, *Jesus Christ being the head corner Stone*, which the Quakers Morals (no more than the Heathens) are not Built upon.

At *Burlington* in *West-Jersey*, Twenty Miles distant from *Philadelphia*, on the other side of *Delaware-River*, there is now a settled Congregation, with a fixed Minister, to wit, the Reverend Mr. *John Talbot*, my Fellow Labourer, where there is a large Congregation, and a considerable Number of Communicants, many of them having been formerly Quakers, and Quakerly affected, or such as were of no particular denomination. And such of them as had not been Baptized in Infancy, have received Baptism, partly by Mr. *Evans*, and partly by Mr. *Talbot*, and some of them by me. Mr. *Talbot* has Baptized most of them who have been Baptized, since our Arrival among them, and particularly all the Children, both Males and Females, of *William Budd*, who formerly was a Quaker-Preacher, but is come over from Quakerism, to the Church, with diverse others of the Neighbourhood, in the Country about the Town of *Burlington*, who come usually to the Church at *Burlington* on the Lord's-Day ; some of them, Six, Eight, and some of them Ten, or Twelve Miles, and some of them more.

In some other Places they are about Building Churches, both in *West* and *East-Jersey.*

The place at *Franckfort* in *Pensilvania,* where the Congregation Assembles on the Lord's-Day, is called, *Trinity Chappel,* it was formerly a Quaker Meeting-House, Built, or fitted by Quakers, but some time ago has been given to the Church, by such who had the Right to it: Some Land adjoining was given by a Person well affected to the Church, for the use of the Minister, who should reside there, for a House, Garden, and small Orchard.

I can say little to any Success we had in *America,* amongst the other sort of Quakers, though, as the above-written Journal sheweth, I Laboured much among them, in true Love, and good Will; but they being misled, and prejudiced by their Leaders, seemed too generally to reject my Labour of Love; however, I am not without hope, that the Seed that God had enabled me to Sow among them, will in some of them, in due time, take Root downward, and bear Fruit upward, though little of it doth yet appear.

There are now Thirteen Ministers in the Northern Parts of *America,* all placed within these two Years last past, and generally Supported and Maintained by the *Honourable Society for the Propagation of the Gospel in Foreign Parts.*

In all the Places where we travelled, the Governours of all the several Provinces, did very kindly treat us, and give us all possible Countenance and Encouragement that we could desire or expect.

Here followeth an Account of the several Treatises I wrote and published in Print, in North America, *within the Time of my Abode there, in the Years* 1702, *and* 1703, *to* 1704.

I. MY Sermon• I preached at *Boston*, on *Ephes.* 2. 20. printed there.
II. My printed Sheet, in a Letter to Mr. *Samuel Willard*, a Preacher at *Boston.*
III. My Reply to Mr. *Increase Mather's* printed Remarks against the Six Rules I gave in my Sermon, on *Ephes.* 2. 20.
IV. My Answer to Mr. *Samuel Willard's* Reply to my printed Sheet.
V. My Answer to *Caleb Pusey* Quaker, his Book against me, which he abusively called, *Proteus Ecclesiasticus.*
VI. The Account of the blasphemous Notions of *William Davis,* who after he left the Quakers, set up for a Sect-Master.
VII. My Answer to a second Book of *Caleb Pusey* against me.
VIII. My Sermon preached at *New-York*, on *Acts* 2. 41, 42.
IX. My Sermon preached at *New-York*, on 1 *Cor.* 12. 13.
X. My Sermon preached at *Annapolis* in *Maryland*, on 1 *Thes.* 1. 5.

All these bound up in one Book, I humbly presented to the Society, soon after my Arrival at *London:* The Book it self may be found at the Library of the most Reverend *Thomas* Lord Arch Bishop of *Canterbury*, by St. *Martins* in the *Fields*, where the Society useth to meet.

APPENDIX.

The Six Rules *above-mentioned, in the first Sheet of the foregoing* Journal, *are these following.*

The First Rule.

WHATEVER is enjoyn'd by our Superiours, if it contradict not God's Commands in Holy Scripture, ought for Conscience sake to be obey'd, according to 1 *Pet.* 2. 13, 14, *Rom.* 13. 5. *Heb.* 13. 7, 17. And if what they enjoyn, be not made a Command of God, or an Article of Faith, or a Means of Grace.

The Second Rule.

Whatever Church holds the Fundamentals of Christian Religion, and has the Word of God duly Preach'd, and the Sacraments of Baptism and the Lord's-Supper duly Administered; such a Church is a true Church of Christ; and to separate from such a Church in external Communion, and in external Acts of Worship, is a Sin, the which Sin is the Sin of Schism, that is very heinous, *Rom.* 16. 17. 1 *Cor.* 12. 25. 1 *Cor.* 1. 10, 13. and nothing can excuse from the Guilt of that Sin, unless when anything is enjoyn'd to Persons that is really sinful and contrary to God's Commands given us in the Holy Scriptures; not what Men, by Prejudice of Education, or by wrong Information, say is Sin, but what really is so, and can be clearly proved to be so out of the Holy Scriptures. And if they cannot join in one or some external Acts of Worship, because sinful; yet in other Acts they ought to join that are not sinful.

The Third Rule.

What Things we see amiss in particular Persons, are not to be charged upon the whole Church, unless the Church do justify those Persons in those Things; and what we can't amend, we ought to bear; for there is no Christian Society upon Earth but has some particular Persons that do amiss; and all Dissenters, when particular Failings of particular Persons are objected to them, give the like Excuse.

The Fourth Rule.

To join in external Acts of Publick Worship, where the Matter is found, tho' there be a great Mixture of unsound Members with others found, is no Sin, but our Duty, for which we are warranted both by the Practice of the Prophets, and other holy Persons in the Ancient *Jewish* Church, who never did separate from the Publick Worship of God when the Matter of it was found, notwithstanding that Things were very much amiss amongst them in Practice: And also by the Example of *Zacharias* and *Elizabeth*, and all other holy Persons that were then in the *Jewish* Church, and by the Example of our Saviour himself and his Apostles, who frequented the Temple Worship, performed in the Synagogues before our Saviour's Passion, that put an end to Circumcision, and Sacrifices, and other Types of the Old Testament.

The Fifth Rule.

Whatsoever Things were commanded of God, or allow'd and practised lawfully under the Old Testament, that were neither any Part of the Ceremonial Law, nor of the Jewish Polity peculiar to that Nation, are still binding to us under the New Testament, or allow'd and practiced lawfully; and a Proof out of the Old Testament, in all such Cases, is as good as a Proof out of the New.

The Sixth Rule.

Set Forms of Prayer and Thanksgiving (where the People pray Vocally with the Minister) are a Duty as well under the New Testament as the Old; and that it was practised under the Old, is clear from *Isa.* 29. 13. *Joel* 2. 17. *Hos.* 14. 2, 3. *Mat.* 15. 8, &c. And under the New Testament our Saviour gave a Form of Prayer to his Disciples, which he commanded his Disciples to say; and *John* the *Baptist* taught his Disciples a Form of Prayer, *Luke* 11. 2. And many of the Dissenters use the Form of *Benediction* after Sermon, *The Grace of our Lord Jesus Christ, &c.* And they use the Form of Words that Christ taught, both in Baptism and the Lord's-Supper. Under the Old Testament they were to pray with the Spirit, and with Sincerity of Heart and Affection, as well as under the New; and therefore if praying in a Form was not then inconsistent with praying by the Spirit, no more is it now.

F I N I S.

[In continuation of the story of the Church's progress, as well as in further illustration of Mr. Talbot's character, we resume here the publication of his letters.]

Mr. Talbot to Mr. Keith.

"N. York, October 20th, 1705.

"REVEREND SIR:

"We received advice from Barbadoes that your Fleet was arrived, a confirmation of which we shall be glad to have from yourself. We the clergy in these Provinces, Pensilvania, N. Jersey, and N. York, being convened here by the directions of my Lord Cornbury and his Excellency Governour Nicholson, to make a representation of the present state of affairs of the Church, which we have drawn up, in a scheme, and transmitted to your venerable Society signed by the twelve apostles, I mean to do in this Letter as I do in my Travels, touch and go from place to place, and tell you such things as I thought not so proper for the Public view. I got some hundreds of Fr. Buggs Books printed, which I had endorsed with a challenge and so was bound to answer it; but I could not provoke the friends to it by no means. No they say, as they used to do, that they will answer in print. Then I offered to take the two Almanacks by Dan. Leeds and Caleb Pusey and prove them by Friends Books. I challenged ye latter at ye head of his Regiment to come forth and see himself proved a Lyar, in ye very same book and page where he most impudently charges G. K. D. L. and ye eight ministers of your Church of England. But all I could get of them at present was this sorry paper, "False News from Gath," which I intend to answer with "true news to Gath," Ashdod and the rest of the uncircumcised, unbaptized Philistines; at length I appointed a meeting at Church, whether they would come or no, and there I exposed their errors before all men, women and children that were there; but none answered a word, though several Quakers were there, whilst I, Mr. Sharpe and Mr. Nichols examined y^e^ "Bomb," and D. L. Almanack by their books, and proved ye quotations true. I have hired a chamber at Burlington, where I keep the present collection of friends books; several of them came to me there and were satisfied, but some desired me to set down my quotations book and page, which I promised to do at my leisure, particularly to one of their friends of ye ministry whom I believe will come off. I have forgot his name, he lives near Peter Chamberlain's in Pensilvania. Mr. Sharpe was very jealous to bring ye Quakers to stand a tryal; he carried one of ye Bombs into their meeting, and read a new challenge which I sent them, to answer what they they had printed; but all in vain. Sam. Jennings stood up and said, 'Friends let's call upon God;' then they went to Prayer and so their meeting broke up. Since, I have read several scandalous Letters from several Quakers, whereby I see they are preparing War against me; one was from W. Bakeshaw, the same villain that pulled ye paper out of your hand last yearly meeting at Philadelphia. He said there was not a word of truth in the Bomb, and he would answer it but none appeared. Mr. Nichol, Mr. Sharp and I preached in our turns, proper sermons to warn ye people of their errors, and heresies; so we kept up ye Christian yearly meeting so happily begun by you at Philadelphia. Mr. Nichols gives his service to you, he is indeed an ingenious man, and will prove in all appearance an able hand against Quakerism. I have promised to set him up with friends, goods, &c.; we mean to go down to Chester and give him a broad side there if the Governour will give us leave. They are all out at Philadelphia as much about Government as ever they were about religion. There is Charter against Commission and Major against Governour. They have 2 sheriffs, Captain Fenny appointed by Governor Evans, and young John Budd by ye Major. Now the Governour proclaimed their proceedings null and void, but G. Jones told him it was not he nor his, neither that should take away their Charter; so much for State affairs, you may hear all perhaps one of these days in Westminster Hall, meanwhile here's a Government divided against itself; God preserve his Church and let them that have the watch look out. There is a new meeting house built for Andrews, and almost finished since you came away, which I am afraid will draw away great part of the Church, if there be not ye greatest care taken of it; Mr. Rudman serves there some times, but chiefly at the Country Church (in Oxford near Frankfort) with good success; but he has met with some disturbance from Edward Eaton, who has been very pevish and scandalous in words and writings, for which he was presented to ye Grand Jury, but it was hard to persuade them to find the Bill; but what will come of it I know not.

"Mr. Sharp and I have gone the rounds several times from Burlington to Amboy, to Hopwell, to Elizabeth Town, to Staten Island in our turns, with good success, God be blessed, in all places. He has gathered a Church himself at Cheesquaks, where he preached several times, and baptized about forty persons. Now I am alone, for my Lord Cornbury has preferred him to be Chaplain of Her Majesty's Fort and Forces at N. York. I saw his Commission signed this day in ye room of Mr. Mott who dyed about 3 months ago. I was loth to part with my good friend and companion in travel, but considering how he had been disappointed at home, I would not hinder his preferment abroad, hoping that the good providence of God and ye venerable Society will supply his place.

"The Assembly sat at Burlington in September, but did nothing that my Lord desired them, so he dissolved them and called another there in October. Now I hear that Mr. Wheeler our good friend is chosen instead of Thomas Gardener. It seems their interest goes down thereabouts. Sam. Jennings complains that a man can't turn friend of truth now but he is ridiculed out of it. I hope the venerable Society will take Mr. Bradford's case into their consideration. It has cost me Ten pounds and more out of my Pocket to print some small books to give away, where I could not stay that the Church might be served and the Printer employed, without setting forth those that are erroneous. I know you will not forget ye Reverend Mr. James, who has been so zealous for ye service of ye Church, since you put him upon it. I count him as my father now you are gone, and indeed our Convocation had been at a Loss for a Foreman had not he supplied the place by his gravity and wisdom. I have drawn another Bill upon Mr. Hodges, not knowing when I should have so good opportunity; besides I have been at more than ordinary charge for horses and cloaths, for I never received any from England since I came out of it. As for that parcel that my Friend Mr. Gillingham sent by Capt. Innifer, I can't hear what is become of it. My horse you know dyed at Burlington and ye Quakers recorded it as a judgment upon me. Ben. Wheat set it down in his Almanack, such a day of ye 1st month, John Talbot's horse dyed, and Barnet Lane haled him into the river. But I was more sorry for the mare that you were so kind to give me, for she dyed before I came over the Bay in Maryland. I hope ye venerable Society will see good to take you into their number, for it may be of use to them to have one there that has been here. I hope the Letter will come safe to your hand by Mr. Robert Owen minister of a church in Maryland who is a very honest Gentleman. And indeed so are all the Missionarys in general, especially the English one Mr. More, the only countryman we have amongst us, a man according to my own heart, I'm sorry he's to go so far off as ye Mohocks, God knows whether we shall see him again. I had ye same call and had gone to the same place, but when I saw so many people of my own nation and tongue, I soon resolved by God's grace to seek them in ye first place, and if we could not recover those that were fallen, yet by God's help we may keep them out of ye pit of Quakers and Hereticks who have denyed ye Faith and are worse than Indians and Heathens who never knew it.

"As for a Suffragan we are all sensible of ye want we have of one, and pray God send us a man of peace, for otherwise he will do more harm than good, as proud, ambitious, covetous men used to do, troubling the State and perplexing the Church, and then they run away, and leave all in the lurch. I saw our honored friend, Coll. Nicholson, last month at Burlington, where he staid a week or ten days. I was obliged to him every way, particularly for his friendly advice in a case that was difficult to me at that time, but I shall not mention names because I am resolved, by God's grace, to take heed what I say of any man, whether good or bad.

"Coll. Nicholson took Bills of Mr. Bass for the money in hand, £70, Pensylvania money, and gave it all to the Churches in these Provinces, with Bills of Exchange to make it up £100 sterling, besides what he subscribed to the Churches to be erected at Hopewell, Elizabeth Town, Amboy and Salem. We have made it appear that he has exhibited to the Churches in these Provinces about £1000: besides, what he has given to particular persons and the poor would amount to some hundreds more, which we did not think fit to mention. He is a man of as much prudence, temperance, justice, and fortitnde as any Governor in America, without disparagement to any, and of much more zeal for the house and service of God. I have seen four of them together at Church in Burlington, but in the afternoon their place had been empty had it not been for the Honorable Governor Nicholson; so that I can't but observe the example of his piety in the Church, is as rare as his bounty towards it; no wonder then that all that love the Church of England are fond of Governor Nicholson, who is a true son, or rather a nursing father, of her in America. I hope you will do him all the service you can at home whereby you will oblige all the Churches abroad.

"Mr. Urquhart is well chosen for the people of Jamaica, and indeed I think none fitter than the Scotch Episcopal to deal with Whigs and Fanaticks of all sorts. Had not Stuttart been allowed to preach he had brought them all to the Church almost by this time; but now they resort most to a barn that is hard by, and will not pay Mr. Urquhart what is allowed by Law, though my Lord Cornbury has given his orders for it. Mr. John Lillingston designs, it seems, to go for England next year; he seems to be the fittest person that America affords for the office of a suffragan, and several persons, both of the Laity and Clergy, have wished he were the man; and if my Lord of London thought fit to authorize him, several of the Clergy both of this Province and of Maryland have said they would pay their tenths unto him, as my Lord of London's Vicegerent, whereby the Bishop of America might have as honorable provision as some in Europe. Ah, Mr. Keith, I have wanted you but once, that is ever since you went. I pray God supply your place with such another, who will pass through all Governments serving the Church, without giving offence unto the State. I hope, good Sir, you will excuse this long Letter. I had not time to write a short one; therefore, *amicitia nostra*, I desire that you would take all in good part that comes from

"Your most faithful friend
"And humble servant,
"John Talbot."

[We next find Mr. Talbot in England, whither he had gone on business of the church, as his letters will explain.]

Mr. Talbot to the Society for Propagating the Gospel.

"London, March 14, 1706.

"*May it please the Reverend and*
Right Honorable Society for Propagating the Gospel:

"After I had travelled with Mr. G. Keith through nine or ten Provinces between New England and North Carolina, I took my leave of him in Maryland. The Assembly then sitting offered me £100 sterling to go and Proselite their Indians; but my call was to begin at home, and to teach our own People first, whose Language we did understand; so I returned to Burlington to finish the Church which was happily begun there. Mr. Sharpe came to my assistance where I left him to supply that hopeful and infant Church, whilst I went to East Jersey for Amboy, Elizabeth Town, Woodbridge and Staten-Island. This we did by turns about half a year till Mr. Mott dyed who was Chaplain of the Queen's Fort and Forces at New York. I was offered this place also, where I should have Board and Lodging and £130 per annum, paid weekly; but nothing could tempt me from the service of the Society who were pleased to adopt me into their service, before I had the honour to know them. Mr. Sharpe was glad to embrace this offer; so I travelled alone, doing what good I could, till last Summer, I met with Mr. John Brook who brought me a letter from my Lord of London and orders to fix at Burlington, as I did till November last. There was a general meeting of the Missionarys who resolved to address the Queen for a suffragan Bishop, that I should travel with it, and make known the requests of some of the Brethren abroad, whose case we had recommended formerly by Letter to the Venerable Society, but without success. It will be four years next June since I associated with Mr. Keith. I was allowed £60 per annum for three years, but for the last I had nothing neither here nor there. I have no Business here but to solicit for a Suffragan, Books and Ministers for the propagating the Gospel. God has so blessed my Labors and Travels abroad that I am fully resolved by his Grace to return, the sooner the better, having done the Business that I came about; meanwhile my Living in Gloucestershire is given away, but I have no reason to doubt of any Encouragement from this famous Society who have done more in four years for America than ever was done before; and your Petitioner will ever pray. God bless all our Benefactors in Heaven and Earth, and reward them for ever, for all the Good they have done to the Church in general and in particular to

"Your most humble servant and
"Obedient Missionary,
"JOHN TALBOT."

Mr. Talbot to the Secretary.

"London, April 16th, 1707.

"HONORED SIR:

"I have received several letters from my friends in America who long for my return, which I was forward to do once and again, but Satan hindered me by raising lies and slanders in my way. But I have cleared myself to all that have heard me, and I hope you will satisfy the Honorable Society that I am not the man to whom that dark character did belong. Mr. Keith has known my doctrine and manner of life some years, what I have ventured, suffered and acted for the Gospel of Christ abroad and at home. I desire his letter may be read to the Honorable Board, and that they will be pleased to dispatch me, the sooner the better, for the season is far spent, and the ships are going out, and if I go at all, I would go quickly. I know the wants of the poor people in America. They have need of me or else I should not venture my life to do that abroad which I could do more to my own advantage at home. I should be glad to see somebody sent to North Carolina. I hope the Planters' letters are not quite forgotten. 'Tis a sad thing to live in the wilderness like the wild Indians without God in the world.

"Your humble Servant,
"JOHN TALBOT."

Mr. Talbot to the Secretary.

[Written after his return to America.]

"Philadelphia, 20th August, 1708.

"HONORABLE SIR:

"I have written several letters to you from Boston and New York by Brothers Brookes and Moore; but I am afraid they are all lost together; they have been nine months gone, and we saw them not since, nor any news of them. I met them at Boston and would persuade them to return, but all in vain; they had been so dragooned that they had rather be taken into France than into the Fort at New York. I have carried on ever since at Burlington as well as I could, and I thank God with success wherever I am; but I cannot stay long at any place, because there are so many that want, certainly the present state of that province is worse than the first; we have lost our labour and the Society their cost, there being several Churches and no ministers in all East Jersey to supply them, so that they fall away apace to Heathenism, Quakerism and Atheism, purely for lack of looking after. Mr. Brooks and Mr. Moore are much lamented, being the most pious and industrious Missionaries that ever the Honorable Society sent over; let the adversaries say what they will they can prove no evil thing against these men. I have heard all sides and parties, what can be said pro or con. Mr. Honeyman is outed, Mr. Nicholls scouted into Maryland; he had come home had I not dissuaded him, and I could have hindered all the rest of these scandals and disorders but that we had no Bishop nor hopes of any; you would not hear of it, therefore I said you must hear worse and worse still, if aught can be worse than that the bodies and souls of men are ruined and undone, and the Bounty of the Society lost, for lack of an overseer of the poor Church in America; without which the Gospel cannot be planted, nor any good work propagated in the World. The Bible you sent to Hopewell I was willing to take to Burlington till more came over, because ours is worn out; they that come I hope will bring Books with them. I shall write more particularly by the next opportunity. God bless all our friends of the Honorable Society, remaining theirs and

"Your humble servant,

"John Talbot."

Mr. Talbot to the Secretary.

"Burlington, 24th August, 1708.

"Honorable Sir:

"It is now nine months ago since I parted with Mr. Brooks and Mr. Moore at Boston; I sent letters by them, but we are much afraid all are miscarried. I was always glad to see them but much surprised to meet them both there; they told me what hardship they met with from the Governors of New York and Jersey, and how they escaped out of their hands; I was for converting them back again, telling them the dangers of the sea and the enemy, but poor Thorogood* said he had rather be taken into *France* than into the Fort at New York; and if they were sunk in the sea, they did not doubt but God would receive them, since they were persecuted for righteousness, that is for Christ's sake and his Gospel, and doing their duty to the best of their knowledge. Truly as it was in the beginning so I find it in the end; all

* The Rev. Thorogood Moore is meant.—Ed.

that will live Godly in Christ Jesus shall suffer persecution; but *somebody* must answer for these things at home or abroad. If I could have given them any hopes of a Bishop or Suffragan to direct or protect them, I believe they would not have gone; nay, I would have hindred them; but, alas! I had no such hopes myself: I came over to be as good as my word rather than on any encouragement to do any good; meanwhile, I am pure from the Blood of all men; ye are my Witnesses that I pleaded with all my soul to send an overseer of this poor Church, but you would not hear; therefore is this evil come upon us. I don't doubt but by God's mercy their souls are not miscarried, they are in peace wheree'r they be I don't doubt; but we Christians in Jersey are most miserable; we have Churches now but no ministers to open them, and if the gate of Heaven be shut, the gates of Hell will soon prevail against us.

"This comes to you in the bosom of Mr. Moore's which he gave me at Boston, which was the last that I had of him; he is much lamented, as indeed they are both; as for Thorowgood, I never knew his fellow of his age, nor ever shall again I fear; nothing can make this country amends for their loss but a good Bishop; but alas! that is *rara avis in terris*, &c. I preached the Gospel at Marble-Head, where the people offered to subscribe some hundreds of pounds to build a Church; but I have resolved to build no more Churches till there are more ministers to serve the Churches that are built. I preached at Stratford as I came along in Connecticut Colony, where was a numerous auditory, and Mr. Muirson had forty Communicants there the first time ever the Holy Sacrament was rightly administered; and upon the Islands, Rhode Island, Long Island, and Staten Island, I preached till the Winter broke up, when I got to Amboy and Elizabeth Town, where had been nobody since Mr. Brook left them, who was an able and diligent Missioner as ever came over; I got home about our Lady day, where I was very welcome to all Christian people, but alas! I could not stay, I am forced to turn Itinerant again, for the care of all the Churches from East to West Jersey is upon me; what is the worst is that I can't confirm any nor have not a Deacon to help me. My Clerk is put in prison, and was taken from the Church on the Lord's day upon a civil action of *meum* and *tuum*. I don't know how soon I may be seized so myself, but I bless God I fear no evil so long as I do none; *Exurgat deus dissipentur inimic*, &c. I hear there is another Governor coming for these provinces; people are sorry it is another Lord, for they say there never came a good one into these parts. I may say of them as the Quakers did of me, 'Thee comest for money,' but I proved them Liars, for I have taken no money of them nor yet of others since I came. I shall say no more on this point but refer all to Mr. Moore's letter, which I hope will have some weight with the Honorable Society, because they are the last words of their best Missioner when he was in prison for the Gospel of Christ and for a good conscience. His humble proposal is that the Honorable Society would use their interest with the Queen that we might have men of morals for Governors, if not of Religion; I say the same, and pray God direct them all for the best; so I desire your prayers for,

"Sir,

"Your most humble servant,

"JOHN TALBOT."

Mr. Talbot to the Secretary.

"Burlington, 30th June, 1709.

"Sir :

"I received your long letter and find *Certamen est de lana Caprina.* For your moderation, which is nothing in the world but a name which St. Paul never used in all his Epistles nor anything like it, but one where 'tis wrong translated ; it should be let your gentleness be known to all men, which I am for as much as anybody, towards man and Beast too ; but if you mean *moderation in Religion,* as one said here, 'I don't care whether I go to Heaven or Hell." Good sir pardon your servant in this thing, but let us not differ about words, but follow the things that are for peace, and things whereby we may plant the Gospel and edify the Church of God. I am very glad to find by the President's letter, that the members of the Honourable Society are convinced, that a head is necessary to the body, but if he don't make haste he will come too late, for here is nothing established, but such a moderation to all that is good, and such a toleration of all that is evil, yea of the most damnable Heresies, which by the way is a damnable Toleration, and worse than the worst persecution that ever was in the world ; for that only destroyed men's bodies, but these destroy body and soul in Hell for ever, which is damnable with a vengeance and will make the last State of poor America worse than the first, if not timely prevented. Is it not strange, that so many islands should be inhabited with Protestants, so many provinces planted by them—so many hundred thousand souls born and bred up here in America ; but of all the Kings, Princes and Governours, all the Bishops and Archbishops which have been since the Reformation, they never sent out anybody here to propagate the Gospel ? I say to propagate it by imparting some spiritual gift by ordination or confirmation. I thought the Society had set up to supply these wants, and to take off this horrible scandal from the Protestant Churches, but truly they would not hear of it till they had lost their best missionaries (may lose all the rest for ought I know before it be legally obtained). What ! is there a law against the Gospel ? Let it be taken out of the way as Popish and Antichristian ; we can't Baptize anybody hardly now for want of God fathers and God mothers, for who will be bound where they are not like to be discharged ? I can't get children here to be catechised, for they are ashamed of anything that is good, for want of school masters to teach them better. There is one Mr. Humphreys come over with my Lord Lovelace, I suppose not unknown to you by Mr. Congreve ; he is a pretty sober young man and graduate of Dublin college ; I have got him £20 subscribed, but that is not enough for one that has a famiiy. If the Society please to add so much to it as they think fit, it will be as good a work as they can do. Mr. Evans liked him so well that he would have had him for a free school at Philadelphia, but that wanderer Mr. Ross, has got in there I believe by this time, for they would not be quiet till they got poor Mr. Chub to resign. I pity Mr. Jenkin's case, and I hope the society will restore him, for he is young enough to move pity and to amend ; or if he cannot live there, let him be Itinerant in this province and I will help him what I can ; the churches in east Jersey are falling to the ground for lack of looking after, I can't go there above once or twice a year to administer the Holy Sacrament that they be not quite starved. It had been better not to have put these poor people to the charge of building churches, than have nobody to supply them, I can't get so much as a Reader here for any of them, and it were to save their souls. You that live at home in ease and plenty, little do you know what they and we do bear and suffer here, and how many thousand souls are legally lost whilst they at home are legally supplying them. Who will answer it to Jesus Christ who will require an account of us all, and that very speedily too, meanwhile He has charged all to take care of his flock not by constraint but willingly, not for filthy Lucre but of a ready mind; then they who don't care whether they go to Heaven or Hell will have no reward for that moderation. I find in your books that one Mr. Sergt. Hooke is willing to give the tenth of his Land to the Church at Hopewell; pray let him send me a power and I will take care of it, and get him a purchaser for the rest. I have got possession of the best house in America for a Bishop's seat; the Archbishop told me he would contribute towards it and so I hope will others; pray let me know your mind in this matter, as soon as may be, for if they slip this opportunity, there is not such another to be had. Our church here does flourish, God be praised, and the town too is much more populous than it was; I hope we shall soon be out of Debt, meanwhile I take nothing of them, there is my moderation; besides I bless God, I have kept the peace where nobody else did or could, and that is no sign of immoderation: now I have shown you my moderation by my works, pray show me yours that I may learn more how to approve myself as I ought.

"Yours &c.

"John Talbot.

"Pray for God's sake send us some books of all sorts, especially Common Prayer books.

Mr. Talbot to the Secretary.

"Burlington, 27th September, 1709.

"Sir:

"Though I have sent you several letters of late, yet I can't omit so good an opportunity as this by Mr. Hamilton of giving my duty and service to the Honorable Society; my comfort is I have always told them the truth both at home and abroad, though I was not believed till it was too late. When I reflect on the progress of the Gospel (I will not say the Church for we never had it here, nor never shall till there comes over a propagator to plant and to build it up) a cloud of melancholy thoughts throngs upon me; for when the Shepherds are smitten the sheep of the flock must need be scattered abroad. Mr. Moore, Mr. Brooks, Mr. Muirson, Mr. Reedman, Mr. Jenkins, Mr. Urquhart, all worthy men, dead in less than two years, and almost all the rest run away, as Black, Crawford, Nichols; Ross is a wandering star, we do not know where he will fix; meanwhile he does not well to supplant and undermine, let him be confined to some place where there is need, and not stay altogether in the town to do more hurt than good; there's Mr. Evans, Mr. Ross, and Mr. Chub all at Philadelphia, and none else in that Province, where the Society have sent most; at Chester there's none, at New Castle none, at Appoquimony none, at Dover hundred none, at the whorekills none, and the people in all these places so abated of their zeal, that I'm sure it had been much better to have sent none at all, than none to supply the death and absence of these men. Here is not one come to supply the loss of these 10 missionaries, and if there does come any what will they do but find great discouragements, and the last state of their several places worse than the first; wherefore my advice is, with humble submission to my superiors, to keep their money and give us leave to come home, and send no more till they think fit to send a propagator of the Gospel; for otherwise their planting the Gospel is like the Indians planting gunpowder, which can never take root, but is blown away by every wind. Poor brother Jenkins was baited to death with musquitoes, and blood thirsty Gal-Knippers,* which would not let him rest night nor day, 'till he got a fever at Appoquimony, came to Philadelphia, and died immediately of a Calenture; my brother Evans and I buried him as well as we could, it cost us above £20 for, poor man! he had nothing, being out of Quantum with the Society, and his bills protested. If you please to call to mind, I told the Society when I was there, that those places must be served by Itinerants, and that it is hardly possible for anybody to abide there, that is not born there, 'till he is musquito proof; those little things are a great plague in some parts, and when a man is persecuted in one place he should have leave to go to another, or else, he has very hard measure, especially in these parts where our life is a kind of Penance both winter and summer, and nobody can tell which is the worst, the extreme heat or cold. I hear Mr. Vaughan is arrived at Boston, but is not yet come into this province, he will have enough to do to supply Mr. Brook's charge at Elizabeth Town, Amboy, Piscataway, who have had none since he left them; but I have done for them, may be once in a quarter or so; somebody occasionally passing by that way, but poor Hopewell has built a Church and have had no minister yet; and he had need be a good one that comes after Mr. Moore; there be many more in England but none so good as to come over and help us, that I can see or hear of. As for the account of what Indians we have converted, truly I never saw nor knew any that were Christians indeed; but I know there are hundreds, yea thousands of our white folks, that are turned Infidels for want of looking after. Let them that have the watch look out and see what they will answer; for he that is higher than the highest regards. I have received nothing from the people in this province, nor will not till they be out of debt for building the church. I leave honest Mr. Hamilton to give you a farther account of our affairs, and how we do; he has been one of our benefactors and given us £10. I hope when he returns, the Society will be so kind as to send us some Common Prayer books which we very much want here and at Hopewell, Maidenhead, and everywhere. I pray God direct and prosper the designs of the sacred Society, that Religion and learning, piety and virtue, may be established among us for all generations: so I rest sir,

"Your's &c. "John Talbot.

* Ganni-nippers, a large species of musquito.

"I hope you will put the Society in mind of what we have often desired, a school master, for there is none in Town nor in all the province that is good; and without, we can't instruct the children as they ought to be in the Catechism, for they will not be brought to say it in the Church till they have been taught at school."

Messrs. Evans and Talbot to the Society.

"Burlington, December 4th, 1712.

"RIGHT REVEREND AND RIGHT HON. SIRS:

"It is with the greatest satisfaction that we received from our brother Henderson the account of your zeal, care and diligence in relation to the Church at Jamaica; your favourable reception of the memorial we signed with the rest of our brethren on that account will encourage us to use the utmost of our efforts for the interest of the Church, though for our reward here, we expect little other than what the effects of the malice and rage of the Church's enemies will afford us. In these parts of the world the great enemy of mankind hath for many hundred years ruled with an uninterrupted sway, and we are sensible that he doth and will use all the means possible to hinder and discourage the Missionaries, whose business it is to promulgate the Gospel, and by that means to deliver his Captives from the greatest slavery into the glorious liberty of the Sons of God. Our Great Master hath, in these parts, raised us up some faithful friends of all ranks who are zealously affected both to us and the work we are engaged in, and nothing now seems more wanting to establish the Church, in a flourishing state, than the residing of a Bishop amongst us in these parts; which we are in hopes it will not be long before we are blessed with, since we are informed the Honorable Society have closed the bargain for the house at the point, and directed the fitting it up for the reception of a Bishop. We are sorry any accident should have altered so charitable and good a design, and therefore you may imagine it was with no little concern that we beheld the damage done by fire, on one part of the house, since the closing of the bargain (though before any possession was given to any person on account of the Society). On the 23d October, in the afternoon, by the foulness of the chimney and carelessness of one Stiles, who kept possession for Mr. Tatham, the fire took on the top of the Roof, but by the industry and care of all sorts of people was extinguished with the loss of part of the Roof of that part of the house that lieth next the Town, and little other damage. His Excellency the Governor, by his letter to Mr. Talbot of the 3d November, 1712, hath directed him to repair the house and make it habitable for a Bishop; which since it could not be done this winter, as your Honours may see by the enclosed certificate, we thought it more advisable to acquaint the Society thereof, as also our opinion that it would be less chargeable and more certain, if the Society would please to give order to some person in this Town to manage that work, and believe Mr. Secretary Bass hath already (without any directions) taken care to provide some things necessary for the covering the House and fencing the Garden, &c., and whose zeal for the interests of the Church, and particularly for the coming over of a Bishop, we believe is not unknown to the Honorable Society, if his letters of the 22d May, 1711, with the enclosed papers, were communicated to the Society. We herewith send the Honorable Society the carpenter's opinion about the repairs, and believe that the sending Glass, Sheet Lead, Nails, &c., from England would be both better and cheaper than to purchase them here. We earnestly pray for a blessing on your pious endeavours for the Glory of God and good of his Church, and remain with all imaginable deference,

"Right Reverend and Right Honorable,
"Your most obedient and faithful
"Humble Servants,

"EVAN EVANS.
"JOHN TALBOT."

Mr. Talbot to the Secretary

"Burlington, October 28th, 1714.

"SIR:

"I sent a letter by Mr. Evans, wherein I desired leave of the Honorable Society to come home. I have been long enough in these parts to see iniquity established by law, and that by some of your own members, and what good can your Missionaries do? I have been sick a long time this fall with a burning fever, which made me so weak that I could scarce speak. I could not preach, nor read prayers, so the service of God ceased. In all this Province of West New Jersey there never was any minister of Christ's Church settled but myself. I have built three Churches since I came here, but have nobody to keep them, nor myself neither. We have had a very sickly time this year; I have buried more than in ten years before; and many Church people died that had nobody to visit them when sick, nor bury them when dead. Let them that have the watch look out, 'tis they must give account; I am clear of the blood of all men, abroad and at home, and so I hope to keep myself. The Society were once upon a good resolution to send Deacons to be School Masters; if they had done so to Burlington, to Bristol, to Hopewell, they might have kept the Church doors open, for they could read the Prayers and Homilies, Baptize and Catechize, they could visit the sick and bury the dead; but now they must bury one another; they have no where to go but to Quakers' meetings, which are as bad as Indians'; there's nothing but powawing and conjuring to raise a Devil they cannot lay again; and now that this wickedness is established by law, what should we do here any longer? They do declare in the presence of God Almighty, they don't swear, call him to witness all they say is no more than yea or nay.

"The Church at New Bristol, over against Burlington, was opened about St. James' day, and so called St. James' Church, by the Rev. Mr. Philips, who preached the first sermon. The Church was full of people from all parts, who were liberal contributors to it. I went now and then to preach there on Sundays in the afternoon before I was sick, but since that I have not been able, so the Church has been shut up, almost ever since it was opened. The Church at Hopewell has been built these ten or twelve years, and never had a minister settled there yet, though they have sent several Petitions and Addresses to the Society; but I understand since, that Hopewell, Maidenhead, &c., were kept under the thumb for Cotton Mather and the rest of the New England Doctors to send their emissaries; and those hirelings have often come there, and as often run away, because they were hirelings, and cared for no souls but themselves.

"As for the Church at New Bristol, it was first begun by the zealous Thorowgood Moore, of pious memory; and when he was taken away by this same cursed faction that is now rampant, I was unwilling any of his good works should fall to the ground, so I crossed the water at my own cost to serve those poor people, who lived in Darkness and the shadow of death, in the midst of Heathenism, Atheism, and Quakerism; but it pleased God by our preaching the word in season and out of season, some came to believe and were baptized, they and their children, and two of the Chief people there, Mr. John Rowland and Mr. Anthony Burton, were willing to undertake to build a Church, which since they have done, and I believe they will endow it too if they get a minister before they die. I gave them five pounds and a pulpit of black walnut, which cost as much more, to encourage them; I promised to lay their case before the pious society, that they may take some care of them, that they be not a reproach to the heathenish Quakers, who are too apt to reflect upon us, 'where is your Priest, where is your Minister, and where is your Church, it may serve us for a meeting house,' &c. *Pudet hæc opprobria nobis dici potuisse et non potuisse repelli.*

"But the History of the Church at Burlington, &c., has been so much better done by Colonel Jeremiah Bass, Esq., Secretary of this Province, and transmitted home, by the hands of the Honorable General Nicholson, that I need say no more at present, but desire the prayers and blessing of the venerable Society for their

"Most humble and faithful Missionary
"And servant,
"JOHN TALBOT."

History of the Church at Burlington, New Jersey, by Jeremiah Bass, Esq., delivered by General Nicholson.

[Mr. Bass was her Majesty's Secretary of the Province of Jersey.]

SOLI DEO GLORIA.

"After a long season of Ignorance, Superstition, and Idolatry had covered this Province, it pleased that Infinite Being whose goodness is over all his works, and who hath promised to give unto our Blessed Saviour, the Immaculate Jesus, the Heathen for his inheritance, and the utmost parts of the Earth for his possession, to illuminate these Provinces with some Rays of his Glory and Goodness, by sending the glorious light of the Gospel amongst us. The first European inhabitants of this River were the subjects of the King of Sweden, who in their first settlement in this River, brought with them the Religion of their country, in which, to their commendation, and the care of their Missionaries, they have yet continued; few of them having at any time from their first settlement to this day, apostatized from their Christian faith, to the envy of Quakerism.

"The next Inhabitants were the Dutch, who having taken the River from the Swedes, introduced their Laws, Government, and Religion, which again suffered an alteration, by the coming in and conquest of these parts by the English, who in their first settlement of this Province, seemed to mind more the business of their Trade and Plantation, than that great concern of their souls. There being in the Western Division, no settled Society or Congregation of any of the Church, or any Dissenters, except Quakers; and although some Reverend Divines, as they occasionally passed through this Province, preached the Gospel and administered the ordinance of Baptism to some few persons, and by that means sowed the seeds of the Gospel, that have since sprung up around us, and excited the desires of some of the inhabitants to make a more diligent enquiry into the true way of worshipping God, and had in some measure taken off those prejudices that most of the inhabitants laboured under, by education, example and reading the Books and hearing the discourses of such as had misrepresented both the Doctrine and Discipline of the Church of England; yet we cannot properly begin any History of the Church but from the arrival of the Reverend Mr. Edward Portlock, who at the desire of several of the Proprietors of the Eastern Division of this Province, came over, ordained by the Right Reverend Henry, Lord Bishop of London, to take the care and cure of souls, as rector of a Church, to be built at Perth-Amboy, the metropolis of the Eastern Divison of this Province, who arrived in this Province, and made his application to the Governor, for the Proprietor, in the year ——; who with the consent and approbation of the Agents, for the Proprietors, called the Council of Proprietors, set apart one of the Houses (that had been formerly built at the charge of the general Proprietors) for the peculiar service and worship of God, according to the Laws of England, which House, by the Contribution of several pious and well-disposed persons, was soon covered, and glazed, and fitted with seats and a Pulpit, and Mr. Portlock put into possession of the same, (which by the way is the only Church they have to this day at Perth-Amboy); in the interim, Mr. Portlock preached sometimes at the Governor's House, sometimes at a House belonging to Mr. Dockaray of London, merchant, sometimes in the neighbouring Towns of Woodbridge, Piscataway, Elizabeth Town, and when the Governor's business called him into the Western Division, accompanied him to Burlington, where the Public Town House was allotted him for that service. This good work was at the same time carried on by the Rev. Mr. Vesey, in the Eastern Division, and the Rev. Mr. Clayton, Minister of Christ Church, Philadelphia. These beginnings of Light, which through the blessing of God were not unsuccessful, and the division that at this time happened amongst the people called Quakers, by Mr. George Keith's opposing some of their principal errors, occasioned several pious and well disposed Christians to think of erecting a place in Burlington, peculiarly dedicated and set apart for the service and worship of God, according to the usage of the best of Churches, the Church of England; who were herein much encouraged and assisted by the pious discourses and sermons of the Rev. Mr. Evan Evans, Rector of Christ Church in Philadelphia, who frequently came over into this Province, preached and baptized both Infants and Adult persons, and the Rev. Mr. John Talbot, our worthy Minister, a Missionary of the Honorable Society for the propagation of the Gospel in Foreign Parts; this good work was very much forwarded by the generous contribution of his Excellency Francis Nicholson, Esq., then Governor of Virginia, who we must own to be our first and best Benefactor, and indeed he gave life and motion to the whole work, by a generous contribution of near £50, to be laid out towards that service; and since, I have the just occasion to mention that worthy patron of our Churches (in whose commendation on this score too much can hardly be said). I may be therefore bold in affirming, that no Church in these parts hath wanted assistance towards its foundation, reparation, or beautifying but hath on application tasted of his bounty; no Missionaries or Ministers, that have had the happiness of his acquaintance, have parted from him without some mark of his favour; nor no devout and pious member, in any exigency or distress, has applied to him for relief or support in vain. On this encouragement, and the assistance of some considerable benefactions of £50, from the members of the Church at Philadelphia; £12 10s. from the Rev. Mr. Myles at Boston, and the courteous care and diligence of Mr. Robert Wheeler, of Burlington, merchant, since deceased, (who has sometimes been in advance above £150, out of his own pocket), and the contributions of several other persons, who though not particularly mentioned, will be rewarded by Him, who has promised a reward for a Cup of Cold Water, given to a Disciple, in the name of a Disciple.

"The Church of St. Mary in Burlington, in the Western Division of the Province of New Jersey, had the foundation stone laid by the Rev. John Talbot, Missionary from the Honorable Society for propagating the Gospel, on the 25th day of March, in the year of our Lord 1703; being a day sacred to the memory of the Annunciation of the Conception of our Blessed Saviour to the Virgin Mary, which gave name to the Church. This beginning was carried on with that Industry and Diligence, chiefly by the said Mr. Wheeler, that it was inclosed, covered, ceiled, and glazed, and the Holy Sacrament administered therein, by the Rev. Mr. John Talbot, on Whitsunday, the 4th of June, 1704; the Divine Service having been read and Sermons preached in the said Church ever since the 22d of August, in the preceding year, 1703. Thus the work of God and his Church was carried on amongst us, with great alacrity. The Burying ground purchased for the Church, containing in all about three acres, being well fenced in, and Pews and Seats in the Church, the members began to think it convenient to form themselves into a regular Society, according to the Law and Customs of England, and therefore addressed themselves by Petition to his Excellency, Edward, Lord Cornbury, (since Earl of Clarendon), Her Majesty's Governor of this Province, and a real friend of our Church, who on the 4th October, 1704, granted his Warrant for a Patent to Incorporate them, under his Privy Seal, with all requisite and necessary powers for their encouragement and support. The Church thus settled, under the care of the Rev. Mr. John Talbot, through the Blessing of God, on his ministry, grew and increased so that we had subscriptions made, and the foundation laid, for a Church at Hopewell, in the upper part of the County of Burlington, which hath been since finished, which was for some time supplied by the Rev. Mr. May, but is now without any minister. We had another begun at Salem, which by some unhappy accidents, hath been since discontinued, though not without some hopes of being revived, when it shall please God to send some one amongst us, that careth for the welfare, and seeketh the good of the Churches; to both of which Churches we find his Excellency, Colonel Nicholson, one of the first and chiefest Benefactors; and here I cannot omit mentioning the Honorable Colonel Cox, then one of Her Majesty's Council for this Province, who was one of the first subscribers to our Church at Burlington, and has given the like assistance to that at Hopewell, together with the assurance of settling 200 acres of Land, out of the nighest and most convenient part of his Land, contiguous to the said Church, for a glebe for the Minister, whenever it shall please God a missionary be sent over, to take care of that Church, or sooner if it be desired. I might also mention the Churches of Chester, New Castle, Dover River, Apoquimony, Oxford, and Bristol, that about the time, were either begun or finished; but designing to confine myself to Burlington only, I purposely omit any particulars of them. Our Reverend Minister's affairs calling him for England, in the year of our Lord 1705, he appointed the Rev. Mr. Thorowgood Moore to serve the Church in his room, a person of morals, exemplary meekness, piety and charity. Our Vestry thought it their duty, by the Rev. Mr. Talbot, to send home Addresses to Her Majesty, and a Letter of Thanks to the Archbishop of Canterbury, the Bishop of London, and the Honorable the Society for the Propagation of the Gospel, which are too large to be inserted in this Essay. Our Church for some time found no considerable alterations by the absence of our worthy Rector; but that enemy of our happiness, who had been many times heretofore sowing the seeds of Division and Dissension amongst us, (which through the care and prudence of our Rector, were not suffered to grow and increase) took advantage of his absence, and stirred up such a flame, that had almost broken us to pieces, and occasioned the unhappy removal both of Mr. Moore and the Rev. Mr. Brooks, Rector of the Church in Elizabeth Town, (erected chiefly by the care and diligence of Colonel Richard Townly, who has given the ground it stands on, and a place for a Burying Ground,) who have not been heard of since their departure from Marble-Head, in the year 1707. But I willingly pass over this subject, too sad to be insisted on, charitably hoping that all who were any ways the unhappy authors of it, have since blotted out their sins by repentance, and I have good cause to believe that had we been so happy, to have enjoyed an Ecclesiastical Governor, to have dispensed the censures of the Church, and to have determined differences, that will sometimes unavoidably occur, betwixt Ministers and Members, and betwixt Ministers and the People, this mischief had been prevented or cured; it is no wonder if our Communicants grew remiss and slack in their duty, if too many fell away in scandalous sins of schism, if error and heresy increased, if scandals were both taken and given (as there were in this case), when the Ecclesiastical sword was wanting, to punish evil-doers, to resist the unruly, to reduce the erring, and to cut off the obstinate and heretics. By this unhappy absence of our Rector, who was then in England, and of Mr. Moore who was gone from us, the number of our Communicants, and the Interest of our Church sensibly decreased, but began again to revive on the return of our Reverend Rector in the year 1708, who acquainted us that he had presented our humble Address to Her Majesty, and the other Letters that we sent; and that Her Majesty had been graciously pleased to give us Lead, and Glass, and Pulpit Cloth, and Altar Cloth, and a Silver Chalice, and Salver for the Communion Table, and a Brocade Altar Cloth; and that she had also sent Lead, and Glass, and Pulpit Cloths, and Altar Cloths for the Churches of Hopewell and Salem, which we received by the hands of the Honorable Col. Robert Quarry. He also brought us an Embossed Silver Chalice and Patten, the gift of Madam Catharine Bovey, of Hacksley; for all which our Vestry returned their thanks by Addresses and Letters of the 6th of November, 1708.

"His Excellency, the Lord Cornbury, being succeeded in the Government of this Province, by His Excellency the Lord Lovelace, whose Commission was published the 20th of December, 1708, all things relating to the Church here, continued much at a stand, His Excellency never coming so far as Burlington, nor as I know of, having ever been at Church in this Province, whilst he enjoyed that Government. By the death of that Nobleman, in the year 1709, the Government devolved upon Colonel Richard Ingoldsby, then Lieutenant Governor of the Provinces of New Jersey and New York, under whose administration, our Vestry (that by some unaccountable neglect, had omitted to pass the charter designed for us, by the Earl of Clarendon) got it now passed, under the Broad Seal of this Province, whereby they became incorporated by the name of the Minister, Church-Wardens, and Vestry, of the Church of St. Mary in Burlington; which was enrolled in the Secretary's Office, the 25th of January 1709. By this Charter, the Rev. Mr. John Talbot, Rector, Mr. Robert Wheeler, and Mr. George Mills, Church-Wardens, and Col. Daniel Cox, Lieut. Col. Huddy, Alexander Griffith, Her Majesty's Attorney General, Jeremiah Bass, Her Majesty's Secretary of this Province, and sundry others, were appointed, constituted and made a Body Corporate and Politic, in deed and in name, to have Community and succession perpetual, with powers to purchase, take and receive Lands, &c., in fee and perpetuity, not exceeding £300 sterling per annum, with power to sue and be sued, implead and be impleaded, to make and use a Common Seal, and the same, to alter at their discretion, to choose New Church-Wardens and Vestrymen, as there shall be occasion, with many other powers and immunities, too large to be here inserted, from which time the members of the Corporation met together, and transacted all affairs, relating to the Church, under that seal and title. And here I cannot forget mentioning the Donation of 250 Acres of Land given to this Church, the last Will of Thomas Leicester, deceased, which by this Charter, we were enabled to receive. We had nothing happened of any great note to us, till the year 1711; and some time in April in that year, the Church received the gift of a large silver Beaker, with a cover, well engraved, being the present of the Honourable Colonel Robert Quarry, for the use of the Communion; in the same month the minister, Church-Wardens, and Vestry, having received advice from the Rev. Mr. Evan Evans, Rector of Christ Church, in Philadelphia, and from the Vestry there, that their Assembly had passed an act directing affirmation, to such, who for conscience sake, cannot take an oath, together with a copy of the said act, and duly considering with themselves, the pernicious tendency of such proceedings to Religion in General, and to the best of Churches, the Church of England in particular, they thought it their duty to give as public a testimony as they could, of their just detestation and abhorrence of such principles and practices, and in order, thereto, at their meeting, on the 4th of April, 1711, they caused the following Resolves to be entered on their minutes:

"'Resolved that the said act is contrary to, and destructive of the Religious and Civil Liberty of Her Majesty's subjects, and contrary to the Laws of Great Britain.

"'Resolved that an address be drawn up to her Majesty against giving her Royal Assent to the said act.

"'Ordered that the Rev. Mr. John Talbot, the Honourable Col. Daniel Cox, Alexander Griffith, Esq., Her Majesty's Attorney-General, and Mr. Secretary Bass, do draw up the said address.'

"According to these Resolves, an Address was drawn, signed and sent home to Her Majesty, together with others, to the Right Rev. Henry, Lord Bishop of London, the Right Honourable, the Earl of Clarendon, &c., which had that good effect at home that Her Majesty was pleased by her order in Council to declare her disapprobation of that act. The gentlemen of this church, were rather induced to this, in that they had just cause to fear that the same enemies of our Church that had, with so much cunning and artifice, obtained that act, in the neighbouring Province, would be restless in their endeavors to obtain the same in this Province; and indeed the party of the same sort of men, having got themselves chosen Representatives of the People, in this Province, in conjunction with some others, who in this too much betrayed the interests of the Church, had at the Sessions of the Assembly, in this Province, in December, January, and February, 1710, obtained a Bill, to pass the House of Representatives, entitled an act for ascertaining the qualifications of Jurors, and enabling the Quakers to serve on them, and to enjoy places of profit and trust, within this Province; which was by the majority of the Council, rejected at the second reading; who in this, as well as in many other instances, showed their zeal and fidelity to the Church, and its interest here in this Province.

"The Church, all this while, had laboured under the burden of a Debt, contracted by several of its members, towards the building and finishing the same, which occasioned a new subscription to be made, which, not answering to a sufficient sum to pay the Debt, we find the same worthy member, Col. Coxe, by the Donation of £25, set us clear of that incumbrance we were uneasy under.

"Our Church now began to have thoughts of providing something in this Town like a Glebe, for the Rector of our Church, for the time being, but were almost discouraged by our paucity and poverty; but Divine Providence, that never faileth those that confide in it, afforded us an unexpected supply, by means wholly unthought of by us. The Rev. Dr. Frampton, late Bishop of Gloucester, having, by his last Will and Testament, left £100 sterling towards propagating the Gospel in America, at the sole appointment of the Right Rev. Henry, Lord Bishop of London, that Worthy and Reverend Prelate, at the instance and desire of Madam Catharine Bovey, of Hacksley, in the county of Gloucester, our worthy Benefactress, by a proper Instrument, in April, before he died, directed the money to be paid into her hands, for purchasing somewhat in America, that may be perpetual to the Church of St. Mary's in Burlington; to which she is pleased in her Letter to promise an addition of her own to complete the purchase. This sum is appropriated towards the payment of the purchase money, for a convenient House, Orchard, and about Six Acres of Land, adjoining to the Church, in the town of Burlington, to the use of the Rector of the said Church, for the time being, for ever; and since I am mentioning these small Benefactors, towards the Church here, I should be justly charged with ingratitude and inadvertency, if I had not remembered that act of generosity in the Right Honorable the Society for propagating the Gospel in Foreign Parts, who have not only constantly supported our Reverend Minister with a salary of £60 per annum, but have, at the expense of £600 sterling, purchased the House formerly built, and belonging to Mr. Tatham, with fifteen Acres of Land, and twelve Acres of Meadow, for the use of a Bishop, when it shall please God to send one hither, and have since repaired the same, at very great additional expense.

"The same General Assembly that had not sat since the 16th of July, 1711, after many repeated prorogations, at last met his Excellency, Colonel Robert Hunter, Governor of this Province, on the 8th of December, 1713, and continued their Session till the 17th of March following, in which amongst other acts, having passed an Act, 'That the Solemn Affirmation and Declaration of the People, called Quakers, shall be accepted and taken instead of an Oath in the usual form, and for qualifying and enabling the said people to serve as Jurors, and to execute any office or place of trust or profit within this Province," the Minister, Church-Wardens, and Vestry, on a due consideration of the danger the Church is in, by the increase of Atheism, Deism, Socinianism, Quakerism, and a new set of people that seem to be a compendium of all the ancient Heresies, known by the name of Free-Thinkers, and perceiving this Act of Assembly to give too great encouragement to these Enemies of our Church, thought it their duty to use their strenuous endeavours to obviate those apparent mischiefs; and, therefore, in an humble manner, made a new application to Her Royal Majesty, (who is not only Titular, but indeed the Defender of the Church) to prevent the giving her Royal Assent to so mischievous an Act; and at the same time addressed the Honourable Society for the propagation of the Gospel, for their countenance and assistance, to all which they are in hopes of a gracious answer. By this Act, the professed enemies of the Church, being made capable to be admitted into all offices and places of profit and trust, it is easy to perceive how hazardous it is for any of the friends of the Church to appear in its defence, or to adventure to put a stop to this foment of evil, by the most regular methods of addressing against it; since some persons, not contented with liberty of conscience, are so fond of licentiousness in Government, that they will leave no stone unturned to obtain their darling Idol. It was for this end that by false suggestions and calumnies, several of the friends and favorites of the interest of the Church, Gentlemen of some of the best estates in the Province, were, to our very great grief, removed from being of her Majesty's Council and their places filled with others, that have been made favorable to their designs and interests; but it is time now to put a period to this Essay, it being sometimes more dangerous to assert Truth than to justify Error. In a word, since the first beginnings of any Established Church in this Province, we may truly say, that the Church never was in more danger, by Enemies from without, and false Brethren, pretended Friends amongst us, and never had so few in public station to appear in her defence.

I have only to add in obedience to your Excellency's commands, the methods in which, your Excellency may be most servicealbe to the Church; your long acquaintance with the interest of the Church in these parts of the world, during your Excellency's Administration of the Government, of the Provinces of Maryland, Virginia, &c., as it makes you a very good judge of all propositions, made for that end, so it might have been a very good reason for me to avoid any such attempt, lest I should too much expose my own weakness; but since your Excellency is pleased to declare that you expect this service from me, I hope my obedience will apologize for my faults. I cannot but think the sending over a Bishop amongst us, to be of absolute necessity, and without which, all other attempts and methods to render the Church flourishing in these parts will be fruitless. Without government, no society or number of men can long be cemented, much less flourish and increase; without the censures of the Church are duly and impartially administered how shall either virtue be encouraged, or vice in all its forms detected and punished? The authors or perpetrators of some crimes may be too great for the Civil government to take hold of in these parts of the world, that might soon be corrected by the Ecclesiastical Governor; we need such an Ecclesiastical Governor that dare reprove and censure any that infringe the just Laws and Constitution of the Church; let us have such a Bishop as St. Ambrose, and we shall soon have such Governors as Theodosius.

I would also humbly propose that no persons be admitted into the Legislature or Executive Power of Government, but such as are in the Communion of the Church, if it be practicable; if in some places, this is not practicable, let them be such at least as are under the sacred tie and obligation of an oath; and, that our youth may not be tainted with erroneous principles, in their tender years, that no schools be permitted for the Education of youth, but such as are Licensed by the Governor's Instructions, that none be licensed but such as have a Certificate of their Sufficiency, Ability, and Sobriety, from the Minister and Church-Wardens of the place, where they last resided, or if no Minister thereof, four of the soberest and most substantial Inhabitants. That all endeavours be used for a legal, regular, and honorable support of an orthodox Clergy.

That no Laws be passed by the Governor and Council, that in any way intrench on the rights and liberties of the Church; or if any such inadvertency should be passed, that they be of no force, until they have received Her Majesty's Royal approbation; that the Laws that enjoin all persons to frequent some public place of Worship every Lord's day, and all Laws for suppressing of Immorality and profaneness be duly and impartially executed.

"That all the Clergy be encouraged to put all the Ecclesiastic Laws and Canons that relate to scandalous offenders, into execution, without any respect of persons whatsoever.

"All which are hereby submitted to your Excellency's judgment by him who is, Your Excellency's most affectionate and very humble servant,

"J. BASS."

Brigadier Hunter to the Commissioners of Trade and Plantations.

[Extract of a letter from Brigadier Hunter, Governor of New York, dated there the 9th of April, 1715.]

"Mr. Talbot has incorporated the Jacobites in the Jerseys, under the name of a Church, in order to sanctify his Sedition and Insolence to the Government.

"If the Society take not more care for the future, than has been taken hitherto, in the choice of their Missionaries, instead of establishing Religion, they'll destroy all Government and good manners."

The Secretary to Mr. Talbot.

August 23d, 1715.

"REVEREND SIR:

"I wrote to you on the 7th of April, in answer to yours of the 28th of October last, which will come by the Rev. Mr. Walker, but because possibly this may come to your hands before his arrival, I have enclosed a copy thereof. I am ordered to acquaint you that at a meeting of the Society, the first of July last, the Right Reverend, the Lord Bishop of London, laid before them an Extract of a Letter, communicated to him by the Lord Commissioners of Trade and Plantations, which was sent to them from Brigadier Hunter, Governor of New York, containing a complaint against you, with respect to your behaviour in those parts. The Society considered the same, and thereupon ordered a Copy of the said Extract, should be sent you, that you may have an opportunity of giving your answer to that charge, a Copy of which Extract is likewise here inclosed. I have nothing more in charge to communiate to you at present.

"I am, &c.,

"W. TAYLOR."

The Church-Wardens, &c., of Burlington to the Honourable Society.

Burlington, 28th, 1715.

"RIGHT REVEREND AND RIGHT HONORABLE:

"We cannot but adore that Divine Providence that has raised up so illustrious a Society, to be the propagators and defenders of the best of Churches, in these dark corners of the world, where the members are so frequently exposed to the malice and rage of those who are declared enemies, both to her doctrine and discipline. We acknowledge with the highest degree of gratitude, the sensible effects of your favour and protection, which we have already received, and hope we shall, by the grace of God, be enabled so to carry ourselves, in this troublesome age, that no calumnies of our enemies, may anyways lessen your opinion of us; we have had the happiness, at your expense, of being educated under the care of a truly Pious and Apostolic Person, the Reverend Mr. Talbot, the fervour and excellencies of whose discourses, and the piety of whose life are the best recommendations of the religion he professes, in now better than this 12 years, that he hath had not only the care of us, but on all emergent occasions, that of all the neighbouring Churches, hath lain on him, and in all that time, we are bound to assert, that we never heard either in his public discourses or private conversation, anything that might tend towards encouraging sedition, or anyways insolencing the government; it was therefore with the greatest surprise imaginable, that we read the following clause of a letter from Brigadier Hunter to the Board of Trade and Plantation, dated the 9th of April, 1715, by the Right Reverend, the Bishop of London, communicated to your Reverend and Honourable Society, in these words, 'Mr. Talbot has incorporated the Jacobites in the Jerseys, under the name of a Church, in order to sanctify his sedition and insolence to the government; if the Society take not more care for the future, than has been taken hitherto, in the choice of their Missionaries, instead of Establishing religion, they will destroy all government and good manners.' What could induce this gentleman to endeavour to fix so barbarous, so calumnious, so very false, and groundless a scandal, is to us altogether unaccountable, to which we think the shortest answer that can be given, is that of Nehemiah to Sanballat, 'there are no such things done as thou sayest, but thou feignest them out of thine own heart."

"The Church at Burlington, Right Reverend and Right Honourable, is the only Church that we know of, incorporated in the Jerseys, which was begun, by that steady protector of our Churches here, the Earl of Clarendon, when he was her late Majesty's Governor of this province, and finished under the administration of Colonel Richard Ingoldsby, and we are therefore, more particularly concerned, to answer to this charge. Our Minister, the Reverend Mr. Talbot, having undertaken his own defence against what the Governor hath charged him with, we shall say no more, than what we have said, on this account."

Mr. Talbot to the Secretary.

"Burlington, November 1st, 1715.

"SIR:

"First I am bound to render thanks to the Right Rev. and Right Honourable Society, for sending honest Mr. Walker, to my assistance; I hope he will answer the good character given of him on all hands; I have offered him my house at Burlington, and all my interest is at his service.

"Next, I am obliged to the Society, for giving me leave to answer for myself, touching the reflections cast upon me by Brigadier Hunter. To be an accuser is bad, to be a false accuser is worse, but a false accuser of the brethren is literally a Devil; I make no difference, for I call God to witness, I know no soul, in the Church of Burlington, nor in any other Church I have planted, but is well affected to the Protestant Church of England and present Government in the house of Hanover; therefore he that accused us all for Jacobites, has the greater sin. I can compare it to nothing more or less, than Doeg, the Edomite, who stabbed the Priests' characters, and then cut all their throats; or Haman, the Agagite, who slandered all the Jews as Jacobites who did not observe the King's Laws; so they were appointed as sheep to the slaughter; but God delivered *them*, and so, I hope he will do *us*, from the hand of the Enemy. The Honourable Colonel Bass, our Chief-Church-Warden, as diligent and faithful a servant of the Church and Crown as any, has been belied out of his Secretary's Office, and fined, and confined in the Common Gaol, for nothing but defending the Royal Law of King George, against an idol of the heathenish Quakers. Mr. Alexander Griffiths died heart-broken, being falsely accused and abused as a disaffected person to the Government; he died at Amboy; poor Mr. Ellis, the school-master, is very much discouraged in his business by a Quaker school-master being set up, in opposition to his license; he has made his complaints oft, not without cause, but without effect; he is a very sober, honest young gentleman, and deserves better encouragement. I wish the Society would take some better care of Burlington House; as for Governour Hunter, he does not come here once in three years, and as soon as he gets his money, spends it all at New York; so that we have only the burden, not the benefit, of Government; therefore we have the greater need of a Chorepiscopus, a Rural Bishop or Suffragan, to impart some spiritual Gift, without which, there never was, or can be any being, or well-being of a Church. This is the burden of all our lamentations, and so it will be, till it is answered; the sooner the better, *Cum bono deo.* So desiring prayers of the sacred Society, I remain,

"Your humble servant,

"JOHN TALBOT."

Mr. Talbot to the Secretary.

"Burlington, 1716.

"SIR:

"I have not had the favour of a letter, though I have sent several since Mr. Walker arrived. I have put him into the Church at Burlington, and into a house, which out of my poverty, I have prepared for the service of the Church, for ever, and for the use of the missionaries, for the time being, from the Honourable Society, if I die in the service, and be not forced to sell it again for pure necessaries.

"I hear that one of my bills was ordered to lie by for a half year. I wish I had known the reason of it, that I might have answered by the bearer, the Honourable Colonel Coxe, who comes home with another gentleman of the Vestry of the Church at Burlington, to clear that Church from the slanders that Colonel Hunter has raised against us, only because we were Christians, and could not serve God and Mammon, Christ and Belial, &c.

"I don't know any thing that I have done, contrary to my duty, either in Church or State; but if it be resolved that no Englishman shall be in Mission or Commission, *apud Americanos*, I don't know what we have done, that we should all give place to Scotch-Irish; but I am content to suffer with Good Company, *ferre quam sortem patiuntur omnes, nemo recuset.* I suffer all things for the elect's sake, the poor church of God, here, in the Wilderness. There is none to guide her, among all the sons that she has brought forth, nor is there any that takes her by the hand of all the sons that she has brought up. When the Apostles heard that Samaria had received the word of God, immediately they sent out two of the chief, Peter and John, to lay their hands on them, and pray that they might receive the Holy Ghost; they did not stay for a secular design of salary; and when the Apostles heard that the word of God was preached at Antioch, presently they sent out Paul and Barnabas, that they should go as far as Antioch, to confirm the Disciples, and so the Churches were established in the faith, and increased in number daily; and when Paul did but *dream* that a man of Macedonia called him, he set sail all so fast, and went over himself to help them; but we have been here these twenty years, calling till our hearts ache, and ye own 'tis the call and the cause of God, and yet ye have not heard, or have not answered, and it is all one.

"I must say this, if the Society don't do more in a short time, than they have, in a long, they will, I fear, lose their honour and character too; I don't pretend to prophesy, but you know how they said the kingdom of God shall be taken from them, and given to a nation that will bring forth the fruits of it. God give us all the grace to do the things that belong to our peace, so God bless you all.

"And yours,

"JOHN TALBOT.

"You may imagine what you please of the Irish missionaries, but I am sure we have lost Mr. Brook and Thoroughgood Moore, two English-men, that were worth all the Teagues that ever came over."

Mr. Talbot to the Secretary. (*Extract.*)

"Burlington, September 17th, 1717.

"SIR:

"I received an Order from the Society, to look after some Lands belonging to the House at Burlington, together with Mr. Vesey, but he is not yet come this way, so I shall say nothing to that point at present, because it is but an acre or two, and that is safe enough.

"The Quakers would have got that, as they have all the rest of the meadow Lands belonging to the Bishop's House, and divided them amongst themselves."

Mr. Talbot to the Secretary.

"Burlington, May 3d, 1718.

"SIR:

"I used to write to you now and then, though I seldom have the favour of an answer, or not to the point. All your missionaries hereabouts, are going to Maryland, for the sake of themselves, their wives and children; for my part, I cannot desert my poor Flock, that I have gathered, nor will I, if I have neither Money, Credit, nor Tobacco. But if I had known as much as I do now, that the Society were not able, for their parts, to send Bishop, Priest, nor Deacon, no Lecturer nor Catechist, no hinter, nor holder-forth, I would never have put the good people in these parts to the charge and trouble of building Churches; (nay, now they must be stalls, or stables for Quakers horses, when they come from market or meeting) as I said before, but some people will not believe till it is too late. Dr. Evans himself is gone to Maryland, for he says nobody will serve the Church for nought, as I do; for my part, I cannot blame the People in these parts, for they do what they are able, and no body can desire more, rich or poor, for those that do them any good. My Duty to the Honourable Society.

"I am your most humble servant,

"JOHN TALBOT."

[It would seem that not long after the date of this letter, Mr. Talbot again visited England, and obtained the interest on Archbishop Tenison's legacy to the oldest American missionary.]

Copy of Order for Mr. Talbot's receiving the Interest of the late Archbishop Tenison's £1000.

"Upon the humble petition of John Talbot, Clerk, this day preferred to the Right Honourable, the Lord High Chancellor of Great Britain, thereby setting forth that Dr. Thomas Tenison, late Archbishop of Canterbury, did by Codicil to his Will, bequeath £1000 towards settlement of Bishops in America; and until such lawful appointments of Bishops, did direct that the interest should be applied to the benefit of such missionaries, being Englishmen of the province of Canterbury, as have taken true pains in the respective plans committed by the Society to their care in the foreign plantations, and have been by unavoidable accidents, sickness, or other infirmities of the body, or old age, disabled from the performance of their duties in the said places, and forced to return to England; and that upon the hearing of this Cause, it was among other things ordered that the £1000 should be placed out at interest, on such Government or other security as Mr. Bennet, by whom the account of the Testator's personal Estate was directed to be taken, should approve of, and the interest thereof is to be applied according to the directions of the Testator's Will, until one month after the appointment and consecration of two Bishops, and that the said John Talbot, who was formerly Rector of Freethorn, in the County and Diocese of Gloucester and province of Canterbury, hath been in the service of the said Society for the propagation of the Gospel in foreign parts, as their Missionary in the foreign plantations, near 18 years, during which time he hath taken true pains in the discharge of his holy function, in the several places committed to his care by the said Society, and by his zeal and exemplary life, and conversation, hath done great service to the Church in America, and therefore is qualified to receive the interest of the said £1000, as by the certificate of the said Corporation, under their Common Seal, hereunto annexed, may appear, and that there having no Bishops been yet appointed in America, and the said John Talbot being the only missionary that is an Englishman, and of the province of Canterbury, hath been so long, and behaved himself so well, in the said service, as by the said certificate appears, the said John Talbot, by the direction of the said Society, applied himself to the said Mr. Bennet, for the said interest, who apprehends he cannot pay the same without the direction of this Court, and thereupon the said John Talbot, on the 22d April 1721, applied himself to your Lordship, that the said Mr. Bennet might pay such interest as was then due to him, which was ordered accordingly, and that the said Mr. Bennet, pursuant to the said Order, did pay unto the said John Talbot, all the interest then received, and the said John Talbot hath applied to the said Mr. Bennet for what interest has been received since, who apprehends he cannot pay the same, without your Lordship's further directions: Therefore, and inasmuch as there is no other person entitled to receive any part of the said interest, it is prayed, that the said Mr. Bennet may be ordered to pay such Interest as is now due to the said John Talbot, or, as he shall appoint, which is ordered accordingly, whereof notice is forthwith to be given.

"RIC. PRICE, Deput. Reg."

Mr. Talbot to the Secretary.

"Burlington, November 27.

"SIR:

"I and Mr. Skinner arrived safe, in six weeks at Philadelphia, never better weather, nor so good a Passage, as the Captain said (who was a Quaker); they and the sailors used to say, they had no luck when the Priests were on Board, but now they are both prettily convinced, and finally converted, to say no more. All sorts and conditions of men, women and children were glad to see us return, for they had given me over. I was yesterday at New Bristol, in Pensylvania, to call the people to Church, but they had almost lost the way; it was so overgrown with Bushes, they could hardly find the Church, having had nothing to do there, for two years and a half. Since I came away the Church there has suffered very much, but the Bishop's house here at the point, is in the worst condition of all; 'tis made nothing but a baudy-house, a sheep's cote and play-house; the boys have broken the windows from the top to bottom; they break the doors, steal the leads and iron bars, they pull down the pales, and cut the Cedar posts, they steal the fruit, and break the Trees; 'tis in vain to repair it any more, unless some family be put in to guard it, I think. I have a house of my own just by the Church, and I would not live in the point House, if they would give it to me, but I am loath to see it fall down, as the Coach House and stables have already; and what will they do for the meadows, they will be lost if not claimed speedily, the witnesses will be dead that know where the Lands lie; if the Society think fit to send any Orders about these things, I hope they will come before it is too late; I thought it my duty to lay these things before the Honorable Body, and hope you will read it to the Committee and Society, that something may be done, before the whole House drops through; this is the last time of asking, so I crave your prayers and remain

"Your most obedient servant,

"JOHN TALBOT.

"P. S.—The Society had better never have bought this House, for some Gentleman or another, such as Colonel Cox, would have done very well with it, but since they have bought, and can't sell it again for the worth, they had better make a Free School or a College; it is very well contrived for that purpose. Several of Mr. Skinner's scholars at Philadelphia are fit for the Academy, but here is no place to send them to; they can't afford to send their children to Europe for Education; sailing is now too dangerous and troublesome and chargeable, something of a College must be had here, the sooner the better. "J. T."

Mr. Talbot to the Secretary.

"Burlington, 20th September, 1723.

"REV. SIR:

"I have more work to do now than I had before, and I have no assistant; they are both gone, and have left me and the Church in the lurch. I have fifteen miles to travel from the Capes of Delaware to the Hills and Mountains in East Jersey, and none to help me but Mr. Lidenius, a Swedish minister, and he is going away. I have been this month at Trenton, at Hopewell, and Amwell, preaching and baptizing nineteen persons in one day. I visited several persons that were sick, who had been Quakers, and who were come off their errors, with Mr. George Keith; they were 80 years of age, and had never received the Holy Sacrament of the Lord's Supper in all their lives, but were loth to die, without the benefit and comfort of it; so I was fain to come back again to Burlington, to get the Elements, then returned to the Mountains, and did administer to their great satisfaction. They are preparing to build a Church in the Spring, but when they will have a minister I cannot tell; but it is a solemn thing (as they say in New England) for the lost sheep to go astray in the Wilderness; to be among Wolves is worse, but for sheep to be without a shepherd, is the most deplorable case of all; meanwhile it is some comfort to see the Bishop's house at Burlington, in repairs again; it is as well finished and furnished, as ever I saw it. The Governour of New York is coming to reside here for a month or two. We have got an honest Churchman, as we suppose, to live there and keep it in good order, now it is so, by care and order of Colonel Coxe; if the account comes not by this ship, "Old Annise," it will by the next this fall, in Captain Richmond. I have set up one Mr. Searle, a schoolmaster, to read prayers, and preach on Sundays, at Springfield; I lent him some sermons of Drs. Tillotson and Beveridge; several Quakers came to hear him, and are much taken with him; they say they never thought the Priests had so much Good Doctrine. I am sure he is a much better Clerk than Mr. H——n, saving his orders, therefore I commend him to the Society for their encouragement; and hope they will count him worthy to be a half-pay officer in their service. I pray God bless all our benefactors, and prosper all the labours of all their honest missioners, especially

"Your &c.

"JOHN TALBOT."

Mr. Talbot to the Secretary.

"Burlington, 7bris 7th, 1724.

"REV. SIR:

"I have been here altogether this last half-year; I preach once on Sunday morn, and Catechize or Homilize in the afternoon. I read the prayers of the Church, in the Church, decently, according to the order of Morning and Evening Prayer, daily through the year, and that is more than is done in any Church that I know, *apud Americanos.* I bought a house and two or three lots of land, adjoining to the Church-yard, and since I came over last, I have settled by deed, upon St. Mary's Church at Burlington, a parsonage and glebe; though there was neither Church, house, nor glebe, before I came, I hope there will be one now, for ever. I design to send the Society some account of the particulars of this in my next; and this is more than any body has done before, that I know, of my own proper cost and charge; so that I have been a good husband, to do this of my poverty, for I have no salary from the people. I had formerly £20 per annum, when there was money, but now, here is neither money, credit, nor tobacco, nothing but a little paper coin, that is nothing but sorry rags, and we can hardly get them to pay the Clerk £10, that is allowed him by the year. We are amongst a set of people called Quakers, who have denied the faith, and are worse than infidels; they serve no God but Mammon, and their own Bellies, and it is against their conscience to let the priest have anything, either by Law or Gospel. I have commonly the Sacrament administered once a month, and at the great feasts two or three days together; the number of Communicants is uncertain, 20, 30, 40, or 50 persons.

"There is no parochial library yet, for I never had any, from the Society, but I design to leave mine, and Mr. Thorogood Moore's, when I die, to that use; meanwhile we want Common Prayer Books very much. If it please the Honourable Society, instead of £5, in small tracts, to let that money be laid out in Common Prayer Books, they would be of great use to the people in all parts, who can't get them here for love or money. Those small tracts were but of small use, for they laid up and did no good, and not being bound, they soon perish in the using, for it costs more to bind books here, than to buy them in Britain. I shall say but one thing more at present, which I omitted when I was in England, for my money was short, or else I would have got some Bells, which we want here very much; I don't mean a Ring of Bells in a Steeple, for idle fellows to make a vain jangling, but one good bell in the Church, that the people may know when to come together to worship God. I pray for you all, as I hope you do for

"Your most Humble Servant,

"JOHN TALBOT."

Mr. Talbot to the Bishop of London.

"Burlington, July 2d, 1725.

"MAY IT PLEASE YOUR LORDSHIP:

"I understand by letters from some friends in England, that I am discharged the Society for Exercising Acts of Jurisdiction over my Brethren, the Missionaries, &c. This is very strange to me, for I knew nothing about it, nor any body else, in all the world. I could disprove it by 1,000 witnesses, but since there is one come home in the Richmond, Mrs. Alexander, relict of the Comptroller in Philadelphia, &c. (she has been many years a member of Christ Church), she can give your Lordship the best account of the present state. As for myself, I shall not turn accuser of the Brethren, but this I will say, those that came last are not better than their fathers, and some of them have given occasion to a proverb of reproach, and been told to their faces, 'The Devil would have the Bishop of London for ordaining such fellows as you.'

"This I take to be the most unpardonable sin, the iniquity of Eli's house, which the Lord said should not be purged with sacrifice nor offering for ever, because his sons made themselves vile, and he restrained them not: But, my Lord, let them be who they will, or what they will, to their own Master they stand or fall, I have nothing to do with them, nor ever had, nor ever will. I am clear of the blood of all men, and will so keep myself. Let them that have the watch look out: as your Lordship has done me the wrong, so I hope you will do me the right, upon better information, to let me be in *statu quo*,—for indeed I have suffered great wrong, for no offence or fault at all, that I know of, a long, long penance I have done, for crimes, alas! to me unknown, but God has been with me, and made all things work together for my good; meanwhile I hope your Lordship will hear the right, and do nothing rashly, but upon your authority, for the edification and not for the destruction of this poor Church *apud Americanos*, which has many adversaries, and none to help her. But this good Lady, Mrs. Alexander, if your Lordship please to give her audience, will give the best information, and answer all objections that can be alleged against

"Your most humble

"And faithful servant,

"J. TALBOT."

Mr. Talbot to the Secretary.

"Burlington, July 8th, 1725.

"REVEREND SIR:

"Yours received March, ult., that I am out of Quantum, with the Society, and also a Bill, protested since that, payable to Mr. Graham, of £30, value received. I heard nothing of this before our Lady Day last past, therefore I have drawn a bill for three quarters' salary, for so long I was actually in their service at my proper cost and charge, in propagating the Gospel, and this is as much due to me, as any I have from them. Sir, I desire the favour of yourself to lay the case before the Honourable Board, and when they consider the thing, as it is, they will please to pay that Bill to my worthy Friend, Mr. Thomas Forey, for I never knew any board discard their officers but they paid them, for the time being, in their service, and knew nothing of their will and pleasure to the contrary. I remain, your most humble and obliged servant,

"JOHN TALBOT."

[Extract from a Memorial to the Society from Churches in Pennsylvania and New Jersey.]

"SHEWETH:

"That the melancholy circumstance of the Church of England in these Colonies, is a subject, we hope, worthy, not only your compassion, but tender regard, having not above one Minister to seven or eight Churches or Congregations, and we bemoan our case, when we behold so many Churches, lately built, lie as desolate around us, convincing arguments of our affection for the Church, and of our great misfortune in being destitute of pastors. When at the same time we daily see Dissenters of all denominations, continually supplied, and increase, through this, our misfortune, and upbraid us with this defect. It is, therefore, with the utmost concern, we express our unhappiness, when we view our circumstances rather decline than flourish. In particular, that Mr. Talbot, who for nigh thirty years past, has behaved himself with indefatigable pains, and good success in his Ministry, among us, under your Honour's care, has by some late conduct (nowise privy to us), rendered himself disagreeable to his superiors and departed from us. We cannot, without violence to the principles of our Religion, approve of any acts, or give into any measures inconsistent with our duty and Loyalty to his Majesty, whom God long preserve; yet in gratitude to this unhappy Gentleman, we humbly beg leave to say, that by his exemplary life and ministry, he has been the greatest advocate for the Church of England, by Law Established, that ever appeared on this shore. This unhappy accident, together with the death and removal of some other clergymen from us, has very much increased the cause of our complaint, and we have no other recourse but to your Honours for relief. Having well-grounded hopes, the same good spirit which prompted you to undertake the glorious work of propagating the Gospel in foreign parts will continue your pious regards to these Colonies, and the rather, since so many stately monuments are erected for God's service, testifying our sincere willingness to embrace your charitable assistance, and to answer the glorious ends you have in view.

"Therefore, your petitioners most humbly beg your Honourable Society will please to extend your wonted charity and necessary supply to the several Churches and Congregations, of which particular accounts are hereto annexed.

"And your Petitioners, as in Duty bound,
"Shall ever pray," &c.

Christ Church, Philadelphia.

SAMUEL HASELL,
ROBERT BOLTON, } *Churchwardens.*

THOMAS LAWRENCE, CHARLES READ,
THOMAS FENTON, BENJAMIN MORGAN,
JAMES TUTHILL, THOMAS TRESSE,
THOMAS LEECH, JAMES BINGHAM, } *Vestrymen, Christ Church, Philadelphia.*

Thomas Polgreen, Thomas Chase, William Fraser, Robert Asheton, George Plumly, Arthur Oliver, Daniel Harrison, John Brooks, Henry Dexter, John Orton, John Knowles, George Meall, R. Asheton.

St. James' Church in New Bristol.

JOHN ABRAHAM DENORMANDIE,
F. GAUDOUETT,
JOHN ALLEN, } *Churchwardens.*

St. Mary's Church at Burlington.

ROWLAND ELLIS,
JONATHAN LOVETT, } *Churchwardens.*

Peter Bard, Samuel Bustill, Richard Allison, James Gould, John Dagworthy, F. Owes, James Trent, Jacob Baillergeau, Edward R. Price, William Cutler, Thomas Fosgate, James Thompson, Anthony Elton, Simon Nightingale, Thomas Skeene, Thomas Hunloke, George Willis.

The Churchwardens of Burlington to the Governor.

"November 4th, 1725.

"Since your Excellency has been pleased to order, that the Rev. Mr. Talbot should surcease officiating in this Church, it heartily grieves me to see the doors thereof daily shut up; but we humbly beg leave to acknowledge your Excellency's favour, and repeated willingness to assist and join with us in this affair. The hurry of country business, that would not admit of our members to meet together, prevented our addressing your Excellency sooner, but we crave leave to acquaint your Excellency, that as it is our unhappiness to be without a Minister, we humbly hope for your Excellency's favourable countenance and good offices to obtain what is so expedient and necessary for the interest of our Holy Religion and the best of Churches, of which we acknowledge ourselves unworthy members.

"We are, &c.,

"ROWLAND ELLIS, and others."

Thus far Mr. Talbot has been permitted to illustrate his own character, by his letters. The reader, however, will, we trust, not be unwilling to trace him to the end of his career; and particularly to be informed of his connection with the Episcopate in the Colonies, derived from the non-Jurors. At the request of the Publishing Committee, therefore, one of their number has prepared the following paper on that subject; and with it conclude our memorials of Mr. Talbot.

NON-JURING EPISCOPATE

IN THE

UNITED STATES,

COMPILED BY THE

REVEREND B. FRANKLIN.

Part of the documentary evidence of the existence of Bishops in America having non-Juring orders, previous to the Revolution, is contained in the preceding letters. Upon referring to the letters written to the Secretary of the Society for the Propagation of the Gospel, by the Rev. John Talbot, anterior to his visit to England, A.D. 1718, it will be observed that he pleads with untiring perseverance, and almost pathetic earnestness, for a Bishop to be sent to America. It will also be observed that at one time he had such hopes of seeing a Bishop here, that he purchased a residence for one by direction of the Venerable Society, at Burlington, N. J. He waited for years in vain. The hopes of the Society were dissipated. Mr. Talbot seems to have despaired of obtaining the Episcopacy from the Established Church, and during his absence, as above, the residence purchased for a Bishop went to decay.

Mr. Talbot had been charged falsely, as it appears, with Jacobinism, even previous to A.D. 1715. This charge might have suggested to him the idea of obtaining the Episcopacy from the Jacobin Bishops of England. It is certain that he went to England about A.D. 1718, and returned late in the autumn A.D. 1722. We have a letter from him to the Secretary of the Society for the Propagation of the Gospel, dated November 27th of that year, which announces his safe return. In this letter, and in all that succeed it, not even a request appears that a Bishop be sent to America, a matter which Mr. Talbot never before omitted strenuously to urge.

It was during this visit that Mr. Talbot received the interest on Archbishop Tennison's bequest.

Mr. Talbot, while in England at this time, made the acquaintance of the Rev. Dr. Robert Welton, who had been deprived of the rectorship of St. Mary's, Whitechapel, London, for his attachment to the non-Jurors. At this time also occurred the first division in the ranks of the non-Jurors themselves. Some adhered to the English Liturgy, as it was in the days of James II., while others wished to introduce what became known as the "*Usages.*" They were four, namely, *mixing Water with the Wine, Prayer for the Dead, the Prayer for the Descent of the Holy Spirit upon the Elements, and the Oblatory Prayer.**

The party which rejected the "Usages," consecrated Ralph Taylor a Bishop in the year 1720. Mr. Perceval, in his book on the Apostolic Succession, states that in the year 1722 Ralph Taylor consecrated Robert Welton a Bishop, and then Taylor and Welton together consecrated John Talbot.

Lathbury, in narrating the history of division among the non-Jurors, writes:

"Being once divided, other minor separations or subdivisions soon followed. Thus in 1723-4,† Robert Welton was consecrated a Bishop by Ralph Taylor, who, contrary to the Canons of the Church, took upon himself to act in his individual capacity. No precedent could be pleaded for such a proceeding, which must, therefore, be regarded as an innovation on the practice of the Universal Church from the Apostolic age. Talbot also was consecrated by Taylor and Welton. These consecrations, therefore, were viewed as irregular and uncanonical. It appears that Taylor [Talbot] and Welton were never recognised as Bishops by the rest of the body; yet both exercised the Episcopal functions in the American Colonies. The Government, at the desire of the Bishop of London, at length interposed, when Welton retired to Portugal, where he died in 1726, and Taylor [Talbot] returned to the Communion of the National Church."

This paragraph has been quoted in full from Lathbury, though it contains some errors which the following documents will show. It con-

* Lathbury's History of the Non-Jurors, pp. 252, 492-494.

† A mistake of a year probably.

firms, if it does not merely repeat, the statement of actual consecration which appears in Perceval's work.

Dr. Welton and Mr. Talbot undoubtedly came to America soon after their consecration, and labored in the cities and vicinities of Philadelphia and Burlington.

The Documents which prove this are given below, with the exception of those which appear in the previous part of the volume.

Letter from an Unknown Person to Dr Bray.

"Cecil County in Maryland, July 29th, 1724.

"Rev. Sir:

"In a former I have acquainted you with my treatment at Philadelphia, how villainously and barbarously I was supplanted by Mr. Talbot, who has been years at Burlington in the Jerseys, some time Itinerant with George Keith, and very famous for his disaffection to the Crown. Ever since the revolution he and one Smith a rigid   took some pains to persuade me not to pray for the King and Royal Family, but to say as they did, only the King and Prince ('tis obvious whom they mean) and since I was not to be wrought on, I was by their contrivance very unhandsomely kickt out, and in order to proselyte that province he, the said Talbot, supplyed the place till some honest hearts addressed the Governour, and he ordered the Church doors to be shut up, but now set open again to your late neighbour Dr. Welton, who I hear is lately arrived there. If more such come of that kidney all the clergy both in and out of the Government will be corrupted, and the people all seduced from their allegiance to his Majesty—there will be no need of popish priests and Jesuits any longer—they who should oppose and resist will effectually carry on and promote the Romish designs. I can't but wonder how my Lord Chancellor was induced to let Talbot when last in England have the interest of the late Archbishop Cant. his legacy towards sending a Bishop over into America, with assurance of having it for the future till one be appointed. I am now settled here in an easy parish well disposed people. I have a fine glebe and between 30 and 40,000 lbs. worth of tobacco yearly; but I fear I shall receive none this year, that and corn all being burnt up with the excessive drought. I am with all humble respects,

"Rev. Sir, Your, &c."

The above letter was undoubtedly written by the Rev. John Urmston, as will appear from its correspondence with the following letter by that clergyman, to the Secretary of the Venerable Society. Though Mr. Urmston uses harsh language, he does not appear to have been able to specify against Mr. Talbot any other charge than that of Jacobinism. The charge of supplanting is at least open to a difference of opinion, particularly as the first part of the letter shows that Mr. Urmston's labors were probably not very acceptable, inasmuch as he came to America after vainly seeking employment in England; and in this country also wandered about seeking employment for a long time in vain. It is thought best to give the letter in full. Though the first third of it does not bear upon the evidence of non-Juring Episcopacy in the American Colonies, it will be seen that the remainder contains almost positive testimony to the fact:

"Cecil County in Maryland, June ult. 1724.

"REV. SIR:

"You may remember that I once had a mind to have gone with the D. of Portland; you were pleased to offer me that letter to a French Marquis who went with his Grace. I thought my Lord D. of Kington who married the other's sister might be more effectual. He spake to his brother and his answer was that he should take no more into his family and yet soon after entertained Charles Lamb. This was one of the many disappointments I met with whilst in England last. I was rude in not acquainting you with my departure, but believe you will be so good as to pardon that and many other liberties particularly this long scroll which with humble respects will give you a further account of my unfortunate circumstances which I the rather communicate to you knowing you to be no half papist, as too many of the clergy now-a-days are.

"You're to be acquainted that I went from London to New England, where I had some hopes of staying but was prevented by the New Converts, one whereof had the offer if he would go to England and be ordained, and forthwith did, and is now minister of the New Episcopal Church in Boston, the only man that could be thought of; he'll do more good there than any other. I left the place very contentedly, and went from New York, where I narrowly missed of being Chaplain to the Fort and assistant to Mr. Vesey. Hearing that the Incumbent of Philadelphia was gone to England for his health, and left the place ill-supplyed, I hastened thither, and was gladly received of the people. About six months after, we had the news of the death of the Incumbent aforesaid. I had written to my correspondent to get some friend to intercede with my then Lord of London to appoint me minister there. I never doubted of my friend's diligence nor his Lordship's favour, but my letters from England must certainly have been intercepted. Mr. Talbot, the famous Rector of Burlington, in the Jerseys, supplanted me here.* Governor Burnet had been long displeased with him by reason he is a notorious Jacobite, and will not pray for the King and Royal Family by name, only says the King and Prince, by which 'tis obvious whom he means. He hath often endeavoured to persuade me to do so too (little less than treason, I

* The counter statement to this will be seen in another part of this volume, in a letter of Talbot, dated at Philadelphia, 9th December, 1723, in the part immediately following the blank, which blank, as the coincidence of dates proves, should contain the name of the Rev. John Urmston.

think, to go about to pervert the King's subjects from their duty and allegiance to his Majesty). He hath poisoned all the neighbouring clergy with his rebellious principles; they dare not pray otherwise than he does when he is present. He caused many of my hearers to leave the Church; at last he gained his point, was accepted, and I kicked out very dirtily by the Vestry, who pretend that the Bishop of London is no Diocesan, nor hath anything to do there more than another Bishop, so that any one that is lawfully ordained and licenced by any Bishop, it matters not who, the Bishop of Rome I suppose Talbot and many more will say, or any other, is capable of taking upon him any cure in America. I was not sorry for my removal from so precarious and slavish a place, where they require two sermons every Lord's Day, Prayers all the week, and Homilies on Festivals, besides abundance of Funerals, Christenings at home, and sick to be visited; no settled salary, the Churchwardens go from house to house every six months, every one gives what he pleases, sometimes liberally, and on the least pretence or dislike, or it may be the persuasion of the Churchwardens and their adherents, they'll give nothing, and so they forced that worthy gentleman, Dr. Evans, and many others to leave the places; they love new faces. I was told that they had eleven ministers within the space of nine years. About three months after Talbot was gotten into his kingdom some had the courage to go to Sir William Keith, who otherwise was well enough pleased with Talbot, and to tell his Excellency that it was a shame such a fellow should be allowed to officiate in the Church, and that if his Excellency suffered him they would write to England against them both, whereupon Talbot was sent away, and the place hath been vacant these four months. What has become of this great Apostle I know not; certainly Governor Burnet will not suffer him to return to Burlington. Some of his confidants have discovered that he is in* orders, as many more rebels are.† I have heard of no ordinations he has made as yet, but doubtless he'll persuade all the clergy who are his creatures to be ordained again by him. To this end he came fraught from England with some of the most virulent and scandalous pamphlets he could pick up; that one I met with by chance, whose title was, 'The Case Truly Stated,' proving that all ordained by Bishops consecrated since or such as conformed and approved of the revolution are imposters, and the divine service is only to be performed by those who have been re-ordained by non-jurors, and that there are enough of them all over England to serve the Church. *Proh mores atque hominum fidem!*

"As oldest Missionary he received the three years' interest of the £2000 the late Archbishop of Canterbury his legacy towards the support of a Bishop in the plantations, and is entitled to the same until a Bishop be appointed. My Lord Chancellor did not know the man, or certainly he would never have admitted him to so great a favour. I went by land from Philadelphia to North Carolina, in order to take a view of Maryland and

* The blank above evidently was filled by, or intended to be understood as if containing, the word *Bishop's*.

† This can hardly be regarded as proof that there were a number of non-juring Bishops in the Colonies. Mr. Urmston was plainly loose, both in his insinuations and assertions. If there had been such numbers as he would seem to assert, we should undoubtedly find other mention of them.

Virginia, and to sell my Plantation, stock, and goods ; that done, I returned to Maryland, and am settled in Cecil County, a very promising, thriving place; the income is between 33 and 34,000, which will be considerable when Tobacco bears a price.

"I am, Reverend Sir,

"Your most obedient

"JOHN URMSTON."

[Extract of a Letter from Mr. Henderson* to the Bishop of London, dated " Maryland, August 16th, 1724.

— " Mr. Talbot, Minister of Burlington, returned from England about two years ago in Episcopal orders, though his orders till now of late have been kept as a great secret, and Dr. Welton is arrived there about six weeks ago, as I'm credibly informed, in the same capacity, and the people of Philadelphia are so fond of him that they will have him right or wrong for their minister.

"I am much afraid these gentlemen will poison the people of that province. I cannot see what can prevent it but the speedy arrival of a Bishop there, one of the same order to confront them, for the people will rather take confirmation from them than have none at all, and by that means they'll hook them into the schism.

"I am well assured they'll get no footing in this province, for I dare say his Majesty King George has not subjects any where in his dominions more zealously attached to him than the Clergy and Protestant laity here, are.

"I question not but your Lordship in your great wisdom will find out some expedient to prevent the ruin that threatens the Church in that province. I need say no more but to beg your Lordship's prayers for,

"May it please your Lordship,

"Your most dutiful son and

"Most obedient humble servant,

"JACOB HENDERSON."

* Mr. Henderson was Commissary in Maryland.

Mr. Stubbs to the Bishop of London.

"Westmer, April 16, 1725.

"My Lord:

"In obedience to your Lordship's commands, just now laid upon me in the Cockpit, I dispatch as ordered by Sir J. Phillips, two paragraphs of a letter just come to hand, signed 'John Urmston,' and dated 'Cecil County, in Maryland, 7ber. 29th, 1724:' 'P. S. Mr. Talbot did me no unkindness in causing me to be turned out of Philadelphia to make room for himself. He convened all the clergy to meet, put on his robes and demanded Episcopal obedience from them; one wiser than the rest refused, acquainted the Governor with the ill consequences thereof, the danger he would run of losing his Government, whereupon the Governor ordered the Church to be shut up.'

"'P. S. He is succeeded by Dr. Welton, who makes a great noise amongst them by reason of his sufferings. He has brought with him to the value of £300 sterling in guns and fishing tackle, with divers printed copies of his famous altar-piece at White Chapel. He has added a scrowl with words proceeding out of the mouth of the Bishop of Peterborough to this effect, as I am told, "I am not he that betrayed Christ, though as ready to do it as ever Judas was." I have met him since in the streets, but had no further conversation with him.'

"Your Lordship's
"Most dutiful
"Philip Stubbs."

Sir William Keith to the Secretary S. P. G.

"May 13, 1725.

"Sir:

"The notice which the Society do me the honour to give by your letter of 15th January, concerning Dr. Welton's character, shall be duly regarded by using all the means that is in my power to prevent the mischief which they apprehend from the Doctor's residing in the Government. But so long as the Vestry here take upon them to be wholly independent on the Governor's authority, and that Clergymen may be indifferently called without either a license from the Bishop or Induction here, I hope I cannot be accountable for irregularities of that nature untill I am better assisted with a proper authority; and if I knew where to make application without giving offence, I think I have some reason to complain that the Church here is so much neglected as that the Governor and those who are truly well affected to our Sovereign Lord King George, and his Royal Family, cannot decently attend the publick worship. The Bishop of London very well knows my sentiments on this matter, and I must entreat that you will be pleased to assure the Society that his Majesty has not a servant in America who is more heartily disposed than I am to rectify abuses of this matter.

"Sir, your most obedient Humble Servant,

"W. Keith."

[Extract from a Memorial of Peter Evans to the Bishop of London.]

"But more especially for your Lordship's goodness in communicating your thoughts concerning the Church Vestry of Philadelphia, of which Vestry your Lordship had received some disagreeable account. Your memorialist, as one (though unworthy) of the said Vestry, humbly begs leave to give your Lordship a true information of the said Vestry's conduct towards Dr. Welton, who at his arrival there, about June 1724, was a stranger, and his coming altogether unknown to every of them. The circumstances of the Church there being not a little melancholy at that time, for that being destitute of a Minister no Divine Service had been performed there for some months before, and a numerous congregation which if kept together were not only able but willing to raise a handsome support for a Missionary which was daily expected from your Lordship.

"But the Church doors being shut, it was evident the congregation would soon dwindle, and be captivated among the many Dissenting Teachers in that growing city, and render them unable to perform their promises to your Lordship. To prevent which inconvenience several members of the Vestry met, and being well assured by some persons of the Doctor's acquaintance, that he was esteemed an orthodox minister, and it appearing by several English printed newspapers that the Doctor had there lately taken the oaths, and conformed to the Government,* but had been deprived of his living, several members of the Vestry asked the Doctor to officiate until such time as they were favoured with a Missionary from your Lordship, which he readily granted, and the Church doors were opened, and for that reason, and from the character of the Doctor's preaching, the congregation resorted to hear him.

"Your memorialist hopes your Lordship will be induced to believe their zeal for the Church (and not for any mistaken principles of the Doctor's) was the true cause of their frequenting the Church. Your memorialist, from his knowledge of and acquaintance with the people there for twenty-two years past, does believe it a piece of injustice to insinuate them as disaffected to his Majesty, for your memorialist well knows that every member of the Vestry and all others of the congregation to whom it was tendered have conformed to the Laws, and given all the proofs of their Loyalty to his Majesty that is in their power.

"But for his and their defence against the information of Sir William Keith, your memorialist begs leave (and he hopes in case of self-defence and

* This was probably an unfounded report.—B.F.

preservation he may be allowed) to observe to your Lordship that Sir William Keith has not been so happy in his conduct, or sincere in his relations as to acquire undoubted credit, as appears from the following Paragraph (taken out of the Lords' proceedings against him for being concerned in the Scottish conspiracy Anno 1703), viz.: 'It was declared by the Lords, spiritual and temporal, in Parliament assembled, that Mr. William Keith (upon his examination by the Lords appointed to examine him by this House) hath prevaricated with this House, and by his behaviour doth not seem an object worthy of his Majesty's mercy.'

"Your memorialist humbly begs leave to observe to your Lordship in vindication of himself and the said Vestry, that the said Sir William has for some years been elected member of the said Vestry, but taking upon him to overrule them, and entirely depriving them of the freedom justly due, he was left out of the Vestry in the time of Mr. Vicary, the last settled Missionary amongst us from your Lordship's predecessors, which was about three years ago, and from that time seemed displeased with the Vestry, and withdrew his subscription from Mr. Vicary, to whom the Vestry shewed all due regard."

The Rev. William Becket, Misssionary at Lewes, Pa. (now Delaware), writes to the Secretary of the Society for Propagating the Gospel, under date of March 13, A. D. 1727. In this letter he mentions Dr. Welton incidentally, as if it were commonly known at that period that he was a non-juror while officiating in Philadelphia. Mr. B. was complaining that marriage licenses were given by the Governor to those who had no right to them, and specially charges Sir William Keith with having granted them "when Dr. Welton, the non-juror, was minister of Philadelphia, to whom it was not fitting to grant them."

[Extract from the Fulham Manuscripts.]

"Queries to be answered by the persons who were Commissaries to my Predecessor:

"Mr. , Minister of , Philadelphia, is desired to answer these queries:

* * * * * *
* * * * * *

"3. Does any Clergyman officiate who has not the Bishop's License for that Government?"

"*A.* One only at present, Dr. Welton at Philadelphia, with whom we have no correspondence nor of whom have we any further knowledge but that we hear he professes to have come into these parts only to see the country."

These queries were signed by

Robert Weyman,	Missionary	at Oxford and Whitemarsh, Pa.
William Beckett	"	" Lewes, Pa., now Delaware.
George Ross	"	" New Castle, "
John Humphreys	"	" Chester, Concord, & Markershook, Pa.

[Letter from Fulham MSS. of Mr. Glentworth to Mr. Cummings.]

"February 14, 1725–6.

"SIR:

"I came from Philadelphia the 4th day of December, at which time Dr. Welton officiated in the Church every Sunday, once at least, but generally twice, and likewise on Wednesdays, Fridays, and Saturdays.

"The order to recall him went over in one Captain Richmond, who sailed the beginning of December, and can hardly be arrived there by this time.

"I am, Sir,

"Your most humble servant,

"THOMAS GLENTWORTH."

Sir William Keith to the Lord Bishop of London.

"Philadelphia, April 8th, 1726.

"MY LORD:

"I am glad to acknowledge the great honour your Lordship was pleased to do me by your letter dated last June, which I received some time ago, and am glad that by your Lordship's great care I can now answer it so effectually as to acquaint you that I have by this conveyance returned an authentic certificate unto my Lord Townsend's office, of Dr. Welton's having been duly served with his Majesty's Writ of Privy Seal, commanding him upon his allegiance to return to Great Britain forthwith; in pursuance of which Order, the Doctor did us the favour about four weeks ago to depart for Europe by the way of Lisbon, so that I doubt not but your Lordship will now more easily find a way to supply this Church with a suitable Incumbent, and as the people's hopes are generally placed on your Lordship's pious care for that purpose, I am fully persuaded that any gentleman who comes over recommended by your Lordship will be handsomely received."

Mr. Cummings to the Bishop of London.

[Extract.]

"Philadelphia, October 19th, 1726.

"My Lord:

"I have been here so short a time that all the account I can give of the place as yet is, that the soil and clime seem to be better and more regular than the temper of the people; however, I have been very well received by those of any note, and am in a particular manner obliged to Mr. Moore, our Collector; he is a sober and pious man, and has all along endeavoured to support the Church, in opposition both to Welton's and the principles of the other Schismaticks and Sectaries, which are indeed here very numerous. I hope in a little time, by proper and moderate methods, to cancel all the bad impressions the angry Doctor had given of his successor. Your Lordship will observe by his favourite sermon, printed here, in what a scurrilous manner he falls foul upon all the Clergy of the present Establishment, charging the people that as they tendered their salvation not to receive but reject any that should be sent among them. He is now in Lisbon; 'tis well if he ben't got into the Convent. I ha'nt seen all the Clergy of this province as yet, but have heard a good character of them all. I have been importuned by numbers of people from Burlington and by some of this province to write to your Lordship in favour of Dr. Talbot; they made me promise to mention him, otherwise I would not presume to do it. He is universally beloved, even by the Dissenters here, and has done a great deal of good. Welton and he had differed and broke off correspondence, by reason of the rash chimerical projects of the former long before the Government took notice of them. If he were connived at and could be assisted by the Society (for I am told the old man's circumstances are very mean), he promises by his friends to be peaceable and easy, and to do all the good he can for the future."

[Extract of a letter from Commissary Chris. Wilkinson to the Bishop of London, dated at "Chester River, in Queen Ann's County, Maryland, June 15, 1726."]

— "I understood Dr. Welton has left Philadelphia and is gone for Lisbon. He and the rest of the non-jurors disagreed very much among themselves, in so much that they avoided one another's company. Mr. Talbot and Mr. Smith (who also differ very much in their sentiments of submission to our established Government) have been with us in Maryland. They behaved themselves very modestly, avoided talking very much, and resolved to submit quietly to the orders sent from England to prohibit their public officiating in any of the Churches, or to set up separate meetings."

Dr. Welton appears not to have returned to England, but to have died in Lisbon.

By reference to the letters of Mr. Talbot during the year 1725, it will be seen that he was discharged from the Society's employment for alleged Jacobinism. It will be observed that he does not deny having received Episcopal orders.

The late venerable Bishop White related a tradition which has been preserved by the Rev. Dr. Hawks in his History of the Church in Maryland. As it is an important link in the present inquiry, it is quoted in full, as it appears in the above work, p. 185.

"The venerable prelate who was so long our presiding bishop, was accustomed to relate a story which he heard from his elder brethren, when he was but a youth, and it may here be most appropriately preserved. The story was this: A gentleman who had been ordained among the Congregationalists of New England, and who had officiated among them as a minister for many years, at length to the surprise of his friends, began to express doubts about the validity of his ordination, and manifested no small trouble of mind on the subject. Suddenly about the time of the arrival of Talbot and Welton, he left home without declaring the place of his destination or purpose of his journey. After an interval of a few weeks he returned, and gave no further information of his movements than that he had been to some of the Southern Colonies; he also said on his return that he was now perfectly satisfied with his ordination, and from that day never manifested the least solicitude on the subject, but continued until he died to preach to his congregation. It was soon whispered by those whose curiosity here found materials for its exercise, that the minister had been on a visit to the non-juring bishops, and obtained ordination from one of them. He never said so; but among Churchmen it was believed that such was the fact."

Both Perceval and Lathbury state, without referring to any authority, that Talbot took the oaths and conformed. If this were the case, it would be difficult to explain why he continued to be deprived of his missionary appointment to Burlington, especially as he was willing to labor, and the people were anxious to have him for their rector.

Thus appears to have ended the only effectual attempt to provide anything like a Protestant Episcopacy for America, until the Revolution having, under the Providence of God, opened a new door, England finally granted to those whom she regarded as successful rebels what she had previously refused to give to obedient children.

The following communication is from Dr. Bray, once Commissary of Maryland. Its precise date is nowhere given, but from facts mentioned in it, it must have been about the year 1740. It presents a view of our condition on the Continent at or about that time :

"*A Memoriall humbly layd before his Grace the Lord A.Bp. of Canterbury, the Lord Bishop of London, and the other Bishops of this Kingdome, Representing the present State of Religion in the several Provinces on the Continent of North America, in order to the providing a sufficient number of proper Missionaries so absolutely necessary to be sent at this Juncture into those parts.*

"MAY IT PLEASE Y^E LORDSHIPS :

"AMONGST other Reasons for my Return at this tyme of Consequence to our Church in America, in Reference to which I have been happy in the approbation of those my Ecclesiastical Superiors, to whom I am more immediately accountable in things relating to my Mission, there is one of concernment to be layd before all your Lordships ; And as I humbly conceive, the Universityes also of this Kingdome. And it is to represent to you the present state of Religion in Maryland, Virginia, Pensylvania, the East and West Jerseys, New York, Road Island, Long Island, North and South Carolina, New England and Newfound Land. And this in order to the Propagation of the true Christian Religion in those Parts at a Crisis when, as many thousands are in a happy Disposition to embrace it, so Infidelity, Heresy, and Schism seem to make their utmost efforts to withdraw, and to fix those people at the greatest distance from it.

"I. And to begin where I am more immediately concerned, with Maryland. Here, through the mercies of God, and after many struggles, we are in a fair way at last to have an Established Church. The law for New England I have brought over along with me for the Royal Assent, not incumbered as formerly with such clauses as hindred the same. And thereby is provided a maintainance for the Clergy of forty pounds of Tobacco per Poll, taxed upon each Comunicable person, which amounts in some parishes to about eighty pounds per annum, according to the Rate which Tobacco has borne these three last years, though that is higher than they can promise themselves the same for the future. But in fifteen of them at least by reason of the thinness of the Inhabitants, not to above a thyrd of that value. And yet these latter parishes having built their Churches, think they ought to have Ministers as well as the rest ; and had I not in my Parochial Visitations given them good words and fair promises speedily to supply them, I fear our Law would have scarcely passed ; and yet how to make good that promise to them I shall be sadly at a Loss, except the Proposalls hereafter given, may find favour with y^r Lordships, and those to whom you shall please to recomend them.

"The Papists in this Province appeare to me to be about a twentieth part of the Inhabitants ; and though the Quakers bragg so much of their numbers and Riches, with which considerations they would incline the Government to favour them with such unprecedented Priviledges, as to be free from paying their dues to the Established Church, or rather would fain overthrow its Establishment, yet they are not above a fifteenth part in number, and bear little Proportion with those of the Church in wealth and trade.

"II. As for Pensylvania, I found too much work in Maryland to be able to visit that Province personally, though most earnestly sollicited thereunto by the People. But there passed letters betwixt myself, and that Church, full of the greatest Respects on their side. And by conferences with some of the Principall Persons of that Country, I was fully made to understand the state of Religion there, where I think, if in any Part of the Christian World, a very great proportion of the People may be said to be Τεταγμένοι, *sive dispositi* ἐις ζωὴν αἰώνιον.

"The Keithites, which are computed to be a thyrd part, are freely such, and so very well affected are they to the Interest of our Church, that in the late election of Assembly men, ever since Mr. Penn came into his Government; they had almost carryed it for the Churchmen, to the great amazement of these latter, so as to let them see that they had been extreamly wanting to themselves in not timely applying.

"There are in Pensylvania two congregations of Lutherans being Swedes, whose Churches are finely built, and their two Ministers lately sent in nobly furnished with £300 worth of Books by the Swedish King, and they live in very good Accord with our Minister and his Church.

"There is but one Church of England Minister as yet, and he at Philadelphia singularly beloved and respected by his People; and they do most importunately sollicite both from thence, and from other Parts of that Province for more, where I am afraid there are at least six wanting.

"There are some Independants, but neither many nor much Bigotted.

"III. Adjoining to this are the two Colonies of the East and West Jerseys, where they have some pretty Towns, and well peopled, but are wholly left to themselves without Priest or Altar. True it is, Mr. Mathers from New England seems now to bestirr himself in sending both there and into the other colonies, where he sees us take footing. His Independent Preachers and the Quakers are very numerous in the Jerseys, but I am credibly informed that the people are more affected to our Clergy, could they have them. The Keithians are alike affected to us, as in Pensylvania, and I think there would be a Reception for six Ministers in both the Jerseys.

"IV. From New York, the E. of Bellamont, the Governor, writes me word, that a Church of England Clergy are much wanted there, and there will be Room for at least two Ministers, besides one which they have already: the one to assist at New York, the other to be placed at Albany, where besides the Inhabitants of the Town, which are many, we have two Companies of Souldiers in Garrison, but all without a Preacher.

"V. In Long Island there are nine Churches, but no Church of England Minister, though much desired, and there ought to be at least two sent into that Colony.

"VI. In Road Island, for want of a Clergy, many of the Inhabitants are said to be sunk down right into Atheism, the new generation being the offspring of Quakers, whose children for want of an outward teaching, which these Enthusiasts at first denyed, being meer Ranters. As indeed the sons of the Quakers are found to be such in most places, and equally to deny all

Religion. And here therefore there will be work enough for two substantiall Divines, at least.

"VII. Ronoak lyes betwixt Virginia and Carolina. It is peopled with English, intermixt with the native Indians, to a great Extent. And as there will be occasion for at least two Missionaries to be sent amongst y^m^, so the Governor, who is now going over to that Colony, being a very worthy gentleman, I dare promise will give the best Countenance and Encouragement which shall be in his power.

"VIII. The last Province that I shall now speak of on the Continent is Carolina, a very thriving Colony, and so large as to want at least three Missionaries, besides one lately sent thither.

"It is no part of my province to speak to Virginia, it being under the Jurisdiction of a very worthy Person, Mr. Commissary Blaire, whose abilities as they fitt him for great Designs, so his Industry has been for some years exercised in doing uncomon services to that Church.

"But the gratitude which all that are well affected to Christianity, do owe, more especially the Clergy, and above all myself, to that admirable Patron of Religion and Learning, Colonel Francis Nicholson, the present Governor thereof, forbids me to pass over in silence those Glorious Works which he is there carrying on with such unusuall application; and which, when accomplished, must render his memory sweet to all succeeding generations.

"The two great Designs which he is now so intent upon for the Good of the Church (not to mention here what a Patron, or rather a Founder he has been to it in most of ye other Provinces, now named) are the Erecting of a Colledge in Virginia, or rather an University for those Parts, which he has almost finished; and the settling of the Church by Law on such a foot, and with the Advice and Assistance of Mr. Blaire, in such a Constitution as will, if they can make the next Assembly sensible of their own Good, reduce the Clergy there from that Servile Dependance on the Vestrys, which would have frightened all men of worth from ever coming amongst them. But the scheme which I have seen these Gentlemen have layd, when accomplished, will render that Clergy and Province mutually happy in one another.

"Considering this Governor's late Heroick Actions in the Conquest of the most desperate of Enemies, the Pyrates, who were so infatuated as to approach his Province, and in whose Reduction his own personall presence and valour had a share, almost to a fault, it's hard to say whether Arms or Letters have the greatest Right to Challenge him for their Generall. But when we consider the extream Disproportion betwixt the numbers of persons in publick Post, who are studious of the Good of God's Church, compared with such as are thought serviceable to the State in Arms, it ought to be the hearty wishes of all the friends of Religion and Learning, not only in his own Province, but all over that Continent, that he would never more expose his person to such Dangers, wherein should he fall, in all human appearance, the Loss would be Irreparable.

"Nor do I think myself obliged to speak here of New England, where Independancy seems to be the Religion of the Country. True it is since a Church was opened at Boston about fifteen years agoe for the English Service, the Congregation of Church People are become very numerous; and the young Students of the College are sayd upon the Reading of our

Episcopal Authors (against which they are narrowly watched by Mr. Mathers) to become not so ill affected to us, but that some of them would gladly receive their orders from the hands of Bishops if they could; and two of them have lately come over hither to be accordingly ordained. But my Design is not to intermeddle where Christianity under any form has obtained possession of the Country, but to represent rather the deplorable fate of the English Colonies, where they have been in a manner abandoned to Atheism, or which is much as one, to Quakerism, for want of a Clergy settled amongst them. And I think I have one remaining Instance of such neglect in this kind, as if it provokes me to some warm Reflections upon our Nation (for the Church I know wants power, and Riches to do much of itself) I conceive the occasion will bear me out.

"And it is with Reference to the last Colony in America that I shall speak to anything at present, named Newfound Land, near whose coast we were drove in my voyage to Maryland; and I could have been very glad if with the safety of our ship and lives, we had been thrown into it, that I might have personally seen the Condition of the place and people. But this Curiosity was in a great measure satisfyd by the account I received from the Master of a Ship on board of us, who had made many Voyages there, and gave me this account of the Island, so farr as it is in the possession of the English; that there are Harbours in it belonging to us 26, Families 274, Inhabitants as well winter as summer on the Island about 1120, workmen about 4200, ships' crews in the Fishing Season 3150, and men in the ships sent at the latter end of the yeare to carry home the Fish 1200.

"And now is it possible to imagine that from a nation possessing Christianity in its Purity, defecate of the least tincture of Dross and Corruption; the sole Tendency of whose Principles is to inspire all its Disciples with the noblest thoughts of God, with an ardent zeale for his Honour and Glory, and with a boundless and unlymitted Love to mankind, a Love as Extensive as the whole World, and as Intensive as that we have to ourselves; Is it credible that in a Colony of so many thousand soules, who are all of them natives from England, from whence our shipping do sail to it during many months in the year, and where so many thousand Families abide perpetually, some 20 years, most the whole course of their Lives, and from whose trade such profit accrues to the Nation as contributes next to the woollen manufacture to turn the Ballance of Europe in Commerce on our side; can any one believe it when he is told, that from such a Nation, with respect to such a Colony, there neither was or is, nor is ever like to be for any measures that have been yet, or are likely to be taken or encouraged by the Publick, any Preaching, Prayers, or Sacraments, or any Ministeriall and Divine Offices performed on that Island; but that they should be suffered to live as those who know no God in the World! Are Rome and Mecca, whose sons are so apt to compass Sea and Land to gain Proselytes to Superstition and Folly, so regardless of their own people? And will it not then be more tolerable for that Tyre and this Sydon than for us in the day of Judgment! for if they had known the things which we do, the most rude and uncultivated of those Parts which we possess, should not have remained uninstructed in the best Religion in the World.

"The truth of it is, this Indifference of ours in propagating the Religion which we profess to believe, in those Parts, where as well our powers do enable us, as our Duty obliges us to take some care thereof, is the Amazement of all whom I ever yet heard make serious Reflections upon it.

"But since for any publick Funds that we are ever likely to get for the Propagation of Christian Knowledge, either in this or the other Colonies, we may complain in vain; and the only hope is from the pious Clergy themselves, and such particular persons amongst the devout Laity, whose hearts are inflamed with a Love of God, and of those souls which he has purchased with his own Blood; I shall rather turn myself to you, my most Reverend Lords, giving you a general Estimate of the number of Missionaries, which we hope to be supplyed withall from y^r^ Paternall Care; and as there will be need of at least two to be sent to Newfound Land, so upon ye whole it appears that there are at present wanting no less than forty Missionaries to be sent into all these Colonies.

"And the necessity that they should be both so many, and singularly well qualified for the purpose, I am next to show you; and that there should be at least that number sent into each of these Colonies, as I have now mentioned, appears from hence, that even then their business will lye extreamly wide, but chiefly for this reason, that there is so great an Inclination to embrace Christianity amongst many Quakers, all over those Parts, where Mr. Keith has been, that it will be a fatall neglect if our Church should not close with that Providence which offers so many Proselytes into her Bosom. For I am to inform your Lordships that this vast accession of perhaps 50000 soules to our Church, if not speedily secured, will fall into the Independents, who being aware of it are very busy at this tyme in sending their Ministers from New England, and those maintained too from thence, which makes it worth our while to examine whether it be not by misapplication of a noble charity. And the Plantations growing now into populous and powerfull Provinces, with all humble submission, in my opinion, ought not to be so neglected, as that it should be indifferent to us, whether they be made True Sons of our Church, or the most soure leavened of all its Enemies, Independants, Ana-Baptists, and Quakers.

"Nor is the necessity less that these Missionaries should be singularly well qualified than that they should be at all sent. And indeed in order to make the better choice, agreeable to what I have observed of the State, the Temper and Constitution of the Country and people, is one great reason that has persuaded me so soon back: and ye persons which alone can do good there, as I conceive, must

"In the first place, be of such nice moralls as to abstain from all appearance of evil, there being not such a calumniating people in the world as the Quakers are every where found to be, and it is the most fault of the Plantations, that they give their Tongues too much Liberty that way, especially if they can find the least flaw.

"Secondly, they must be men of good Prudence, and an exact Conduct, or otherwise they will unavoidably fall into Contempt with a people so well versed in Business as every the meanest Planter seems to be.

"Thirdly, they ought to be well experienced in the Pastorall Care, having a greater Variety both of Sects and Humours to deal with in those parts than are at home; and therefore it would be well if we could be provided with such as have been Curates here for some time.

"Fourthly, more especially, they ought to be of a True Missionary spirit, having an ardent Zeale for God's Glory, and the Salvation of men's soules. And

"Fifthly, of a very ACTIVE SPIRIT, and consequently not so grown into years as to be incapable of Labour and fateigue, no more than very young, upon which account they will be more lyable to be despised.

"And lastly, they ought to be good, substantiall, well-studied Divines, very ready in the Holy Scriptures, able with a sound Judgment to explicate and prove the great Doctrines of Christianity, to state the nature and extent of the Christian duties, and with the most moving considerations to enforce their Practice, and to defend the truth against all its adversaries; to which purpose it will be therefore absolutely requisite to provide each of them with a Library of necessary Books, to be fixt in those places to which they shall be sent, for the use of them, and their successors for ever. This to be a perpetuall Encouragement to good, and able Divines always to go over and to render them useful when they are there; a design, of whose usefulness, of whose necessity I am now so fully persuaded, since I have been in and know ye wants of these Parts, that I am resolved to have no hand in sending over any one, the best Missionary, who shall not be so provided.

"Well, but the great quere will be how we may be able to procure so great a number of such able Missionaries, how to maintain them, and how to furnish them out with such Libraries; in order to all which I crave leave to offer these following considerations:

"First, that the Colonies now named, consisting chiefly of Quakers, or such as for want of the Gospell being preached amongst them, are in a manner of no religion; they are in that respect to be considered as so many Heathen Nations. And it will seem unreasonable to expect that a people before they are converted and made to understand the goodness and advantages of true Religion, should be induced to maintain its Ministry, and especially in this case of the Quakers, the persons chiefly to be proselyted; who above all other rights of the Church of Christ, have been deeply prejudiced against the maintenance of the Clergy.

"Secondly, that if the Missionaries, which shall be sent into each of these Colonies, shall be well chosen and duly qualified, I am persuaded they will find the work of God to prosper so well in their hands, that in three years' time the people will, out of pure Devotion, subscribe or settle a very plentifull maintenance both for them and their successors; to support me in which Conjecture we have two very eminent and late Instances: the one in Pensylvania, the other in Carolina; in the former of which Mr. Clayton, who at his first going over three years agoe, and whilst his Congregation was not above sixty persons, had scarcely £50 per annum maintainance, yet upon the accession of new Converts to upwards of 700 (for so is that Church increased in three years) has brought the maintenance of the Minister of Philadelphia to £150 per annum; and in Carolina, Mr. Marshall, through his excellent Preaching and singular conduct, so gained upon ye people, that from a poor subscription maintenance at first, they settled upon him and his successors within two years after his being amongst them, what amounts to £300 per annum; and at his death, the General Assembly of the Province were so kind to his widow, as to present her with £300 upon her Return home.

"Thirdly, I conceive, therefore, that in the interim, and during the first three years, it will be absolutely necessary that these Missionaries should be subsisted from hence; and it shall be my utmost care in that time to have them so provided of Glebes, and the same so stocked, as that they may thenceforward live comfortably upon the Emoluments of their own places.

"Fourthly, the method by which I would humbly propose to have these Missionaries, which I desire, both well chosen and supported from home in their service for the first three years, is as follows:

"I. As to the choice, that every Bishop be pleased to pitch upon some proper person within his own Diocess, such as his Lordship shall judge best qualified, as aforesaid, for the Mission. And then

"II. As to his support, that his Lordship having subscribed to the following Proposall, the sum his Lordship shall think fitt to contribute towards such a Design, he be pleased to recommend it to the Dignifyed and others the most considerable Clergy within his Diocese, and they to the well-disposed Laity, within their respective parishes, to make up the sum proposed.

"III. That the sum subscribed for each Missionary be £50 per annum for three years, and as less will not be sufficient to encourage a person of Learning and worth to undertake the Mission, so it will not suffice to subsist even a private Minister in these parts, where every thing is very dear, which must be bought for money, and not bartered for by the product of the country, which no Clergyman will be Master of till he can have a Glebe, and shall have cultivated his Plantation.

"IV. That the subscriptions be payd into the Arch Deacons at their Easter Visitation, and be forthwith returned by them to the hands of the Bishop of the Diocess, or to such person or persons in London as his Lordship shall appoint to receive it, and to pay it to the order of the Missionary sent by such Diocess.

"V. That besides the £50 per annum allowed each Missionary for his subsistence, £20 a year be also subscribed towards raising a Library of necessary and useful Books, both for himself and his successors in the Town, or other place wherein he shall be settled.

"VI. That the first payment of the £50 and £20 be advanced at his first going off (which I could wish might be before Christmas next), that so being sufficiently furnished with all necessaries, he may not appeare to come as an Indigent person into the place where he shall be appointed, and as one that is to have free quarters upon those he is to proselyte; the Quakers being very prying into the Condition of those who come over, whom, if they find poor, they proclaim hirelings, and to come over meerly for Bread. But if otherwise, they have been found at a loss what to say against them. And to be well provided at first will succeed the better to the advantage both of the Missionary himself and the Church, to the support and countenance of which he will undoubtedly lay a good Foundation, who coming first shall be happy in his conduct.

"And indeed, my Lords, could we but have such men as by their reall worth might be able to gain the affections of those people, I do not in the least doubt, from what I have already found, but that in my next Visitation, I could obtain large Tracts of Glebes, and good Houses built by the respective parishes in Maryland, and the Proselyte Churches in the other Colonies, so as both those, who shall now go over, will themselves in few years be in a comfortable condition, and their successors after them in a happy settlement.

"And as neither the Clergy's Condition can be comfortable, nor can it be properly called a settlement, till they shall be in Houses, and on Glebes of their own; so now is the time to endeavour both, or it will be too late hereafter to think of obtaining either, for as yet land may be taken up, or had upon easy terms. But should the Plantations continue to increase as they have done of late, within seaven years, Land will not be purchased at treble the Rate as now.

"For my own part, I take this to be so happy a Juncture to lay the Foundation of lasting Good to the Church of God in those Provinces, that though after the Expence already of above a thousand pounds in its service, and though it must be still at my own charge that I can again go, yet I shall not make the least difficulty in accompanying your Lordships' Missionaries, which from your respective Dioceses you shall please to send into those Parts. And being therefore so little interested myself in the Mission, that it will go near to sacrifice the remainder of my small Fortunes to Embarque again in it, I hope I may with a better Countenance, through your Lordships' Patronage, presume to offer the following Proposalls to the Very Reverend Dignitaries and wealthier Clergy of the Church, for a small subscription from each of them towards the maintenance of those Missionaries, their Brethren, whom your Lordships shall please to send."

"*Proposalls for the Propagation of the Christian Religion, and for the Reduction of the Quakers thereunto in the several Provinces on the Continent of North America.*

"Whereas severall English Colonies on the Continent of North America, now growing into populous Provinces, are however, to the no small scandall of our Church and Nation, as yet, destitute both of Churches and of persons to Minister in Holy Things, to preach to them the word of God, to offer up the Prayers of the People, and to administer the Holy Sacraments.

"And whereas, to the great Dishonour of God, and the Destruction of a multitude of souls, as well as the great Scandall of the Reformed Religion, many thousands of the people in those Parts have been sadly deluded by Quakers into a Total Apostacy from the Christian Faith, and giving themselves up to the Conduct only of the Light within, or mere Natural Conscience, have rejected the Holy Scriptures from being the Rule of Faith and Practice.

"Whereas again, notwithstanding the strong prejudices and great obstinacy of that sort of Unbelievers, yet through the blessing of God upon the Labours of such, who have hitherto endeavoured the Reduction of that people, many of the Quakers are returned to the Christian Faith, and others amongst them are so staggered as to doubt that they are in a dangerous state of Unbelief, so that now there wants only under God more Labourers to be sent into those fields, which seem to be white for Harvest.

"And Lastly, whereas we, the Clergy and others of the Diocess of ————————, in concurrence with such as are piously disposed in other Diocesses, being sensible of the infinite mercies of God towards us in affording us the Light of his Holy Gospell; and thinking ourselves obliged out of Gratitude to God, and Compassion to those People, who are not yet happy in the like, to provide, so far as in us lyes, for the Propagation of the same Holy Faith amongst those of our own Nation, though never so far remov'd from us into Foreign Parts, Do subscribe the severall sums to our names annexed, to be payd yearly, at the Easter Visitation, to the Reverend the Arch Deacon of ————————, to be immediately returned by him to the Right Rev. Father in God, the Lord Bishop of this Diocess, for the maintenance, support of, and to provide a Library for such Missionary as his Lordship shall think fit to send into those Parts.

A List of Persons Licensed to the Plantations by the Bishops of London from the year 1745 inclusive.

[From the Fulham MSS.]

	AFRICA.				
M	Philip Quaque, a Moor	May	4	1765	Gold Coast
	ALBANY.				
M	Harry Munro	July	21	1770	
M	William Stanford	July	8	1775	Went to Jamaica
	AMERICA IN GENERAL.				
	John Jones	June	19	1750	
	Gideon Castlegrave	Jan.	11	1750	
	Thomas Browne	July	28	1764	

	Name	Month	Day	Year	Remarks
	David Fullerton	June	20	1767	
M	John Sayre	Sept.	29	1768	Now in Nova Scotia
	Thomas Fielde	Aug.	2	1770	Dead
M	Daniel Batwell	Oct.	16	1773	
	Myles Cooper	Jan.	4	1774	
	ANTIGUA.				
	Alexander Grant	Dec.	21	1748	
	Robert Moncrief	Feb.	27	1748	
	John King	Sept.	1	1750	
	William Shervington	Dec.	23	1753	
	Henry Byam	Oct.	20	1754	
	Samuel Lovely	Oct.	3	1758	
	John Bowen	Dec.	23	1759	
	James Somerville	March	5	1768	
	Francis Massett	Sept.	29	1768	
	James Coull	Dec.	26	1772	St. John's Parish
	John Shepherd	March	8	1773	
	Josiah Weston	Dec.	21	1774	St. Mary's Parish
	James Lindsay	Feb.	17	1783	Falmouth Parish
	Samuel Jefferson	Dec.	30	1783	St. John's Parish
	BAHAMA ISLANDS.				
	Richard St. John	Sept.	25	1745	
	John Snow	May	26	1746	
M	William Duncanson	Sept.	8	1760	Dead
M	George Tyzard	Jan.	19	1767	Dead
	Richard Moss	Feb.	16	1767	Dismissed
M	John Hunt	Nov.	4	1769	Dead
M	James Brown	March	15	1779	Providence, went to Pensacola
	BARBADOES.				
	Kenneth Morrison	Oct.	21	1745	
	Thomas Barnard	Dec.	22	1746	
	Robert Braithwaise	Sept.	27	1750	
	John Edwards	Dec.	26	1750	
	Edward Brace	Dec.	28	1750	
	William Duke	Dec.	21	1753	
	John Shepley	Feb.	12	1754	
	Isaac Hunt	Feb.	4	1755	
	Robert Boucher	Dec.	21	1756	
	Thomas Harris	Feb.	7	1757	
	Richard Saer	March	17	1757	
	Wm. Duke	May	21	1758	
	Jonathan Downes	March	30	1759	
	Richard Harris	Dec.	23	1759	
	Thos. Duke, a Deacon	June	1	1760	License endorsed Sept. 22, 1765
	Thomas Wharton	June	12	1760	
	William Dunlap	Feb.	25	1766	
	William Ferrill	Aug.	31	1766	
	Robt. Boucher Nicholls	April	5	1768	
	Joseph Hebson	Sept.	29	1768	

	Name	Month	Day	Year	Remarks
	Benjamin Spry	Oct.	27	1768	
	Michael Mashart	Jan.	1	1771	Catechist
	Joseph Hutchins	June	13	1771	
	Samuel Dent	Dec.	26	1772	Christ Church Parish
	Henry Quintine	Feb.	22	1773	
	Robert Jackman	Dec.	28	1777	St. George's Parish
	John Duke	Aug.	24	1779	License endorsed June 16, 1783
	Hugh Williams Austin	Aug.	24	1779	
	Henry Evans Husband	March	14	1781	
	Francis McMahon	Sept.	25	1782	St. James's Parish
	Henry Evans Holder	Oct.	28	1782	St. Joseph's Parish
	Timothy Blenman	June	24	1783	St. George's Parish
	Hugh Williams Austin	Sept.	8	1784	St. Peter's Parish
	BERMUDAS.				
	James Holiday	July	15	1745	
	John Danvers	May	9	1746	
	Alex. Richardson	June	16	1755	
	John Feveryear	Oct.	12	1755	
	Thomas Lyttleton	March	30	1767	Now in England
	Benjamin Blackburn	Dec.	27	1773	St. George's Parish
	Ludlow Holt	Feb.	25	1777	
	CAPE BRETON.				
	Benj. Lovell	Sept.	9	1784	Military Staff
	CANADA.				
	David Cabran de Lisle	April	15	1766	
	Leger Jno. Baptiste Noel Veyssiere	March	5	1768	
	David Francis de Montmollin	March	5	1768	
	CARRIBEES.				
	James Ramsay	Nov.	24	1761	St. John's Capisterre
	William Scott	June	29	1764	
	John Symes	Sept.	21	1767	
	Benj. Wm. Hutchinson	June	24	1768	
	Hy. Erskine Kirkpatrick	July	18	1768	
	John Pogson Crook	March	25	1769	
	William Taylor	Dec.	24	1769	
	Thomas Wilson	Sept.	22	1771	Did not go
	NORTH CAROLINA.				
	John Reid	April	1	1745	
	John Rowan	Sept.	21	1747	
	Robert Cumming	Jan.	19	1748	
	William Pow	Jan.	23	1748	
M	Alexander Stewart	June	18	1753	
M	John McDowel	July	5	1753	

	William Fanning	March	25	1754	
	William Miller	March	31	1755	
	Samuel Laird	Oct.	12	1755	
M	Daniel Earl	Sept.	19	1756	
	William Harrison	Dec.	21	1756	
	William Teale	Dec.	6	1762	
M	John Barnett	May	2	1765	Bad Man!
M	James Cosgreve	Feb.	25	1766	
M	George Meiklejohn	March	12	1766	
M	Charles Kupples	June	11	1766	
M	Samuel Fiske	Aug.	31	1766	
M	John Cramp	Sept.	21	1767	
M	Hobart Briggs	April	5	1768	
	James Macartney	July	25	1768	
	Francis Johnston	Sept.	29	1768	
M	Henry John Burgess	Nov.	1	1768	
M	John Wills	Jan.	30	1769	Dead
M	Theodorus Swain Drage	May	29	1769	Never heard of him after
	Edward Jones	May	29	1769	
M	Peter Blin	Sept.	29	1769	
M	Charles Edward Taylor	Jan.	1	1771	Now there
M	Nicholas Christian	Aug.	13	1773	
M	Nathaniel Blount	Sept.	21	1773	St. Thomas's Parish
	Hezekiah Ford	Sept.	29	1774	St. Jude's Parish
C	Charles Pettigrew	March	1	1775	
	John Lott Phillips	June	11	1776	St. Margaret's Parish
	SOUTH CAROLINA.				
	Alexander Keith	June	26	1745	
	David Garrow	July	15	1745	
	Bolton Simpson	Aug.	26	1745	
	Robert Beetham	Oct.	16	1745	
	Robert Stone	June	30	1749	
	Jn. Utrick Geisendauner	Sept.	24	1749	
	Wm. Langhorne	June	5	1750	
	Alexander Douglass	Aug.	24	1750	
	Charles Martin	Sept.	13	1751	
	Michael Smith	April	14	1752	
	James Harrison	June	22	1752	
	Robert Barron	Feb.	2	1753	
	Alexander Barron	June	17	1753	
	Richard Clarke	July	16	1753	
	John Andrews	July	16	1753	
	Jno. Cheshire Heyborne	Aug.	7	1753	Did not go
	Clement Brooke	Jan.	29	1755	
	Jenkin Lewis	July	5	1755	
	Winwood Serjeant	Dec.	19	1756	
	Samuel Fenner Warren	Jan.	12	1758	Afterwards My. in N. England
	Robert Cooper	May	1	1758	
	John Tongue	Sept.	8	1759	Dead
	Abraham Immer	Jan.	28	1760	Dead
	Joseph Dacre Appleby				

	Wilson	Oct.	26	1761	Dead
	Offspring Pearce	Oct.	26	1761	
	Joseph Stokes	Oct.	30	1761	Dead
	George Skene	Dec.	7	1761	
	John Green	March	16	1762	Dead
	John Evans	March	24	1762	Dead
	Joseph Edwards	June	29	1762	Did not go
	John Hockley	Sept.	12	1765	
	William Lonsdale	Jan.	16	1766	Dead
	Paul Turquand	April	28	1766	
	Charles Woodmason	April	28	1766	Came to England
	George Spencer	April	24	1767	Dead
	Samuel Ward	Dec.	14	1767	Did not go
	Thomas Straker	Jan.	28	1768	Dead
	John Lewis	July	21	1768	
	Richard Farmer	Nov.	16	1768	Dead
	Francis Hoyland	March	26	1769	Did not go
	Robert Purcell	April	5	1769	
	Thomas Morgan	May	29	1769	Dead
	Robert Smith	Oct.	3	1769	
	James Pierce	Oct.	3	1769	Dead
M	Saml. Frederick Lucius	Nov.	1	1769	
	William Jones	Feb.	8	1770	
	Henry Purcell	March	31	1770	
	John Hinde	Jan.	29	1771	
	Nathl. James Martin	May	29	1771	
	Christ. Erust Schab	May	29	1771	Dead
	John Villette	Sept.	2	1771	Came home. Prince Frdk's parish
	Thomas Walke	Feb.	18	1772	St. Mark's Parish
	Haddon Smith	Aug.	22	1772	
	Edward Jenkins	Aug.	29	1772	Ashley Parish
	Charles Fredk. Moreau	Feb.	8	1773	
	John Dundays	June	6	1773	Dead. Prince Frederick's Parish
	Wm. Eastwick Graham	June	11	1775	Prince William's Parish
	ST. CHRISTOPHERS.				
	William Topham	Feb.	24	1745	
	Thomas Jones	May	4	1748	
	Robert Roberts	Sept.	6	1753	
	Francis Hoyland	Dec.	23	1753	
	Delahay Reece	Feb.	9	1760	
	John Clerkson	Sept.	30	1760	
	Hnry. Robt. Duckworth	Dec.	26	1772	
	John Roberson	June	11	1775	
	Wm. John Julius	Sept.	21	1781	
	Wm. Thomas	May	19	1783	SS. George & Peter's Parishes
	CONNECTICUT.				
M	Matt. Graves	Oct.	22	1747	
M	Richard Clark	Feb.	25	1767	
M	John Tyler	June	29	1768	
	John Rutchers Marshall	July	28	1771	Woodbury

	James Nicholls	Feb.	3	1774	Northbury & New Cambridge
	DOMINICA.				
	Henry McLeane	July	1	1764	
	James McIntosh	Dec.	29	1771	
	Austin Leigh	Feb.	16	1771	
	Joseph Miller	Sept.	21	1773	
	Isaac Mann	Aug.	24	1774	SS. Paul's & George's Parishes
	George Green	March	26	1778	
	EAST FLORIDA.				
	John Forbes	May	5	1764	St. Augustine
	John Frazer	March	23	1769	
	John Leadbetter	Nov.	8	1773	St. Augustine
	John Kennedy	Dec.	24	1776	St. Mark's
	WEST FLORIDA.				
	Samuel Hart	May	5	1764	Mobile
	William Dawson	July	2	1764	Pensacola
	William Gordon	Aug.	8	1767	
	Nathaniel Cotton	March	2	1768	
	George Chapman	May	3	1773	Pensacola
	GEORGIA.				
	Barthol. Louberbuhler	Nov.	2	1745	
M	Jonathan Copp	Dec.	28	1750	
M	Samuel Frink	Nov.	17	1763	
	John Alexander	April	28	1766	
M	Edward Ellington	May	5	1767	
	Alexander Finlay	Sept.	23	1770	
M	James Seymour	Aug.	24	1771	Augusta
M	John Holmes	Aug.	1	1773	St. George's Parish. Dismissed
	John Rennie	Dec.	17	1773	
M	James Browne	June	24	1779	St. George's Parish. In England
	John Stewart	March	31	1781	Christ Church, Savannah Parish
	GRANADA.				
	George Bowdler	July	6	1764	
	John Cumming	Dec.	24	1769	
	John Findlater	June	13	1771	
	Francis McMahon	Sept.	9	1784	
	GUADALOUPE.				
	Gaspar Joel Monard	Aug.	25	1759	
	JAMAICA.				
	Joshua Peat	Sept.	22	1746	
	Patrick McCullock	June	7	1748	

George Evans	Jan.	12	1749	
Joseph Stoney	Nov.	22	1750	
Henry Caaffe	Sept.	22	1751	
Colin Campbell	Sept.	22	1751	
Robert Harris	Jan.	28	1752	
Robert Atkins	July	5	1753	
John McAuley	Sept.	22	1754	
Isaac Teale	May	13	1755	
Anthony Davis	Sept.	25	1757	
John Ramsay	Sept.	23	1759	
John Perney	Nov.	26	1761	
Michael Smith	June	19	1764	
Hadden Smith	Dec.	21	1766	
William Clarke	Dec.	22	1767	
John Walcot	June	25	1769	
Inglis Twing	June	25	1769	
John Usher Tyrrel	Dec.	24	1769	
Thomas Pool	Aug.	1	1773	St. George's Parish
William Morgan	Sept.	21	1773	
Alexander Robertson	March	1	1775	Clarendon Parish
Middleton Howard	Oct.	1	1775	
Richard Johnson	Oct.	1	1775	
Philip Anglin	Oct.	28	1776	
Peter Miller	Sept.	28	1777	Kingston Parish
Thomas Bradshaw	March	26	1778	
James Steel	April	8	1782	
Thomas Simcocks	Sept.	13	1784	Westmoreland Parish
ST. JOHN'S ISLAND.				
John Caulfield	Aug.	17	1769	
LEEWARD ISLANDS.				
Matt Towers	May	26	1746	
MARYLAND.				
John Houston	Sept.	21	1747	
Hamilton Bell	Oct.	19	1747	
George Cooke	Dec.	21	1748	
Alexander Adams	Dec.	21	1748	
Richard Brown	July	9	1750	
John Macpherson	April	17	1751	
Thomas Johnston	June	16	1751	
Matthew Harris	March	26	1753	
Thomas Thornton	Sept.	22	1754	
John Ross	Sept.	22	1754	
Alexander Williamson	Dec.	27	1755	
Philip Walker	March	25	1756	
William Barrell	March	4	1760	
Samuel Keene	Sept.	30	1760	
Joseph Mather	Dec.	29	1760	
Daniel Maynadier	Dec.	29	1760	
Francis Lander	Nov.	24	1761	

	William Dowie	April	2	1762	
	Samuel Howard	May	2	1765	
	Samuel Sloane	Dec.	23	1765	
	Thomas Alkin	Feb.	25	1766	
	Benet Allen	Sept.	30	1766	Come home
	Henry Fendall	Feb.	25	1767	
	Edward Edmiston	March	30	1767	
	Thomas John Clagett	Oct.	11	1767	
	John Porter	June	11	1768	
	John Patterson	June	11	1768	
	Jeremiah Berry	Dec.	22	1768	
	Daniel McKinnon	Dec.	22	1768	
	John Scott	March	25	1769	
	Jcb Henderson Hindman	Dec.	24	1769	
	Edward Gaunt	Feb.	2	1770	
	George Gowndril	March	31	1770	
	John Montgomery	July	23	1770	
	John B. Gowie	July	28	1771	Prince George's Parish
	Thomas Lendrum	Feb.	2	1773	
	obert Graham	March	8	1773	St. Paul's Parish
	James Wilmer	Sept.	21	1773	
	Thomas Reid	Sept.	21	1773	
	Hamilton Bell	Feb.	28	1774	Somerset Parish
	George Mitchell	April	6	1774	Stepney Parish
	William Duncan	May	29	1774	St. Michael's Parish
	Thomas Harrison	Aug.	24	1774	Trinity Parish
	Walter Hanson Harrison	Aug.	24	1774	Durham Parish
	Robert McKormick	April	11	1775	St. James's Parish
	Thomas Braithwaite	Jan.	6	1776	
	MASSACHUSETTS.				
M	Willard Wheeler	Dec.	21	1767	
M	Mather Byles	June	29	1768	
M	William Clark	Dec.	22	1768	
M	Gideon Bostwick	March	14	1770	
M	Daniel Fogg	Aug.	19	1770	
	MONTSERRATT.				
	William Blair	Sept.	27	1750	
	John Symes	Sept.	21	1767	
	George Young	Dec.	28	1775	
	MOSQUITO SHORE.				
M	Thomas Warren	June	24	1768	Gone to Jamaica
M	Robert Shaw	June	29	1774	
	NEVIS.				
	Edwin Thomas	Sept.	11	1747	
	William McHenley	Feb.	24	1773	St. John's & Thomas's Parishes

	NEW ENGLAND.				
	Barzillai Dean	Nov.	21	1745	
M	William McGilchrist	Oct.	10	1746	Dead
	William Hooper	June	10	1747	
M	Jerem. Leaming	June	21	1748	
M	Richard Mansfield	Aug.	11	1748	
	Jonathan Coulton	March	26	1752	
	Ichabod Camp	March	26	1752	
M	John Fowle	May	24	1752	Dead
M	Edward Bags	May	24	1752	
M	Peter Bowers	March	18	1753	
M	John Troutbeck	May	7	1754	Dead
M	Solomon Palmer	Oct.	20	1754	Dead
M	Marmaduke Browne	Jan.	29	1755	Dead
M	William McClenachan	March	31	1755	Dead
M	Edward Winslow	March	31	1755	Dead
M	John Graves	June	4	1755	Dead
M	Christopher Newton	July	28	1755	
M	Samuel Fairweather	March	25	1756	Dead
M	James Scovil	April	4	1759	
M	Samuel Peters	Aug.	25	1759	In England
M	James Greaton	Jan.	28	1760	Dead
M	Jacob Bailey	March	17	1761	Nova Scotia
M	Thomas Davies	Oct.	26	1761	
M	Samuel Andrews	Oct.	26	1761	
M	John Beardsley	Oct.	26	1763	Nova Scotia
M	Joshua Wingate Weeks	April	17	1763	Ejected himself
M	Roger Viets	April	17	1764	
	William Walter	Feb.	28	1764	
	Abraham Jarvis	Feb.	28	1764	
M	Bela Hubbard	Feb.	28	1764	
M	John Lyon	June	29	1765	Dead
M	John Wiswell	Feb.	11	1767	Nova Scotia
M	Richard C	Feb.	27	1770	
M	Luke Babcock	Feb.	2	1770	Dead
	Samuel Parker	Feb.	28	1774	Trinity, Boston
	NEWFOUNDLAND.				
M	Benjamin Lindsay	March	30	1751	Dead
M	Edward Langman	Jan.	10	1752	Dead
M	William Fotheringham	June	8	1762	Dead
M	James Balgour	June	29	1764	
M	Laurence Couglan	April	26	1766	Removed
M	Isaac Hunt	March	4	1777	Trinity Bay. Never went
	Walter Price	March	22	1784	St. John's Parish
	NEW HAMPSHIRE.				
M	Moses Badger	Feb.	23	1767	Dead
M	Kanna Cossit	March	27	1773	Haverill Parish
	William Aldington	June	11	1775	

	NEW JERSEY				
M	Thomas Thompson	March	25	1745	Dead
M	Thomas Wood	Sept.	29	1749	Removed to Nova Scotia. Dead
M	George Craig	Sept.	1	1750	Dead
M	Samuel Cooke	June	3	1751	
M	Thos Bradbury Chandler	Aug.	20	1751	
M	Samuel Seabury	Dec.	23	1753	
M	Robert McKean	April	26	1757	Dead
M	Andrew Moreton	March	17	1760	Removed
	Agur Treadwell	April	30	1762	
M	Leonard Cutting	Dec.	21	1763	
M	Nathaniel Evans	Sept.	22	1765	Dead
M	Jonathan Odell	Jan.	19	1767	
	George Spencer	Jan.	19	1767	
M	Abraham Beach	June	14	1767	
M	William Frazer	Dec.	21	1767	
M	William Ayres	Dec.	21	1767	
	David Griffith	Aug.	19	1770	
M	Robert Blackwell	June	11	1772	Gloucester County. Dismissed
M	Samuel Tingley	March	8	1773	St. John's in Elizabeth Town. Removed to Maryland.
M	Uzal Ogden	Sept.	21	1773	Sussex County
	NEW PROVIDENCE.				
M	Robert Carter	Sept.	23	1749	Dead
	NEW YORK.				
	Joseph Lamson	June	10	1745	
	Samuel Auchmuty	July	20	1747	Dead
M	Epenetus Townsend	Dec.	21	1767	Dead
M	Joshua Bloomer	Feb.	28	1769	
M	William Andrews	June	10	1770	
M	John Stewart	Aug.	19	1770	
M	John Doty	Jan.	1	1771	
	John Vardill	April	6	1774	
	John Ogilvie	June	30	1749	Dead
	William Johnson	March	25	1756	Dead
	John Milner	Feb.	25	1761	Dead
M	Harry Munn	Feb.	11	1765	Come to England
M	Ephraim Avery	June	2	1765	Dead
	John Bowden	May	29	1774	Shenesboro'. Refused it
	Benjamin Moore	June	29	1774	Charlotte, &c. Precincts
	Jas Sayre	Sept.	21	1774	Fredericksburgh Precinct
M	William Stanford	July	8	1775	Albany. Mosq. Shore
	Thomas Lambert Moore	Sept.	21	1781	Islip, in Suffolk County
	NOVA SCOTIA.				
M	William Tutty	April	17	1749	Dead
M	William Anwyl	April	27	1749	Dead
M	Peter Christian Burger	Jan.	15	1752	Dead
M	John Breyntow	April	23	1752	

M	Joseph Bennet	March	10	1762	
M	Paulus Byrzelius	Feb.	25	1767	
	James Adam de Martel	July	2	1767	
M	John Eagleson	March	23	1768	
M	Peter de la Roche	March	11	1771	
M	William Ellis	Feb.	28	1774	
	Nathaniel Fisher	Sept.	25	1777	Annapolis and Granville. Removed to Boston.
	PENNSYLVANIA.				
M	Philip Reading	April	7	1746	Dead
M	William Sturgeon	June	20	1747	Dead
M	Hugh Neill	March	26	1750	Dead
M	William Smith	Dec.	23	1753	
M	Thomas Barton	Jan.	29	1755	Dead
	Aaron Cleveland	July	28	1755	
M	Charles Inglis	Dec.	24	1758	Went to New York
	Jacob Duchè	March	11	1759	
	William Thompson	Dec.	23	1759	In England
M	Alex. Murray	June	7	1762	
	Jacob Duchè	Sept.	12	1762	St. Paul's, Philadelphia
	Richard Peters	Sept.	16	1765	Christ Chh. & St. Peter's, Phila.
	Samuel Giles	Dec.	23	1765	
	Hugh Wilson	Dec.	23	1765	
M	John Andrews	Feb.	19	1767	Went to Maryland
M	Samuel Magaw	Feb.	19	1767	Has a Church in Philadelphia
	Walter Chapman	July	7	1768	Did not go
P	Thomas Coombe	Oct.	17	1771	
	William White	April	25	1772	
	Bernard Page	Aug.	24	1772	Wyoming Parish
	Fraugott Fred. Illing	Aug.	24	1772	Junietta
P	William Stringer	March	8	1773	St. Paul's, Philadelphia
	Thomas Hopkinson	Sept.	24	1773	
	Sydenham Thorn	Aug.	24	1774	Mispillion and St. Paul's
	QUEBEC.				
	Lewis Guerry	April	11	1775	
	RHODE ISLAND.				
M	Thomas Pollen	Feb.	9	1754	Dead
	George Bissett	May	6	1767	
	TOBAGO.				
	John Stephen	Sept.	30	1764	
	John Trotter	Dec.	22	1768	
	VIRGINIA.				
	John Robertson	Jan.	21	1745	
	Alexander Campbell	Jan.	21	1745	
	William Yates	April	1	1745	Dead

	Alexander White	June	10	1745	Dead
	William Proctor	July	1	1745	
	William Coles	Feb.	2	1746	
	William Webb	March	16	1746	
	Joseph Simpson	June	2	1746	Dead
	John Hindman	Sept.	22	1746	
	William Stuart	Sept.	26	1746	
	Robert Dickson	Oct.	22	1746	
	Musgrave Dawson	Feb.	1	1747	Dead
	Robert Innes	July	6	1747	Dead
	Isaac Campbell	July	6	1747	Dead
	Thomas Warrington	Sept.	21	1747	Dead
	Roscow Cole	Jan.	19	1748	
	John Smelt	March	28	1748	Dead
	John Dixon	Aug.	4	1748	
P	Alexander Cruden	March	14	1749	
	John Andrews	April	12	1749	
	Richard Locke	May	13	1749	
	Archibald Spencer	Aug.	30	1749	
	William Douglass	Sept.	24	1749	
	Robert McLaurin	Aug.	24	1750	
	Adam Menzies	Dec.	28	1750	Dead
	James Fowlis	Dec.	28	1750	Dead
	Peter Davis	June	11	1751	
	John Ramsay	July	13	1751	
	Miles Selden	Jan.	15	1752	
	John Nivison	Feb.	25	1752	
	Joseph Bewsker	March	2	1752	
	John Brumskill	Sept.	29	1752	
	Thomas Smith	Feb.	2	1753	
P	John Agnew	June	17	1753	
	Thomas Wilkinson	July	31	1753	
	James Pasteur	Dec.	23	1753	
	Thomas Davis	Sept.	22	1754	
	James Garden	Sept.	22	1754	
	James Craig	March	31	1755	
	Joseph Davenport	Oct.	12	1755	
	James Maury	Dec.	27	1755	
	William Meldrum	June	13	1756	Dead
	Rice Hove	Dec.	21	1756	
M	Gronow Owen	Oct.	21	1757	
	Jacob Rowe	Feb.	13	1758	Dead
	Robert Read	April	10	1758	
	Isaac William Giberne	Sept.	30	1758	
	James Craig	Sept.	30	1758	
	John Brander	March	11	1759	
	Andrew Burnaby	April	7	1759	
	Alexander Rhonnald	Aug.	25	1759	
	Patrick Lunen	Dec.	23	1759	
	Joseph Collinson	Dec.	23	1759	
	Thomas Price	Dec.	23	1759	
	Richard Hewitt	Sept.	30	1760	
	James Semple	Sept.	30	1760	
	Arch. McRobert	Feb.	25	1761	
	James Horrocks	Nov.	5	1761	Dead

	William West	Nov.	24	1761	Gone to Maryland
	Leonard Watson	March	10	1762	Did not go
	Jonathan Boucher	March	26	1762	
	Archibald Dick	March	26	1762	
	Devereux Jarratt	Dec.	28	1762	
	Richard Collinson	Dec.	28	1762	
	William Buckham	April	17	1763	
	James Maury Fontaine	Oct.	10	1763	
	John Lyth	Oct.	10	1763	
	Henry Skyring	Oct.	10	1763	
	John Mathews	June	29	1764	
	John Wishart	June	29	1764	
	Walter Jameson	June	29	1764	
	Robert Renney	July	1	1764	
	Thomas Lendrum	April	3	1765	Dead
	Townsend Dade	Aug.	13	1765	
	Charles Mynn Thruston	Aug.	13	1765	
	Christopher Mackae	Dec.	23	1765	
	George Goldie	Feb.	25	1766	
	William Hubard	April	28	1766	
	Thomas Floyd	May	9	1766	
	Josiah Johnson	July	10	1766	Dead
	William Halyburton	Aug.	28	1766	
	Benjamin Sebastian	Sept.	21	1766	
	Lee Massey	Sept.	21	1766	
	James Stuart	Sept.	21	1766	
	Arch. Aven	Feb.	2	1767	
	William Bland	June	24	1767	
	Thomas Martin	June	24	1767	
	Thomas Lundie	Dec.	21	1767	
	William Coutts	June	7	1768	
	Samuel Clug	June	11	1768	
	Arthur Hamilton	June	11	1768	
	Walter Macgowan	June	24	1768	
	Robert Yancey	July	25	1768	
	William Agar	June	21	1768	
	James Stevenson	Sept.	29	1768	
	Arthur Emerson	Sept.	29	1768	
	James Thompson	Feb.	28	1769	
	Charles Clay	June	7	1769	
	Mathew Maurey	Aug.	24	1769	
	Thomas Baker	Aug.	24	1769	
	Isaac Avery	Oct.	18	1769	
	Samuel Henley	Dec.	24	1769	
	Alexander Lunen	Dec.	24	1769	
	Thomas Gwatkin	Jan.	5	1770	
	John Kynaston	Aug.	9	1770	
	James Herdman	Sept.	23	1770	
	William Selden	March	11	1771	
	Spence Grayson	May	29	1771	
	Abner Waugh	March	11	1771	St. Mary's Parish
	John Wingate	Sept.	22	1771	Dale Parish
	William Vere	Sept.	22	1771	
P	James Ogilvie	Sept.	22	1771	Hampshire.
	Daniel Sturges	Nov.	11	1771	Norborne

Benjamin Blagrove	March	5	1772	Elizabeth City
William Leigh	March	16	1772	Shelburne
Nathaniel Manning	March	16	1772	Hampshire
Robert Buchan	March	16	1772	
John Braidfoot	April	25	1772	
Peter Muhlenberg	April	25	1772	
Joseph Messenger	May	7	1772	Stafford County
William Hannah	June	11	1772	Culpepper County
William Holt	June	11	1772	Amelia County
John Bracken	July	6	1772	Amelia County
Francis Wilson	Aug.	24	1772	Drysdale Parish
Saml. Smith McCrosky	Sept.	21	1772	Christ Church Parish
Rodham Kenner	Sept.	21	1772	Hampshire
John Hyde Saunders	Sept.	21	1772	James City
Alexander Balmain	Oct.	11	1772	Cople Parish
Jesse Carter	Oct.	21	1772	Southampton Parish
Robert Andrews	Dec.	26	1772	Ware Parish
William McKenzie	June	6	1773	
John Campbell	June	6	1773	Stratton Major Parish
John McLean	Aug.	1	1773	Botetourt Parish
Thomas Davis	Sept.	21	1773	Norfolk Parish
Thomas Hall	April	6	1774	St. Martin's Parish
Emanuel Jones	Sept.	21	1774	St. Bride's
Samuel Shield	Dec.	21	1774	Drysdale Parish
John Hurt	Dec.	21	1774	Trinity Parish
John Brace	March	1	1775	Elizabeth Parish
John Leland	April	11	1775	Wicomoco Parish
Christ. Todd	April	26	1775	Brunswick Parish
William Gordon	June	11	1775	
John Buchanan	Aug.	13	1775	Henrico Parish
James Madison	Oct.	1	1775	
John White Holt	June	11	1776	Russell Parish
ISLAND OF ST. VINCENT.				
Thomas Load	Dec.	28	1777	

A List of the several Parishes or places where Divine Service is performed according to the rites of the Church of England, in South and North Carolina, Pennsylvania, New Jersey, New York, Connecticut, and New England, with an Account of the present Income belonging to each Parish, or place, taken from the Books of the Society for the Propagation of the Gospel in Foreign Parts, July 1, 1724.

[From the Fulham MSS.]

Names of the Parishes and Places.	Allowance from the Society sterling.			Allowance by Act of Assembly reduced to sterling.			Voluntary contributions reduced to sterling.
SOUTH CAROLINA.	£	*s*	*d*	£	*s*	*d*	
St. Phillips's, Charlestown.—There is a house and glebe; the Rev. Mr. Garden the present Minister - -	00	0	0	120			Besides considerable perquisites for weddings, christenings, funerals.
St. James's, Goose Creek.—A house and glebe; the Rev. Mr. Ludlam, Minister - - - - - -	50	0	0	80	0	0	
St. Andrew's.—A house and glebe; the Rev. Mr. Guy, Minister - - -	50	0	0	80	0	0	
St. George's.—A house and glebe; the Rev. Mr. Varnod, Minister - -	50	0	0	80	0	0	
St. John's.—A house and glebe; the Rev. Mr. Hunt, Minister - -	50	0	0	80	0	0	
St. Thomas's.—No house, two glebes, money allowed out of the Treasury, now at interest for building a house; the Rev. Mr. Hasell, Minister - -	50	0	0	80	0	0	
St. Dennis's, a French Conformist Church.—No house nor glebe; the Rev. Mr. Lapiere, Minister - -	00	0	0	80	0	0	
Christ Church.—A house and glebe; the Rev. Mr. Pownall, Minister -	50	0	0	80	0	0	
St. James's, Santee, a French Conformist Church.—A house and glebe; the Rev. Mr. Pouderons, Minister - -	00	0	0	80	0	0	
St. Paul's.—A glebe but no house; the money allowed by the Treasury at interest for building one; the Rev. Mr. Standish lately appointed Minister there - - - - -	60	0	0	80	0	0	
St. Bartholomew's and St. Helen's. Depopulated by the Indian war; have neither Churches nor Parsonage houses; when they shall be supplied they will be allowed each - -	50	0	0	80	0	0	

Names of the Parishes and Places.	Allowance from the Society sterling.	Allowance by Act of Assembly reduced to sterling.	Voluntary contributions reduced to sterling.
NORTH CAROLINA	£ s d	£ s d	
Is divided into several precincts or parishes, and an allowance settled out of each precinct, by Act of Assembly, of about £70 Carolina money, which amounts to about £15 sterling. A particular account of the state of the Church there is daily expected from Mr. Mosley, a gentleman of that country. There is at present but one Minister, the Rev. Mr. Newnam, who supplies four or five of the parishes by turns, and is allowed by the Society - - - - - -	80 0 0	About £60, which he is supposed to receive for his service.	Not known to the Society.
PENNSYLVANIA.			
N.B.—Twenty shillings this country money is about 15s. sterling. No provision made in this government for the Church by the Assembly.			
Christ Church, in Philadelphia.—A handsome parsonage, and the minister is maintained by the voluntary contributions of the people; besides which there is an allowance from the Crown of £50 sterling per annum if it can be recovered, which will make it a comfortable living. There is at present no settled minister; there is no allowance from the Society.			
There is also £30 a year allowed by the Crown to a Schoolmaster, which, with the encouragement he might meet with there, would be a handsome subsistence for a Schoolmaster.			
New Castle.—There are three Churches in this county, viz., one at Newcastle, one at Whiteclay Creek, and one at Apoquinomy, now all supplied by one minister. There is an estate left to the Church at Newcastle forever, worth about £20 per annum sterling. The Rev. Mr. Ross is the present Minister. There is no glebe or parsonage house that the Society have any account of.	70 0 0	00 0 0	About £48 per annum, Pensylvania money.
Chester.—There are three Churches in			

Names of the Parishes and Places.	Allowance from the Society sterling.			Allowance by Act of Assembly reduced to sterling.			Voluntary contributions reduced to sterling.
	£	s	d	£	s	d	
this county, viz., one at Chichester, one at Chester, and one at Concord, all supplied by one minister; there is a valuable piece of ground given for a minister's house, garden, and other conveniencies at Chester, but the house not yet built. The Rev. Mr. Humphrey is the present Minister - - - - - - -	60	0	0	00	0	0	Formerly about £30 per annum, Pensylvania money, and have promised to increase it.
Oxford.—There is no glebe nor parsonage house, but the people have promised to purchase a house and 110 acres of land, and £80, that money has been left for that purpose. The Rev. Mr. Wayman is the present Minister, who also supplies	60	0	0	00	0	0	About £20 Pensylvania money, and some presents of provisions.
Radnor, a Welsh Congregation, about twenty-five miles distant from Oxford, who are very pressing to have a minister reside among them, though they say they are not able to do anything for him. They have built a Church, but have no parsonage nor glebe.							
Sussex.—In this county there are three Churches, all supplied by one minister. A great number of people, who have subscribed sufficient sums to the minister for support of himself and family, so that he may lay by the Society's allowance. The Rev. Mr. Becket is the present Minister -	60	0	0	00	0	0	The sum is not known to the Society.
Apoquinomy.—There is no glebe nor parsonage house, but the people have promised to provide a house for the minister, and to contribute to his maintenance according to their capabilities. There is no minister there at present - - - - - -	60	0	0	00	0	0	About £30 Pensylvania money subscribed to the former minister.
Kent County.—The Church here has not been supplied with a settled minister for many years past. The people are very desirous of an Episcopal Minister, and promise to contribute according to their abilities. There is no glebe nor parsonage house.							
The Churches at *Bristol*, *Perquihomen*, *and another new Church* lately built in this Province, being but small							

Names of the Parishes and Places.	Allowance from the Society sterling.			Allowance by Act of Assembly reduced to sterling.			Voluntary contributions reduced to sterling.
	£	s	d	£	s	d	
congregations, are supplied by the neighbouring clergy, and the ministers of the Swedish congregations there, for which they receive some small allowance from the Society.							
NEW JERSEY.							
N.B.—20s. money of New York and of this Province is about 13s. 4d. sterling. No provision is made in this Province for the Church by Act of Assembly.							
Burlington.—There is no house nor glebe. Mr. Talbot is the present Minister - - - - -	60	0	0	00	0	0	Formerly about £20 per annum, New York money, now uncertain.
Hopewell, Maidenhead.—Two Churches supplied by one minister, now vacant. There is no house nor glebe, but Colonel Coxe has promised to give one hundred acres of land to the Church at Maidenhead - -	60	0	0	00	0	0	Small and uncertain.
Salem.—A new congregation. There is no parsonage house nor glebe, but the people have promised to make a handsome provision for their minister, who is the Rev. Mr. Holbrook -	60	0	0	00	0	0	The sum not known to the Society.
Elizabeth Town.—The minister whereof also supplies some neighbouring towns. There is no house nor glebe. The Rev. Mr. Vaughan is the present Minister - - - - - -	60	0	0	00	0	0	About £30 per annum, New York money.
Amboy.—The minister whereof also supplies Piscatoqua and Woodbridge, two other Churches in that neighbourhood. There has been lately given to the Church at Amboy some ground for a glebe and building a parsonage house; and a lady has left by her will, for the use of the minister forever, a house and land worth £400 sterling. The Rev. Mr. Skinner is the present Minister -	60	0	0	00	0	0	About £30 per annum, New York money.

Names of the Parishes and Places.	Allowance from the Society sterling.	Allowance by Act of Assembly reduced to sterling.	Voluntary contributions reduced to sterling.
NEW YORK.	£ s d	£ s d	
Trinity Church, in that city.—There is a house and garden, and besides the allowance by Act of Assembly, the perquisites and presents are very considerable, in so much that this living is computed to be worth above £200 sterling per annum. There is nothing allowed by the Society to the Minister, who is the Rev. Mr. Vesey.	00 0 0	100 N. York money.	The amount of the voluntary contributions & perquisites is unknown to the Society.
But the Society allow to a catechist for the negroes in New York (the Rev. Mr. Wetmore) £50 sterling per annum, who is also an assistant to the Rev. Mr. Vesey, for which the people have promised to allow him £50 per annum, New York money -	50 0 0	00 0 0	£50 per annum, New York money.
West Chester, to which is annexed East Chester, Yonkers, and the Manor of Pelham, all served by one Minister. There is a house and glebe of twenty three acres. The Rev. Mr. Barton is the present Minister - - -	50 0 0	50 N.York money.	About 40s. per annum, New York money.
New Rochell.—A French Conformist Congregation, part of the parish of West Chester aforesaid, to whose minister the people are rated, so that there is nothing by Act of Assembly settled on the minister here. There is a house and glebe and one hundred acres of land let out for the benefit of the Minister, who is the Rev. Mr. Stoupe - - - - - - -	50 0 0	00 0 0	Formerly £25 per annum, New York money, now precarious, the people providing fire wood & some presents.
Rye.—There is a parsonage and glebe, and to this parish is annexed Mamaroneck and Bedford, where the minister occasionally officiates. The Rev. Mr. Jenney is the present Minister -	50 0 0	50 N.York money.	The minister says he receives nothing this way.
Richmond, on Staten Island, has a parsonage house and glebe of sixty acres, and Mr. Duxbury has lately left to the Church there a very handsome plantation, the value of which has not been certified to the Society. The Society allowed £50 sterling per annum to the late Incumbent, but the Governor has lately collated			The late minister received none except some

Names of the Parishes and Places.	Allowance from the Society sterling.	Allowance by Act of Assembly reduced to sterling.	Voluntary contributions reduced to sterling.
	£ s d	£ s d	
to that living one Mr. Harrison, who is well contented without the Society's allowance - - - - -	00 0 0	40 N.York money.	few necessaries for his house.
Jamaica, on Long Island, the minister whereof supplies two other towns in that neighbourhood. There is a parsonage house and glebe. The Rev. Mr. Poyer is the present Minister -	50 0 0	60 N.York money.	Small and uncertain.
Hempstead, on Long Island, the minister whereof also supplies the adjacent towns. There is a parsonage house and glebe; and the Rev. Mr. Thomas is the present Minister -	50 0 0	60 N.York money.	Nothing.
CONNECTICUT.			
N.B.—No provision is made in this Province or Government by Act of Assembly.			
Stratford.—A congregation supplied by the Society for some time past. There is a Church now building, but the members are for the most part poor, and their contributions to the minister precarious. A gentleman has lately given four hundred acres of land for a perpetual glebe for an Episcopal minister there, of a considerable value. The Rev. Mr. Johnson is the present Minister - -	60 0 0	00 0 0	The sum not known to the Society.
There are several other congregations in this Government, who have conformed to the Church of England, and are very desirous of having ministers, particularly New Town, where there are thirty Communicants, and the Conformists being the major part of the Town, the Episcopal Minister, if chose by them, will be entitled to a maintenance by the laws of the country. They have laid out two hundred acres of land for a glebe for an Episcopal Minister.			
If the Society should think fit to send a Missionary to New Town he might also supply *Ripton*, as Mr. Johnson might *Fairfield*. Two other Conformist congregations, those of Rip-			

Names of the Parishes and Places.	Allowance from the Society sterling.	Allowance by Act of Assembly reduced to sterling.	Voluntary contributions reduced to sterling.
	£ s d	£ s d	
ton, having also agreed to lay out a glebe for an Episcopal Minister.			
NEW ENGLAND.			
N.B.—No provision is made by Act of Assembly for the Church in this Province.			
In *Boston* there are two Churches, one called			
The King's Chapel, of which the Rev. Mr. Myles is the present Minister, who is supported by the voluntary contributions of the people, the amount whereof is not known to the Society. The Rev. Mr. Harris, who is called the King's Chaplain, is afternoon preacher, for which he receives from the Crown £100 sterling, paid in England, and has one of Sir Leoline Jenkins's Fellowships at Jesus College. The Society allow nothing to this Church.			
The other, called *Christ Church*, lately built. The present Minister is the Rev. Dr. Cutler; he has an allowance from the Society, which, together with the voluntary contributions of the people, is a comfortable maintenance for him and his family - -	60 0 0	00 0 0	The Society have had no account of the particulars or gross sum.
Newbury.—There is no house nor glebe yet provided, but the people, by voluntary contributions, pay the minister as much or more than the usual rate was, for the maintenance of a dissenting teacher, besides which he has £60. The Rev. Mr. Plant present Minister - - - - - -	60 0 0	00 0 0	The sum not known to the Society.
Marblehead.—There is no house nor glebe; the voluntary contributions very precarious. The Rev. Mr. Mossom, Minister - - - - -	60 0 0	00 0 0	About £20 per annum, New England money.
Bristol.—A new settled Church, built by voluntary subscriptions, and the people have promised to contribute to the utmost of their ability towards the maintenance of their minister. There is no house nor glebe. The			The sum not known

Names of the Parishes and Places.	Allowance from the Society sterling.			Allowance by Act of Assembly reduced to sterling.			Voluntary contributions reduced to sterling.
	£	s	d	£	s	d	
Rev. Mr. Ussher is the present Minister - - - - - - -	60	0	0	00	0	0	to the Society.
Providence.—A new Church, likewise built by voluntary subscriptions. There is no house nor glebe, but the people have promised to assist the minister by voluntary contributions to the utmost of their power. The Rev. Mr. Pigot is the present Minister - - - - - - - -	60	0	0	00	0	0	The sum not known to the Society.
Newport, on Rhode Island, the minister whereof occasionally officiates at Tiverton, Swansey, and Little Compton. There is no house nor glebe. The Rev. Mr. Honeyman is the present Minister - - - - - -	70	0	0	00	0	0	About £40 per annum New England money.
Narraganset, in the Colony of Rhode Island, the minister whereof also occasionally officiates at Tiverton, Swansey, and Little Compton in conjunction with Mr. Honeyman. There is no parsonage house, but some lands laid out for the ministry in general, which the present minister, the Rev. Mr. Macsparren, is endeavouring to recover out of private hands, who have gotten possession thereof. The people have promised to contribute handsomely towards his maintenance, and to provide him a house - - - - - - -	70	0	0	00	0	0	The sum not known to the Society.

[From the Lambeth MSS.]

[A Copy of Mr. Whitefield's letter to the Society against their Missionaries, November 30, 1740; and also a letter from Dr. Bearcroft on that subject, June 27, 1741.]

"On board the Savannah, bound from Philadelphia to Georgia, Nov. 30th, 1740.

"HONOURED GENTLEMEN:

"I hope a single eye to God's glory, inclines me to trouble you with this. I have been now through the greatest part of America, and have had an opportunity of seeing the state of the Church of England. I think it is at a very low ebb, and will in all probability be much worse, nay, at last dwindled into nothing, unless care be taken to send over Missionaries that are better qualified for the pastoral office. It is too evident that most of them are corrupt in their principles and immoral in their practices, and many of them such as could not stand their Trials amongst the Dissenters, or were discarded by them for their profaneness and irregularities. Our Church seems to be their last refuge, so that it is almost become a saying, that anything will make a Church Parson. None but those who are here present can tell into what contempt our Church is brought. The accounts given in to the Society by the Missionaries are the subject of common ridicule. I read some of them lately. I was ashamed to see how the nation was imposed on, and therefore thought it my duty to inform you of it. But perhaps I have said too much already however. I have delivered my soul. I write out of the simplicity of my heart. I leave the consequences to God, for the stones would cry out against me if I did not speak. If you had a mind only to establish the form of religion, sending such *ungodly despicable* Ministers would render even that ineffectual; for though the Dissenters have lost much of the power of Godliness, yet they have enough left to shame us. I speak not this out of prejudice or resentment, for I am as much opposed by their as our own Carnal Clergy, but I do it to prevent your being imposed on for the future, and to entreat you, if you would not have our tottering Ark fall quite down, that you would not employ such unhallowed hands to keep it up; they will meet with a Curse instead of a Blessing.

"I am,

"Honoured Gentlemen,

"Your very humble servant,

"GEORGE WHITEFIELD."

"Charterhouse, June 27th, 1741.

"MY LORD:

"Mr. Whitefield hath wrote three letters about the Missionaries, but the Society would not answer them, the two first directed to the Secretary, and the last directed immediately to the Society, which is so extraordinary an one, that I thought it proper to transmit a Copy to your

Lordship. The stroke under ungodly despicable, is in the original, though there are several of them, I will venture to affirm, as worthy as, and I am sure, much more regular than himself. His first letter was levelled chiefly against Mr. Arnold, who had debated with him in Print, and the single fact charged by Mr. Whitefield on Mr. Arnold is this, in Mr. Whitefield's own words: 'He hath borrowed four or five pounds from one Owen Owens, and said that Mr. Cummins would pay it; when the man applyed to Mr. Cummins, he said he knew nothing of the matter, but rather than have Mr. Arnold exposed, he paid the sum for him. This is to be attested by numbers of witnesses, and Mr. Frame, Brother-in-Law to Mr. Proprietary Pen, told me yesterday the Governor informed him how he had been chiding Mr. Cummins for not suffering him to be pursued and apprehended.' I wrote upon this to Mr. Cummins, the Commissary of Philadelphia, whose answer is this: 'As to that silly story which you tell me Mr. Whitefield wrote against Mr. Arnold, 'tis true his giddy admirers made a noise with it here, but without any just grounds, for Mr. Arnold, the night before he left this place, asked me to lend him £5. I told him I could not tell if I had so much at that time in the house, but desired him to breakfast with me next morning and I could then give him an answer. He was obliged, it seems, to set out very early, and having borrowed the money of Owen Owens gave him a letter to me, desiring I would pay that sum, and promising to remit it me in a little time from New York. When Owen came demanding his money that morning, after asking him a few questions, I found, though I promised to see him paid, he was ready, and I doubt not, instigated by Whitefield's votaries, to follow after and arrest Mr. Arnold because he had dared to contradict their oracle. I therefore directly paid him the money, and Mr. Arnold soon after very honestly and without my asking sent me payment of it from New York. I shewed your letter to Mr. Frame, the Proprietor's Brother-in-Law, before some Gentlemen; he affirmed what related to him is false.' I may perhaps have tired your Lordship, but have mentioned these things as they may afford some little light to Mr. Whitefield's full thoughts about the Missionaries, and if I can be any way serviceable.

"I am, my Lord,
"Your most obedient and
"Most humble servant,
"Philip Bearcroft."

Letter from Mr. Whitefield to the Bishop of Oxford.

"On board the Mary and Ann, bound from London to Scotland, July 28th, 1741.

"My Lord:

"Want of leisure not respect has been the occasion of my not sending your Lordship my letter, which I promised some time ago. Being now on board on my way to Scotland, I have time to write my thoughts more freely. I would first then observe to your Lordship that you have too good an opinion of the Missionaries in general that are employed by the honourable Society. Your Lordship says, p. 31, 'that it hath been pretended indeed that immoral and negligent men are employed as Missionaries.' This can be too easily proved. I could mention several instances. Whether this be from want of care I will not take upon me to determine, but that it frequently and commonly happens is certain. I have lately received a letter from Jonathan Belcher, Esq., late Governor of New England, wherein he writes thus: 'It is now about thirty-seven years ago that I dined with the late Dr. Compton, then Bishop of London, at his Palace at Fulham, and there were several Bishops and other dignified Clergy at Table; and knowing me to be a young gentleman of Interest and Figure in my Country, they urged me much to conform to their Church, and asked me how the Church of England got forward in New England. I told their Lordships that they were greatly deceived in what money was sent hither in that service, for that the general rise of the Church in New England was from dissolute livers, such as quarrelled with their Ministers, but that it was "*Rara Avis in terris*" for any man to go over to the Church, from a principle of religion and conscience, or to improve himself in a pious, serious life; and this really, Sir,' adds this worthy gentleman, 'is the case of this country at this day.' I hope this will have more weight with your Lordship, as coming from a gentleman without my knowing anything of it, a gentleman also of figure and good report, and who declares himself unprejudiced in another part of his letter. For speaking of a particular thing, he writes thus: 'Not that I have any squeamish prejudices against that excellent Church' (meaning the Church of England), 'although I have been born and bred a Dissenter; and pray what do we differ in doctrine? Would they preach and live their articles, there would be a more general coalition among them and the Dissenters.' And then he afterwards says: 'From long observation I find no persons going off from our Church to that of the Church of England, who thereby become more vitally pious. If I found they did, I should, I hope from a wise and judicious choice, immediately conform.' Thus far the worthy Governor Belcher, and indeed, my Lord, this is too true. Those at a distance cannot well conceive how contemptible our Church is abroad, and that owing to the unworthy, immoral, and negligent lives of the generality of the Missionaries, several of which have come over to us, because they could not stand tryal among the Dissenters, or had lived too loosely among them. Your Lordship is pleased to say, p. 32, 'That the most earnest requests, the most solemn adjurations are sent, that all who can would give any useful intelligence relating to them.' This is certainly right and good, but I fear your Lordship hath been misinformed if your Lordship was told that great regard is always paid to such intelligence, for I myself have sent over two letters to the Honourable Society for this purpose, and no regard has been paid to them. If your Lordship pleases I will send you copies of them both. I could not but further observe in looking over the list of the Missionaries, that there are no less than twenty employed in preaching and teaching school in the Province of New England (where certainly the Gospel is preached with greater purity than at home), and but two settled Missionaries in all North Carolina, and one of those, viz., Mr. Garzia, can scarce speak English. Does not this look too much like making a party of religion? I have a letter now by me somewhere amongst my papers, wrote by Dr. Mather to the late Lord Chancellor King, in which he gives sad proofs of the immorality of our Missionaries, and also complains of this seeming partiality. If the people of New England impose taxes on the Members of the Church of England, whilst others are exempt, it is certainly wrong. But as the first settlers went over there to worship God in their own way, Independency I think may well be reckoned the Established Worship there as well as Presbytery the Established Worship in Scotland: and surely it would more answer the design of the Institution of the Honourable Society to send Missionaries to North Carolina, where there are inhabitants enough and nobody to teach them, than to New England, where they have a Minister of their own every five or ten miles. Your Lordship, I am persuaded, is more noble than to be offended with this plainness of speech. The Searcher of Hearts knows from what principle I write. Your Lordship is pleased to say, page 31st, 'that exact accounts are required from the Missionaries twice a year.' And when they are brought in, what accounts do they generally give? That they have baptized so many, and had so many Communicants. A poor account this, and in other respects so very bad, that when I was last at Philadelphia, many that were really Friends of the Church upon reading the accounts were ashamed to see how the Honourable Society was imposed on by the account of the pious labours of the Missionaries. Indeed your Lordship says, page 17th, and I doubt not your Lordship was informed so, 'that multitudes of Negroes and Indians have been brought over to the Christian Faith.' This, for all that I know to the contrary may be matter of fact. I pray God it may be found true at the great day; but your Lordship says, page 9, 'the success of one of the Catechists has been so great in the Plantation belonging to the Society, that out of two hundred and thirty, at least seventy are now believers in Christ.' I should be glad to know what Plantation your Lordship means: that seventy may have learned to repeat their Creed, the Lord's Prayer, and Ten Commandments in the Vulgar Tongue, and been baptised, is probable enough. But that seventy are now believers in Christ, I cannot help questioning. I fear your Lordship hath been misinformed; and now I am mentioning the Negroes, I beg leave to object against the method lately proposed for their Conversion, especially in the Province of Carolina, where the Governors are so exceedingly jealous over any that shall undertake publicly to teach them. I believe it will be a work of a long time to find out two or three young Negroes, and to instruct them so as to qualify them to instruct others. Besides, few, I believe, will submit to be taught by a young Negro. I question whether the Assembly will permit a slave to learn to write. And, after all, this way of converting them will only be teaching them to write and read. These are good things, but without setting over them truly pious people, that may have more authority over them than any young negroes whatsoever, and may lead them to a knowledge of themselves and God; however good the intention of the Honourable Society may be, I fear their good intention will prove abortive and of none effect. Pensylvania, in my opinion, is far preferable to Carolina for the instruction of the Negroes. The Quakers, however blameable in other respects, are certainly praiseworthy in this: I mean their lenity to their poor slaves. Your Lordship is pleased to urge these people's forbidding to assist his Majesty (whom I truly love and honour), as one reason why Missionaries should be sent over to instruct the people in better principles. But at the same time, your Lordship takes notice of many other pernicious errors that took early root in the Provinces abroad, that are not yet extirpated, and perhaps in part newly revived; some dissolving the obligations of moral duties; some destroying the inward peace of every pious and good person, and making life gloomy and uncomfortable; some leading men to ascribe every folly or wickedness that possesses the fancy to Divine inspiration; some inconsistent with our present happy establishment. All these, my Lord, are errors, and, as your Lordship hath been pleased so particularly to mention the Quakers, would it not have been right in your Lordship to have pointed out the others also who are thus erroneous, that people might the better beware of and so avoid them. I suppose your Lordship has been informed of the persons that broach such errors, otherwise I suppose your Lordship would not have mentioned them; and if so, I would humbly submit it to your Lordship's judgment, whether you are not bound in conscience to write to them or plainly name them, that they may either clear themselves or take shame for holding and preaching things contrary to the Gospel of the ever-blessed Jesus. Thus, my Lord, I have freely wrote to your Lordship what was upon my heart. I think I have no sinister end in view; I think I write purely out of a zeal for God, and the good of souls. I heartily pray for the coming of Christ's Kingdom, and would therefore willingly have all things taken out of the way that may obstruct its progress. I am persuaded your Lordship would not wilfully continue in any error, nor be above receiving information from the meanest servant of Jesus Christ. This persuasion encouraged me to write to your Lordship. You may depend on it, my Lord, that I shall not mention what I have wrote, and if your Lordship is so condescending as to send me a line by way of answer, it shall be kept quite secret by,

"My Lord,
"Your Lordship's dutiful
"Son and Servant,
"George Whitefield.

"P. S. I hope to be in London in about six weeks. If your Lordship pleases to direct a letter to me, as before, it will come to hand. The Lord be with your spirit."

Letter from the Lord Bishop of Oxford to Mr. Whitefield.

"Cuddesden, September 17th, 1741.

"Sir:

"It being now about the time that you proposed to be in London, I send this to return you thanks for your last letter. I am not sufficiently acquainted with Governor Belcher's character to know how far his account of his own impartiality may be relied on. We often deceive ourselves in that matter, and all sects of Christians are too apt to think hardly of those who are not of their own Church, and especially those who leave it; and as there is but too much room for all parties to reproach one another with want of inward religion, very well meaning persons may mistake in making comparisons. To his testimony you add your own, and I believe you speak as you think. But you must permit me to say, and I do it with sincere good will to you, that I am persuaded you are much too severe in what you have printed concerning your Brethren of the Clergy in this Nation, and therefore you may have been too severe in what you have written concerning those abroad, especially as I find that many accounts different from yours are sent to the Society, concerning their Missionaries, by persons in all appearance well deserving credit. Still what you and the Governor have said, may and I hope will give occasion for stricter enquiries, but you cannot think it reasonable that we should pay regard to your accounts only. I have seen one, if not both your letters to the Society. They consist, as I remember, of general Charges, without mentioning any particular, and therefore all that can be done upon them is to enquire. Your objection against the number of Missionaries in New England I have endeavoured to answer in my Sermon, and if they can be proportioned better, I wish they were. But I have always understood that the reason of there being only two in North Carolina, was the bad reception of those who were sent, of which you may read very discouraging accounts in Humphrey's History of the Proceedings of the Society, and the difficulty of finding Persons to undertake that Mission; which difficulty I suppose must have been the reason of sending a Person not sufficiently acquainted, by your account, for I know not the fact, with our language. I believe the accounts of the Missionaries are as regularly sent to the Society as can be expected from that distance, or proper notice taken of the neglect. They may indeed, and frequently, if not constantly, do give further accounts than of their Baptisms and their Communions, which however are such marks of Christian profession as deserve to be particularly mentioned; nor do the accounts which we publish by any means consist of these only. But it may be very improper for us to print everything which it may be proper for them to write. If any part of their information which we print is false, we designedly put it in the power of all abroad who are really Friends of our Church or of Religion, to prevent our being imposed on by it, and if they will not, the blame is not ours; for making these things the subject of their discourse instead of informing us, is only doing harm. But I hope all good persons will consider how very licentious common discourse upon such subjects usually is, and will therefore examine carefully before they take up accusations. The only Plantation belonging to the Society, I mean as their Property, is in Barbadoes, and when I say that seventy of the Negroes there are believers in Christ, I use that expression as I apprehend it is commonly used in speaking of Countries where different religions are professed, to signify that so many profess themselves Christians. I do not see reason to suspect their being hypocrites in that profession, and I hope their faith produces good fruits. The method lately proposed for instructing Negroes continues to appear to me very promising, at least highly fit to be tried. There is a prospect that the young Negroes designed for teachers will, by the blessing of God on their education, become truly pious, as well as qualified in other respects. The disadvantage of their youth will be lessening every day, and they will gain authority by degrees if they are duly supported. It is not that I know of, proposed that their scholars should learn to write, and I do not at all understand why you say that this method will be only teaching them to write and read. Whether Pensylvania is preferable to Carolina for Instruction of the Negroes I know not, but wish it were tried every way. What errors took early root in our Colonies, and are not yet extirpated, you may see in Humphrey's, and as I have only spoken doubtfully concerning the revival of any of them, and that not upon any intelligence communicated particularly to me, but from such accounts as lie before the Society, I do not apprehend myself obliged to go further than I have done in this matter. I have accused no person, nor designed to make any person otherwise thought of than he was before. If I have given occasion to any one to ask himself whether he is blamable or not, I have only put him upon doing what we all ought to do more frequently, and God grant we may do it, to his Glory and our own Good.

"I am, Sir,

"Your loving Brother

"And Servant,

"THOMAS OXFORD."

"Mr. Whitefield."

EFFORTS

TO OBTAIN

THE EPISCOPATE

BEFORE THE REVOLUTION.

BY FRANCIS L. HAWKS.

THE following article was published some twenty years ago in a then existing Church periodical of but limited circulation, and has probably fallen under the eye of comparatively few of the members of the Society. As time and care were bestowed in the collection of facts necessary in its preparation, the Publishing Committee have thought it worth reprinting, and have therefore obtained the consent of the author, who is one of their number, to preserve it in the pages of the Society's collections :—

Among a body of Christians, in whose system of ecclesiastical government episcopacy held a conspicuous place, it would follow, of course, that efforts would not be wanting to obtain an officer so essential as is a Bishop. Hence, at a very early period, the subject of an American Episcopate seems to have occupied the minds of Episcopalians, both in the colonies and in the mother country.

The Bishop of London, "by customary usage (which seems to have taken its rise from accidental connexion"*), exercised spiritual jurisdiction in the plantations, from a period commencing soon after the settlement of Virginia; and to him was confided the supervision of a diocese, which it was neither expected or required that he should ever see.†

* *Archbishop Drummond's* paper upon the present state of the Church of England in the colonies, drawn up in June, 1764.—MSS. of Gen. Convention.

† There is some difficulty in tracing satisfactorily the origin and progress of the "accidental connexion" of the Bishop of London with the church in the American colonies. The best account which we can furnish on this subject is the following :—

The first royal grant made of lands in America was by King James I. in the year 1606, to what was then termed the second Virginia Company; and pursuant to the provisions of this grant, it was ordered that "the true word of God should be preached, planted, and used, according to the rites and doctrines of the *Church of England.*"

It was not long ere the evils resulting from such an arrangement were sensibly felt in the colonies, and readily suggested themselves to the minds of churchmen in England. Nay, the necessity of a Bishop to an Episcopal

In 1620, the number of clergymen in Virginia was less, by one-half, than the number of parishes, and it was the duty of the "Virginia Council," which sat in London, to supply the deficiency. The Bishop of London was a member of the council, and had taken a deep interest in the prosperity of the plantations, having raised £1000 toward building a college in Virginia. The council, therefore, very naturally applied to him as one of their body, *for his help in procuring ministers.* And this is the first instance to be met with of the connexion of the Bishop of London with the Church in the colonies.

This was probably the origin of the jurisdiction exercised for many years over the American church by the successive prelates of the see of London. This jurisdiction was unquestioned for a long period of time, and of course gained strength with its age. At length, in 1675, the Committee of Trade and Plantations "desired that inquiry be made touching the jurisdiction which the Bishop of London hath over the foreign plantations." What caused the inquiry is unknown, but no return was made to it. In 1679, however, the instructions given to *Lord Culpepper,* at that time appointed governor, clearly show that the Bishop of London was not supposed to have any *jurisdiction,* for he has nothing but a mere ministerial office assigned him : the *Governor* has the power to prefer to ecclesiastical benefices in the colony, and the only notice taken of the Bishop of London is in requiring of the person preferred a certificate from that prelate that the candidate is "conformable to the doctrine of the Church of England."

In 1681, *Sir Thomas Lynch* was appointed Governor of Jamaica, and he was instructed to report to the *Bishop of London* all ministers who officiated in the island without "being in due orders."

In 1685, the Bishop of London proposed to the Committee of Trade, that he should have all ecclesiastical jurisdiction in the West Indies, *except the disposition of parishes, licenses for marriage, and probate of wills.*

This was approved of, and the governor was directed to give all countenance and encouragement to the exercise of ecclesiastical jurisdiction in the island, by the Bishop of London, except in the particulars enumerated, as to which the power was conferred on the governor.

Similar instructions were given to all the other colonial governors, and under this authority, Bishops *Compton* and *Robinson,* and for a few years, Bishop *Gibson,* exercised jurisdiction in the plantations. But, in 1725, Bishop *Gibson* desired more explicit authority and direction, and for that purpose applied by petition to the king in council. The petition was referred to the attorney and solicitor general, who stated as their opinion that the Bishops of London had all acted by an authority which was *insufficient,* and that the ecclesiastical jurisdiction of the colonies did not rightfully belong to any Bishop in England, and that the most proper mode of conferring on any person the right to exercise such jurisdiction was by *patent.*

A patent was accordingly granted to Dr. *Gibson,* but it was to him *personally,* and not as Bishop of London; his successors were not named in it, so that the patent expired with his life: nor did any of his successors ever obtain another, but acted without one.

From the first exercise of jurisdiction up to the period of Bishop Gibson's patent, there were several circumstances which had a tendency to strengthen the opinion that the Bishop of London was the rightful diocesan of the American church. Thus, in 1679, some of the inhabitants of Boston, who were members of the Church of England, petitioned Bishop *Compton,* then in the see of London, for his help in obtaining for themselves the services of the church. The bishop procured the consent of the king that a church should be allowed. This application called the attention of Dr. *Compton* more particularly to the state of the church in the colonies, and resulted in his proposing to various parts of America to supply them with clergymen ; and on his application to the king, his majesty granted a bounty of £20 to each minister who would go over to the colonies, and instructed the governors to permit none authoritatively to serve any cure of souls "unless he was licensed to do so *by the Bishop of London.*"

Church was so obvious, and its propriety so unquestionable, that it seems to have engaged the unsolicited attention of even the irreligious monarch, Charles II. And it is but an act of justice to the prelates who successively occupied the see of London, to remark, that among the dignitaries of the English church, none seem to have been more generally anxious than were they to furnish the colonies with a bishop. We meet with no record of any whose lust of power was such as caused them to covet the exercise of an authority, which, while it conferred honour, imposed also a fearful responsibility.*

In most of the earlier efforts which were made for procuring the Episcopate in America, the *laity* seem to have co-operated with the clergy; though in the *first* step taken towards effecting the object, it does not appear that either clergy or laity in the plantations had any agency; but in the subsequent applications, for several years, there is abundant evidence that a bishop was solicited alike by *all*.

The first proposal of an American Episcopate, of which we have any authentic record, was in 1672 or the year following.† In one of these years

Another circumstance, which doubtless confirmed in public opinion the authority of the Bishop of London, was the following:—Sir *Leoline Jenkins*, observing the wretched state of the colonies as to religious instruction, by his will (after remarking on the small number of clergymen in the fleets and plantations of the king) founded two new fellowships at Jesus College, Oxford, upon condition that the fellows and their successors forever, should take priests' orders, and go out as chaplains in the navy when thereto required by the Lord High Admiral; and in case there should be no use for them at sea, then they were "to be called *by the Lord Bishop of London* to go out into any of his majesty's foreign plantations." The selection by the testator of the Bishop of London to make the call was probably founded on the opinion, then prevalent, that the spiritual care of the plantations belonged to that prelate.

In 1701, the charter of "the Society for the Propagation of the Gospel in Foreign Parts" was obtained; and by this society, missionaries were furnished to all the colonies except Maryland and Virginia, up to the period of the American revolution. But, as all the clergymen who had come over prior to 1701, had been licensed by the Bishop of London, the practice continued after the society was established, and the missionaries always considered that prelate as their diocesan. For the statements in this note, see Bishop *Sherlock's* memorial to the king in council, presented in February, 1749–50; Dr. *Kennett's* account of the society; *Humphrey's* History of the Society; and Bishop *Gibson's* petition and commission, among the MSS. of the General Convention.

* We find one of the English prelates using the following language on this subject: "No one who has any experience or sense of these things [the duties of a bishop] can ever say that the Bishop of London could at any time take a competent care of the plantations as a bishop; nor did the ablest prelate that ever filled that see ever think that he could, or ever wish to continue in so irksome and fruitless an office."—Thoughts upon the present state of the Church of England in America, by *Archbishop Drummond*—MSS. of Gen. Convention.

Again, another thus expresses himself: "I am very sensible (and in this I speak the sentiments of my brethren) that nothing can more effectually contribute to the happy and prosperous state of the colonies, in a civil as well as a religious view, than the appointment of resident bishops. A bishop of London, however inclined to do his duty, is too sensible of the importance of the charge which long usage and custom has committed to him, and too conscious of the little service he can do to a clergy at this distance from him, not to feel very anxiously the necessity of a more immediate inspection and government."—Original letter from the Bishop of London to the clergy of Connecticut, February 18, 1765—Johns. MSS.

† A letter of 1662, sent from England to Massachusetts, would seem to show that a

a resolution was taken by the king (Charles II.) in council to send a bishop to Virginia, and the individual was actually selected on whom the proposed honour should be conferred. Dr. *Alexander Murray*, who had been the companion of the king in his travels, was the person nominated to be the first bishop in America; and a draught of letters patent was prepared, which Bishop *Gibson* in 1723 stated, was then extant among the records of the see of London.*

Of the causes which led to the failure of the intended design, it is not possible at this distance of time to speak with certainty. In the manuscript already referred to, it is suggested by Bishop *Gibson* that the plan was defeated because "the endowment was to be out of the public customs." In an extract from a letter written by Dr. *Murray* himself,† a different, and probably more correct reason is assigned. In October, 1673, the plan of establishment for the bishop was referred to the then Bishop of London (Dr. *Compton*), and the Lord Keeper (Sir *Orlando Bridgman*); and very soon after, through the instrumentality of the celebrated ministry, known as the *Cabal*, Sir *Orlando Bridgman* was displaced before an opportunity had been afforded him of reporting on the proposed establishment; and the subject was not again resumed.

The next mention which we find made of an American Episcopate is in the abstract of the proceedings of the Society for Propagating the Gospel, in the year 1703. It is there said that the society had received "addresses from divers parts of the continent, and islands adjacent, for a suffragan, to visit the several churches; ordain some, confirm others, and bless all."

Indeed, about this period, the pressing want of a bishop seems to have been very sensibly felt, and the applications to the society appear to have been urged with an almost importunate frequency. They received a respectful hearing, and at length a committee prepared a statement of facts, entitled "the case of suffragan bishops for foreign parts briefly proposed," which was submitted to the queen's attorney-general for his opinion.‡

bishop was appointed in that year. Its language is: "There was a General Governor, and a Major-General chosen, and *a Bishop with a suffragan*, but Mr. Norton writes that they are not yet out of hopes to prevent it." See *Hutchinson's History of Massachusetts*, vol. i. p. 225, *note*. There is no evidence which throws light on this appointment, if it ever was made. It is perhaps not improbable, that in transcribing, a mistake may have been made in the year; 1662 having been written for 1672.

* Bishop *Gibson's* letter and memorial on sending bishops to the English plantations abroad. MSS. of Gen. Convention.

Address from the clergy of New York and New Jersey to the Episcopalians in Virginia, p. 11.

† Chandler's Appeal further defended, p. 148.

‡ Dr. *Kennett's* account of the Society, published at London in 1706, but without the author's name. By the beneficence of many individuals, a fund for the support of a bishop in America had been gradually accumulating, and it is probable, that had one been appointed, the colonists would have been entirely relieved from the burthen of his maintenance. It deserves too to be remembered, that the larger portion of this fund was contributed by gentlemen who were themselves in the episcopal office; among whom Bishop *Butler*, of Durham, holds a conspicuous place. Indeed, such was the anxiety of the English prelates on the subject, that it was said the Bishop of London, in 1745, "offered to the king and council, on condition that an American bishop might be sent

The plan was not, however, brought to a speedy conclusion, for in 1710 we find the society alluding to the want of a bishop in America, stating that the subject is yet under the consideration of the society, and informing the public that they were endeavouring to find a commodious and central place in which to fix the residence of the bishop.* Nor was it long after this representation, before the society purchased at Burlington, in New Jersey, at an expense of £600, a convenient mansion house and lands for the use of the future bishop.†

We have said that in the earlier efforts which were made to procure the episcopate, the laity co-operated with the clergy. In an address of the society to the throne in 1712, the subject is thus represented to the queen: "We cannot but take this opportunity, farther to represent to your majesty, the earnest and repeated desires not only of the missionaries, but of divers other considerable persons that are in communion with our excellent church, to have a bishop settled in your American plantations."‡ And again, in 1714, by way of apology for such continued importunity, the society stated that it acted "upon renewed instances from governors of provinces, ministers, vestries, and private persons in the plantations, for settling ecclesiastical superiors there," and "after a loud call for fifteen years together."§

Nor is it surprising that such should have been the fact: at the period of which we are now writing, the jealousy of ecclesiastical power, and the dread of prelatical tyranny, seem not to have been awakened. There appears at this time to have been very little effort made to play upon the prejudices, or to alarm the fears of men: the political aspect of affairs, which at a subsequent period arrayed in opposition to an American Episcopate all who were not, and many who were churchmen, furnished at this time no exciting cause. The colonies were in tranquillity. In many parts, the inhabitants were almost entirely of the Church of England; these individuals looked toward the mother country with the confiding feelings of a child towards a parent. Too feeble to think of independence, and probably too loyal to desire it, the institutions of the land of their fathers were invested with a sacredness which they wished not to violate. They had been educated in the faith of the Church of England. That church deemed

over in his time, that he would give towards his support ten thousand pounds."—Original letter from Dr. *Chandler* to Dr. *Johnson*—Johns. MSS.

* Abstract of the society's proceedings, 1710.

† Address from the clergy of New York and New Jersey to the Episcopalians of Virginia, p. 13. It has been stated in a life of Dean *Swift*, by Sir *Walter Scott*, that "there was a plan suggested by Colonel *Hunter*, Governor of Virginia, to send out Dr. *Swift* as bishop of that province, to exercise a sort of metropolitan authority over the colonial clergy; but the appointment did not take place." If the statement of the biographer be correct, it is probable that the plan was contemplated about this time. Dr. *Dalcho* (alluding to the circumstance in his History of the Church in South Carolina) observes, that the known intimacy between Colonel *Hunter* and Dr. *Swift* affords some confirmation to the statement. Colonel *Hunter* was appointed Governor of Virginia in 1708, but was captured by the French on his voyage out. In 1710 he was sent out Governor of New York and the Jerseys. See *Dalcho's History*, pp. 90, 91.

‡ Dr. *Kennett's* anniversary sermon, 1712, p. 29, note.

§ Abstract, 1714.

bishops necessary for ecclesiastical government. The colonists looked around them, and saw the number of Episcopal clergymen in this country, *exceeding* the number in many of the dioceses of England.* They felt that if supervision was needed at home, the necessity for it abroad could not be diminished, where the number to be overlooked was larger than that at home.

The representation of the Society for Propagating the Gospel, to which we have already alluded, experienced at the hands of the queen the most favourable reception. In the abstract of the proceedings for 1715, it is stated that "her majesty was pleased to give a most gracious answer, highly satisfactory to the Society, and a draught of a bill was ordered, proper to be offered to the parliament for establishing bishops and bishoprics in America." The object so earnestly desired appeared at this time on the eve of accomplishment; but the friends of the measure were destined to witness the destruction of their hopes, in the death of the queen, before the bill had been introduced into parliament.

Disappointed, but not in despair, the advocates of an American Episcopate renewed their efforts early in the reign of the queen's successor. They were favourably received by *George* I., and once more did they look forward to the successful termination of their persevering labours: once more too were they doomed to disappointment: scarcely was the new monarch seated on his throne before his attention was absorbed by the single object of retaining his sovereignty. The friends of the house of Stuart, by their efforts to place the pretender upon the throne, furnished for a time ample employment to the king and his advisers. It was not a period to devote much attention to the comparatively unimportant application of a few episcopalians in the colonies, when the existence of the government itself was threatened by an extensive and dangerous rebellion.

Thus interrupted in their designs, the friends of an American Episcopate seem not to have renewed their application for many years. It was not until the second George had been upon the throne for thirteen years, that in 1740 the necessity of a bishop over the churchmen of America was again *publicly* alluded to. In that year, Dr. *Secker*, who was then Bishop of Oxford, preached the anniversary sermon before the Society for Propagating the Gospel, and depicting in lively colours the inconveniences of the Church in America, pleaded with affectionate earnestness for a resident bishop, as the only remedy for its manifold spiritual privations.

Whether any measure proposing relief resulted from his representation, we have not the means of discovering; it is probable, however, that, discouraged by repeated failures, the society preferred patiently to wait until some opportunity, decidedly favourable to their wishes, should present itself.

This opinion derives countenance from the fact that, from the period just alluded to, up to the year 1750, we have met with no record of any attempt, direct or indirect, for the attainment of the object in view.

There seems to be reason too for supposing that during this interval, the efforts of English churchmen were suspended upon the intimation of those in authority. In the manuscript of Archbishop *Drummond*, prepared in 1764,

* Abstract, 1715.

and already referred to, he remarks, that "in the late reign, the fears of disturbing his majesty's governors, particularly in New England, so influenced the ministry, that they not only, perhaps very wisely, hesitated about the proposal of settling bishops in America, but *finally* postponed it."

However, about the year 1750, some of the leading members of the Society for Propagating the Gospel* entered upon the subject with a zeal which seemed only to have gained strength from previous disappointments.

We have remarked that in 1713 but little opposition had been made to the proposed measure by such of the colonists as were not of the communion of the Church of England.

To say that there was no opposition would not be true: there probably never was a period when the unhappy feelings engendered by differences of opinion in religion, did not produce an opposition, in which conscience had less to do than party feeling. But at the early period which we have named (1713) the opposition which was made, principally in New England, was by no means formidable. Indeed, uncommon pains seem to have been taken to remove all just ground of apprehension from the minds of those to whom Episcopacy was most abhorrent. In a letter to Dr. *Colman*, a congregational minister of Boston, written by Dr. *Kennett* in 1713, we meet with the following language in reference to an American Episcopate: "I hope your churches would not be jealous of it, they being out of our line, and therefore *beyond the cognizance of any overseers to be sent from hence.*"†

But at the latest period of which we have spoken (1750), the state of things was materially different from what it had been when efforts to obtain a bishop in the colonies were first made. An opposition, by no means general in its origin, and, so far as we can discover, not marked by violence in the commencement, had in the lapse of time attained to a magnitude not to be despised: the question had from time to time been agitated, discussion had provoked warmth, to minds heated by controversy objects assumed an undue magnitude, dangers were apprehended more imaginary than real; religious *prejudices* assumed their unholy sway, and religious toleration was not at all understood.‡ The gradual increase too, both of

* Bishops *Sherlock, Secker,* and *Butler.* Free examination of Critical Commentary, p. 2.

† *Turell's* Life of Dr. *Colman,* p. 127.

‡ As a matter of curiosity, there is subjoined the following passage on the subject of religious toleration; it is to be found in an article contained in Gaine's N. York Gazette of May 2, 1768, and is there given as an extract from some work on the subject: "Toleration is a city of refuge in men's consciences for the devil to fly unto—a toleration of soul murder: for establishing whereof damned souls in hell will curse men upon earth—a transcendent catholic, fundamental evil,—the abomination of desolation: all the devils in hell, and their instruments, are at work to promote a toleration."

Another instance of how little was understood of religious toleration is furnished by the following incident. When Governor *Dudley* of Massachusetts died, there was found in his pocket a copy of verses written by himself, containing these lines:

"Let men of God in court and churches watch
O'er such as do a *toleration* hatch,
Lest that ill egg bring forth a cockatrice,
To poison all with heresie and vice."

"This (says *Hutchinson*) was the prevailing doctrine many years, and until their eyes

Episcopal congregations and clergymen in New England, doubtless, contributed not a little to give fierceness to the opposition. The number of the Episcopal clergy in New England had been enlarged from six or seven to twenty; and of these twenty, several had deliberately renounced their ordination in the congregational mode, from conscientious scruples as to its validity. This latter fact alone was sufficient to provoke the hostility of the descendants of the pilgrims. It was not to be endured, that Episcopacy should, unmolested, rear its mitred head among the children of men who had said to the world: "Let all mankind know that we came into the *wilderness*, because we would worship God without that *Episcopacy*, that *Common Prayer*, and those unwarrantable *ceremonies*, with which the *land of our forefathers' sepulchres* has been defiled; we came hither because we would have our posterity settled under the pure and full *dispensations* of the gospel; defended by *rulers that should be of ourselves*."*

But whatever may have been the causes which led to the opposition, the fact is undeniable, that among such of the colonists as were not of the Church of England, the resistance to the measure was so determined, that in the steps taken in 1750, uncommon care was manifested to remove the apprehensions and disarm the hostility of American anti-Episcopalians.

The plan which, after much deliberation, was at that time digested was designed to pay a due regard to the necessities of the church on the one hand, while it should offer neither injury nor offence to any portion of the colonists on the other. This plan, we presume, will lose nothing of its interest with the reader, when he is informed that it is from the pen of the justly celebrated Dr. *Butler*, Bishop of Durham. It is in these words:

1. That no coercive power is desired over the laity in any case, but only a power to regulate the clergy who are in Episcopal orders, and to correct and punish them according to the law of the Church of England, in case of misbehaviour or neglect of duty, with such powers as the commissaries abroad have exercised.

2. That nothing is desired for such bishops that may in the least interfere with the dignity, or authority, or interest of the governor, or any other officer of state. Probates of wills, license for marriages, &c., to be left in the hands where they are; and no share in the temporal government is desired for bishops.

3. The maintenance of such bishops not to be at the charge of the colonies.

4. No bishops are intended to be settled in places where the government is in the hands of dissenters, as in New England, &c.; but authority to be given only to ordain clergy for such Church of England congregations as are among them, and to inspect into the manners and behaviour of the said clergy, and to confirm the members thereof.†

were opened by a fresh persecution coming upon themselves from King *James*. This made his declaration for a general liberty of conscience welcome, and they thanked the king for allowing to them what they before thought themselves bound in conscience to deny to others."—See *Mather's Magnalia*, book ii. chap. v.; *Hutchinson's History*, vol. i. p. 75, *note*.

* *Mather's Magnalia*, book iii. part i. sect. vii. p. 219, vol. i. Hartford edit.

† The manuscript copy of this plan, in the handwriting of Bishop *Butler*, and dated

At the present day, when an experience of many years has shown that the liberties of our country are not jeoparded, even though we have bishops among our citizens, it is somewhat difficult to sympathize with our ancestors in their excited apprehensions of a tyrannical prelacy. With the restrictions which the plan just stated would impose upon the bishops of America, it surely seems difficult to imagine that there was any serious cause of alarm. And yet it would probably be most unjust to suppose that the alarm expressed was not in many cases truly felt. There doubtless were some whose only apprehension was, that the Church of England in America would increase at the expense of the denominations which were around it: they probably knew that the claim of American Episcopalians to a bishop was perfectly unanswerable; nor were they ignorant of the distinction which existed between the ecclesiastical rights of a spiritual kind appertaining to a bishop, and the accidental appendages of temporal power, which had been conferred by man, but which formed no necessary part of the Episcopal office.

There were others, however, less informed, who honestly dreaded the introduction of bishops, as a measure pregnant with danger to their liberties. The very name was associated inseparably in their minds with spiritual courts and tithes, and a long et cetera of grievances, which from boyhood had formed the subject of unalterable hatred and pious anathema. With them, bishop and tyrant were synonymous terms.*

The prejudices implanted by early education disqualified them from viewing the subject dispassionately. They were not sufficiently informed upon the point to make a sober decision. The claim urged by Episcopalians to enjoy equally with all their fellow-citizens the exercise of their peculiar religious opinions and practices, was an equitable claim; honest men felt it to be so; had they but understood that it was possible for a bishop to be one divested of all *temporal* power, and that immense wealth was not *essential* to the Episcopal office, their hostility to bishops would probably have been less sturdy in its character.

Let then the declaration, that their opposition finds its best apology in their ignorance, be viewed rather as the judgment of charity than as evidence of disrespect.†

in 1750, was in the possession of the Rev. Mr. *Apthorp*, of Massachusetts, and was first published by him. A copy of it may also be seen in the Address from the Clergy in New York and New Jersey to the Episcopalians in Virginia, pp. 21, 22.

* A striking instance of the truth of this remark is furnished in the following extract, which was published in Parker's New York Gazette of April 4, 1768:

"Those apostolical monarchs who are to chastise us with scorpions, right reverend and holy tyrants, who want to plunge their spiritual swords into the souls of their fellow creatures:—of all who will not be so senseless as to adore the mitre and surplice:—blood-suckers who obliged our ancestors to abandon their native land, and leave behind them what is the very heaven of persecutors and temporizing conformists."

† The equity of the demand made by the Episcopalians of America cannot be better exhibited than in the following forcible language of Bishop *Lowth:*

"These unhappy churches labour under the singular distress of not being able to minister to their own spiritual wants: their situation and circumstances deprive them of the common benefit which all Christian churches, in all ages, and in every part of the world, have freely enjoyed: and which in that country [America] Christians of every other denomination do at this time freely enjoy. If any easy remedy can be applied to

There was, too, a third, though not very numerous, class, perfectly acquainted with the distinction between powers purely Episcopal, and those which were not, who yet doubted, either the honesty of intention of those who proposed to separate between them, or questioned the practicability of making such a separation. As to their motives, they were probably pure. Evidence is not wanting to justify the charitable inference of the venerable senior Bishop of the church, with respect to this class of opponents.* As they laid aside their resistance to an Episcopate purely religious, as soon as American independence had quieted their apprehensions of supposed political danger, it ought to be believed that they were sincere in the apprehensions previously professed.

But to resume the narrative. On the 21st of February, 1750, Bishop *Sherlock*, then in the see of London, presented to the king in council "Considerations relating to Ecclesiastical Government in his Majesty's Dominions in America."† A copy of this document is appended to Dr. *Chandler's* "Free Examination of the Critical Commentary on Archbishop Secker's letter to Mr. Walpole," and it manifests a studious care to avoid giving just offence to any of the inhabitants of this country. It expressly disavows any intention of sending a Bishop to New England or Pennsylvania; it proposes to confide to the American prelates no powers but such as are purely Episcopal; and, in direct terms, protests against any tax or imposition upon the people of this country for the support of the proposed Episcopate.

The period selected for bringing the subject before the king seems to have been an inauspicious one. His Majesty was at that time preparing for a visit to his German possessions on matters of great political moment; and on this account the consideration of the subject was deferred until his return from Hanover; and thus was defeated the *third* application which had been presented to the throne.

During the absence of the king, Bishop *Secker*, in reply to a letter from Mr. *Walpole*, (addressed to Bishop *Sherlock*, but meant also for Bishop *Secker*,) drew up an answer, which produced no effect upon the proposed measure, so far as we can discover.

We are now approaching that period in our history when the hostility of the colonists to a resident bishop had assumed a systematic form, and was by

this grievance, surely in charity it will not be denied to their petitions: *in justice it cannot be refused to their demands.* The proper and only remedy hath long since been pointed out:—the appointment of one or more resident bishops for the exercise of offices *purely Episcopal* in the American Church of England:—offices, to which the members of the Church of England have *an undeniable claim,* and from which *they cannot be precluded without manifest injustice and oppression.*" And again—"Unless groundless fears, invidious surmises, injurious suspicions,—unless absurd demands of needless and impracticable securities against dangers altogether imaginary and improbable, are to set aside *undoubted rights, founded upon the plainest maxims of religious liberty, upon the common claim of mutual toleration,* that favourite but abused principle, the glory and the disgrace of Protestantism, which all are forward enough to profess, but few steadily practise; and which those who claim it in its utmost extent for themselves are sometimes least of all inclined to indulge in any to others."—Anniversary Sermon before the Society for Propagating the Gospel in 1771, pp. 14, 18.

* See Bishop *White's* Memoirs, p. 7.

† Letter from Bishop *Sherlock* to Dr. *Johnson,* dated September 19, 1750. Johns. MSS.

no means confined to those who were not Episcopalians. The *causes* which led to the determination of the parent country to impose upon the colonies the odious stamp duty of 1764, belong to the province of the civil historian: our subject has no connexion with them. But the *effect* produced by the obnoxious measure upon our ancestors falls within the range of our investigation; for the political aspect of affairs at that day had an important bearing upon the question of an American Episcopate.

Wounded by the unkindness of the mother country, insulted by a contemptuous neglect of respectful representations, and deeply injured by what was deemed oppression, it is not wonderful that our forefathers should abate nothing of their prejudices against bishops, when they thought of the ecclesiastical establishment of England, intimately blended as it is with the machinery of her civil government. From the oppressions of the government, the transition was easy to apprehended oppressions by the Hierarchy which it sustained. The cordial hatred which was felt by many towards that Hierarchy, it was not difficult to transfer to those who might be sent hither clad with Episcopal authority, communicated by the bishops of England. These circumstances were favourable to those who had long resisted the proposed measure. To them it was an easy task to awaken a determined opposition in minds predisposed to view with suspicion any thing which, in its fortunes, was so linked to the British government, that it could not but be the upholder of its measures.

In England, too, the large body of the dissenting interest readily cooperated with their brethren in America. The different denominations concentrated their forces in a committee in London, and a constant correspondence was carried on with a society in this country, composed principally of the Congregationalists of New England and the Presbyterians of New York and New Jersey. The venerable Bishop of Pennsylvania informs us that at a subsequent period, in 1771 and 1772, he was acquainted with a member of the English Committee, and knew that he had free access to the ministry. It was deemed an object of importance to avoid giving offence to the dissenters, and exciting thereby their political opposition, as they possessed an influence in the elections to Parliament which was too powerful to be despised.*

Unpropitious as were the times for agitating the question of an American Episcopate, it may well be supposed that the discussion would not *wilfully*

* Bishop *White's* Memoirs, p. 50. The following extracts also exhibit the influence which the dissenters exercised on the subject:—

"—— From him I first learned the true reason of the Bishop of London being opposed and defeated in his scheme of sending us bishops. It seems that the Duke of Newcastle, Mr. Pelham, and Mr. Onslow, can have the interest and votes of the whole body of the dissenters upon condition of their befriending them; and by their influence on those persons, the ministry was brought to oppose it."—Manuscript letter of Dr. *Chandler* to Dr. *Johnson.*—Johns. MSS.

—— "We must wait for more favourable times; which I think it will contribute not a little to bring on, if the ministers of our church in America, by friendly converse with the principal dissenters, can satisfy them that nothing more is intended or desired than that our church may enjoy the full benefit of its own institutions, as all others do. For so long as they are uneasy, and remonstrate, regard will be paid to them and their friends here by our ministers of state."—Letter from Bishop *Secker* to Dr. *Johnson.*

be provoked by the Churchmen in this country. Accident, however, appears to have brought it forward in the following manner:

The Society for Propagating the Gospel in Foreign Parts had from the commencement been the chief source of support to the Episcopal ministers on this continent. In every colony but Virginia and Maryland all the clergy of the church were, or had been, missionaries of the Society. Without the aid of this institution, the Church could not possibly have been sustained in the greater part of what was British America. Under its auspices, houses of worship had been built, congregations had been collected, and ministers sustained, until the Society, by its annual bounty, was now upholding more than eighty missionary stations, and supporting seventy-two missionaries, exclusive of those employed in Newfoundland, Nova Scotia, and the West Indies.* Of these, thirty were employed in New England, and truth compels us to add, that they were deemed *intruders* by the descendants of the first settlers. This state of things produced repeated attacks on the Society by those who viewed with jealous apprehension its successful operations. The chief subject of complaint was, that, unmindful of the purposes of its institution, instead of sending the Gospel and the ministry to the *destitute* parts of the continent, it sought out the better settled and more comfortable portions of the country, and there stationed its missionaries, to make converts *to the Church of England*, of men who already had the Gospel preached among them by ministers of other denominations.† It was

* Abstract of the Society's proceedings for 1764.

† With the venerable English Society for Propagating the Gospel, the church in this country has no connexion, save that created by the bonds of a common faith; but there is not an Episcopalian in the United States acquainted with the labours of that Society in planting the Church on this continent who must not feel that *he*, at least, owes to it a heavy debt of gratitude. We would endeavour, even at this distance of time, to pay a small portion of that debt by repelling a calumny. The growth of the Church in New England, particularly, was a perpetual source of irritation and hatred to the bigoted Congregationalists: hence the charge of making "converts to the Church of England" was often repeated. And yet, upon the best inquiry we have been enabled to make, we cannot find a *solitary instance* of a Missionary having been sent by the Society into New England but *upon the request of the people themselves.* It was the practice of the Society not to send a missionary to any place before the inhabitants applied for him. Nay, in some instances, in New England, the people not only asked for a missionary, but at their own expense actually erected Church edifices before the Society sent any clergymen to them. The Society was in operation for several years before it sent *any missionary to New England,* as the abstracts will show. This course of conduct is not consistent with the design "to *episcopise* dissenters," as it was termed. The truth seems to be this: the Church grew, notwithstanding opposition; and the cause of its increase is furnished by an eye-witness (the excellent Dr. *Johnson,* of Stratford), in a manuscript now before us. "The true causes and occasions of the being and growth of so many congregations of the Church of England in these provinces are as follow:—

"1. As the country continued to increase, and there were many accessions from Great Britain and Ireland, there were, among others, many of the established Church came over to settle in these colonies, as well as others, so that there was, fifty years ago, scarce a town of considerable standing but what had some scattering among them, in some several families. In Stratford, for instance, the first in Connecticut that applied to the Society, there were, in the beginning of this century, fifteen families.

"2. So the case has been ever since Church people have settled in this country, many dissenters have treated them with much clamour, and contempt, and frequent disputing, which occasioned many of them to procure books wherewith to defend themselves, such not to be expected that a charge of this kind, often repeated as it was, would be permitted to pass unnoticed. The Society had in its employment gentlemen who were prompt to repel this unfounded imputation. Among these was the Rev. *East Apthorp*, the missionary at Cambridge, a clergyman deservedly respected, both for his piety and ability, who published a small pamphlet, entitled "Considerations on the Institution and Conduct of the Society for Propagating the Gospel in Foreign Parts." It was not long before this production found an antagonist, of no mean ability, in Dr. *Mayhew*, a Congregational minister of Boston, who gave to the world his answer, with the following motto prefixed, sufficiently expressive of the nature of the work:—"*Brethren unawares brought in, who came in privily, to spy out our liberty which we have in Christ Jesus, that they might bring us into bondage; to whom we gave place by subjection, no, not for an hour, that the truth of the Gospel might continue with you.*"

In this angry production, (for such it must be deemed,) Dr. *Mayhew* not only considered the subject introduced in Mr. *Apthorp's* pamphlet, but interspersed many injurious reflections on the Church of England, and particularly inveighed against the plan of appointing bishops for America; and thus the matter was once more presented as a subject of controversy.*

An anonymous production, published originally in London, and reprinted in this country, contained an answer to Dr. *Mayhew*, remarkable for its strength of argument, fairness of discussion, and Christian temper. Such was its effect, not only upon those who took no part in the discussion, but even

as "the London Cases," "Hoadly against Calamy," "Archbishop Potter on Church Government," and some even "Hooker's Ecclesiastical Polity," not to mention some others; and their thus defending themselves occasioned many inquisitive candid dissenters to read those books, which reconciled them to the Church. So that the dissenters themselves, by thus censuring and disputing, have occasioned the increase of the Church.

"3. Another thing, and what has of late chiefly occasioned the accession of multitudes of proselytes to the Church, was the wild enthusiasm that long obtained among themselves; on which occasions their own managements were in many instances so extravagant and ridiculous as tended vastly more to drive their people into the Church than any thing we ever did to draw them over to it; particularly that monstrous enthusiasm that was at first encouraged by themselves, fifteen or twenty years ago, in consequence of Mr. Whitfield's rambling once and again through the country, who was followed by a great many strolling teachers, who propagated so many wild and horrid notions of God and the Gospel, that a multitude of people were so bewildered, that they could find no rest to the sole of their foot, till they retired into the Church as their only ark of safety. And many of these continue among great numbers to this day, and have occasioned many separate meetings among the dissenters themselves, and these have occasioned much hot contention among them in settling ministers, and often the prostitution of discipline upon the merest trifles, which have caused many people to conclude, that if they must separate from their former brethren, who are in endless contentions and confusion, their best way will be to retire into the Church, which is in peace. Now these are all known facts."—Johns. MSS.

* That we may not be suspected of doing injustice to Dr. *Mayhew*, we would add that his work was condemned by those of his own persuasion. In reply to an inquiry made of Dr. *Samuel Chandler*, a Presbyterian divine of London, whether he could or did approve of the bitter and injurious publications against the Society, he answered, that "he was truly sorry to see what Dr. *Mayhew* had published, and had wrote to him, signifying the same, with his desire that he would desist."—Original letter from Rev. Mr. *Jarvis* (afterwards Bishop *Jarvis*) to Dr. *Johnson*.—Johns. MSS.

upon Dr. *Mayhew* himself, that he frankly acknowledged his adversary to be "a person of excellent sense and a happy talent at writing; apparently free from the sordid, illiberal spirit of bigotry; one of a cool temper, who often showed much candour, was well acquainted with the affairs of the Society, and in general a fair reasoner."* Dr. *Mayhew* published *two* answers to the tract, in which he abated much of his former acrimony; he persisted, however, in affirming, that he was not "wrong in any material point," and so far indulged in reproach, that he was animadverted on by Mr. *Apthorp* in a very sensible and polite review, entitled, "A Review of Dr. Mayhew's Remarks," &c. This terminated the controversy. Dr. *Mayhew*, on reading it, declared he should not answer it, and in the following year he died.†

At the time Dr. *Mayhew* answered the "anonymous tract," he was not aware of the fact now well established, that the author of that production, whom he characterized as a "worthy answerer," was Archbishop *Secker*, the President of the Society for Propagating the Gospel. If the character of this prelate, as given by Dr. *Mayhew* in the extract already quoted, be honourable to the memory of the Archbishop, it is honourable also to the character of Dr. *Mayhew*, that, notwithstanding the warmth of controversy, he candidly acknowledged the merits of an antagonist whom he must have felt that it was difficult to answer. The incident is one which reflects honour on both the gentlemen concerned.

At the same time that the Archbishop was engaged in England in the preparation of his tract, the Rev. Mr. *Caner*, of Boston, and Dr. *Johnson*, of Stratford, were occupied on the same subject, and their several productions were afterwards published in the same volume, Dr. *Johnson's* observations forming an appendix to Mr. *Caner's* fuller vindication.

The reasons assigned in the writings both of the Archbishop and Mr. *Apthorp*, for desiring the proposed establishment of bishops in the colonies, furnish perhaps the best picture of the disadvantages which retarded, at that day, the growth of the Church. The principal reasons are the want of *confirmation*, the need for *superintendence* of the conduct of the clergy, and especially the saving candidates the trouble, cost, and risk of a voyage to and from England in procuring *ordination*. While all other denominations had the means within themselves of perpetuating their ministry—while bishops were not denied to another Church of Protestant Episcopalians, the Moravian Brethren—the members of the Church of England alone were excluded from a right, the exercise of which was, in their view, essential to their existence as a Church. The expense of the voyage to and from England was not less than £100; nearly one-fifth of those who had taken that voyage had lost their lives; and, in consequence of these discouragements, one-half of the churches in many of the provinces were destitute of clergymen. These reasons were forcibly and unanswerably urged, and common justice and common humanity, it was truly said, pleaded strongly for a remedy of these evils.

To guard too against the fears of those who were known to be opposed to the measure, it was stated in the publication of the Archbishop, that the

* *Mayhew's* remarks on an anonymous tract, &c., p. 3.

† Review of the Life and Character of Archbishop *Secker*, by Dr. *Porteus*.

proposed bishops should "have no concern in the least with any persons who do not profess themselves to be of the Church of England, but may ordain ministers for such as do; may confirm their children when brought to them at a fit age for that purpose; and take such oversight of the Episcopal clergy as the Bishop of London's Commissaries in those parts have been empowered to take, and have taken without offence. But it is not desired in the least that they should hold courts to try matrimonial or testamentary causes, or be vested with any authority now exercised either by provincial governors or subordinate magistrates, or infringe or diminish any privileges or liberties enjoyed by any of the laity even of our own communion." And as to the place of residence of the American bishops, it was declared, "that it neither is, nor ever was intended or desired to fix one in *New England;* but Episcopal colonies have always been proposed." "To such a plan as this," says the venerable Bishop *White*, "it is difficult to perceive how hindrance could have been attempted by any description of persons without an avowal of intolerance."* Dr. *Mayhew* very candidly remarked, with reference to it, "that if such a scheme as this were carried into execution, and only such consequences were to follow as the proposer had professedly in view, he could not object to it, except upon the same principle that he should object against the Church of England in general."†

And yet, such was the state of excitement produced in the colonies by political considerations, that the scheme of sending bishops to this country, however restricted in their powers, met with but little countenance from the great mass of the inhabitants: the opposition was not confined to those who were not of the Church of England; there were Episcopalians, both of the clergy and laity, who had caught the temper of the times, and learned to look with a suspicious distrust upon the scheme of an American bishop, as but another plan for riveting chains which they already thought were scarcely to be tolerated longer.

The character of the distinguished prelate who had so successfully encountered Dr. *Mayhew*, gained nothing thereby in the eyes of a large majority, but was assailed with a virulence of invective seldom surpassed. With unrelenting rancour, and unexampled wantonness of abuse, he was attacked in pamphlets and newspapers, and escaped not the malevolence of his enemies even after he had descended to the grave.‡

When it is recollected that the chief, if not the sole cause of this insatiate hate, was the aid which the Archbishop had rendered to the measure of an American Episcopate; in other words, his demand for *religious toleration* in America, it is difficult not to concur in the sentiment expressed by his affectionate and pious biographer. "What an idea (says Bishop *Porteus*)

* Bishop *White's* Memoirs, p. 53.

† Remarks on an anonymous tract, &c., p. 59.

‡ The following specimen is from the pen of an *Episcopal* clergyman in Virginia, whose name we deem it most charitable to his memory to withhold. The extract was published in Purdie and Dixon's Virginia Gazette of July 18, 1771:

"As to *Secker*, he is laid in the grave: disturb not his slumber. His character, no more than his body, can endure *the keen question of the searching air*. Unless you would give another specimen of your friendship, cause him not to STINK to futurity."

must it give mankind of his grace's character to have such a circumstance singled out by his bitterest revilers as the most exceptionable part of it!"*

Scarcely had the controversy which has been detailed been brought to a conclusion before it was again renewed, under the following circumstances:—At the annual meeting of the Society for Propagating the Gospel, held in 1767, the Bishop of Landaff preached the anniversary sermon, in which he alluded to the state of religion on some parts of the continent. Certain expressions which he used, representing the condition of some of the colonies as but little better than heathenish, were supposed by some to refer particularly to *New England*, though candour compels us to add, that such does not seem to have been a fair inference. On the contrary, New England is particularly designated as being worthy of great commendation for the attention which religion had there received from its earliest settlement.

Among those who professed to entertain this singular opinion of the bishop's sermon was Dr. *Charles Chauncy*, of Boston, a Congregational divine of much celebrity. He published "A Letter to a Friend, containing Remarks on certain Passages" in the sermon, and as the necessity of a resident Episcopacy was one of the points urged by the Bishop of Landaff, the door was open for a renewal of the war of pamphlets.

That Dr. *Chauncy* was justly entitled to the reputation which he possessed is evident from his publication, for it is not wanting in ability, and especially in ingenuity. The ground which he took was, that the introduction of bishops was not to be dreaded as a measure at all likely to convert Presbyterians into Churchmen; nor was it on that ground opposed; but from the fear of hurtful consequences both to the bishops and people; and he thus expresses his views:—

"Such consequences would certainly be the effect, if these bishops should make use of their SUPERIORITY, as most probably they would, sooner or later, to influence our great men here, and much greater ones at home, to project and endeavour to carry into execution measures *to force the growth of the Church.* It may be relied on, our people would not be easy if restrained in the exercise of that 'liberty wherewith Christ hath made them free;" yea, they would hazard everything dear to them, their estates, their very lives, rather than suffer their necks to be put under that yoke of bondage, which was so sadly galling to their fathers, and occasioned their retreat into this distant land, that they might enjoy the freedom of men and Christians."†

Nor did the Society for Propagating the Gospel escape the rebukes of the author of the letter. The sole design of the institution was stated to be "to *episcopise* the colonies."

Dr. *Chauncy* was followed by Mr. *William Livingston*, a lawyer of New York, who, in 1768, published in that city, "A Letter to the Right Rev. Bishop of Landaff," &c. It must be deemed most unfortunate for the literary reputation of Mr. *Livingston*, that he had ever seen the production of Dr. *Chauncy*. That he had seen it is proved by a quotation from it, accompanied with a very slight acknowledgment of his obligation for the quotation. From beginning to end, his letter is but a repetition of the arguments of Dr. *Chauncy*, presented in the gaudy trappings of a more florid style. Every

* Life of *Secker*, by Dr. *Porteus*.

‡ A Letter to a Friend, &c., p. 47.

passage of the sermon commented on by Dr. *Chauncy*, is commented on by Mr. *Livingston, and none other is;* nay, these passages are considered in precisely the *same order*, and not unfrequently answered, in part, in the *very same words;* nor is there a solitary thought worthy of note, which had not already been given to the world by Dr. *Chauncy.* It would be difficult to conceive of a more palpable plagiarism, unless it were a *verbatim* copy.

We should be the less disposed to record this instance of literary theft, if it were not prefaced by the affectation of a modesty which becomes ridiculous as soon as the theft is known. The advertisement to Mr. *Livingston's* "letter" contains a disclaimer of any desire to come before the public as an author, and an expression of diffidence, resulting "from the business of his profession, and a sense of inability."

The next production, and that which terminated the discussion on the bishop's sermon, was an anonymous pamphlet, entitled "A Vindication of the Bishop of Landaff's Sermon." This is now known to have been written by Dr. *Inglis*, an Episcopal clergyman of New York.* Extensive research, a familiar acquaintance with facts, a skilful arrangement of them, manly argument, and a keen and biting sarcasm, are characteristics of this production.

Before the discussion elicited by the sermon of the Bishop of Landaff had been brought to a close, the point in debate was presented anew, and new combatants were ready to enter the field of controversy.

Early in 1767, the Rev. Dr. *Johnson* of Stratford, in Connecticut, suggested to Dr. *Chandler* of Elizabethtown, in New Jersey, the propriety of addressing the public on the subject of an American Episcopate. It has indeed been intimated that the suggestion came from a higher source, and that the measure originated with the Archbishop of Canterbury. Of this, however, no proof has been met with, and as it was positively contradicted by Dr. *Chandler*, the insinuation was probably without foundation. Very soon after the proposition by Dr. *Johnson*, a voluntary association of the Episcopal clergy of New York and New Jersey,† at which were present some of their brethren from the neighbouring provinces, after discussion of the subject, were unanimous in the opinion "that fairly to explain the plan on which American bishops had been requested to lay before the public the reasons of this request, to answer the objections that had been made, and to obviate those that might be otherwise conceived against it, was not only proper and expedient, but a matter of necessity and duty."

The performance of this duty devolved on Dr. *Chandler*, and gave birth to "an Appeal to the Public in behalf of the Church of England in America," published in June, 1767. This production consisted substantially of a short but perspicuous view of the evidence in favour of Episcopacy, the hardships of the case of the Church, deprived of an officer deemed essential to its existence, the plan proposed, with an answer to the fears and objections of those who opposed it.

* Afterwards Bishop *Inglis*, and father of the late Bishop of Nova Scotia.

† Among the names of the clergy then assembled are to be found those of Dr. *Auchmuty*, Dr. *Chandler*, Dr. *Myles Cooper*, Dr. *Ogilvie*, Mr. *Charlton*, Mr. *Seabury* (afterwards Bishop of Connecticut), Mr. *Ingles* (afterwards Bishop of Nova Scotia), and Mr. *Abraham Beach*.

It was not to be expected, after the previous discussions of the subject, that the author could present much of *novelty* to attract his readers. The object of Dr. *Chandler* was to satisfy the American public, that the apprehensions which were entertained by many were groundless—that the claim of Episcopalians was founded in the most obvious justice, and that their peculiar opinions on the subject of Church Government were built upon apostolic and primitive usage. The work is marked by a sound judgment and lucid argument, and upon its first appearance was treated by many, even of those who were not Episcopalians, with the respect which was due to the talents and standing of the author. The more candid acknowledged that to resist such claims as were there presented, upon the ground of apprehended evils, which were all guarded against by the plan proposed, savoured more of intolerance than of Christianity.

The first opposition to the "appeal," there is reason to think, had its origin in disappointed feelings. An application for a charter by the Presbyterians of New York had been rejected by the authorities of the mother country, and the Bishop of London was supposed to have been active in defeating the application. These facts are stated repeatedly in the subsequent newspaper publications on the part of the Church, and are not contradicted in the replies of its adversaries; but of the precise nature of the application, or of its merits, we have no evidence on which to speak.

The attack on the Appeal commenced simultaneously from various quarters, thus giving rise to a very natural suspicion, that a combination had been entered into for the purpose of effectually crushing the plan of an American bishop. A series of essays appeared in the New York Gazette, under the name of the "American Whig;"* while the Pennsylvania Journal in Philadelphia gave to the world the lucubrations of the "Sentinel," and Dr. *Chauncy* of Boston (in his proper name) published the "Appeal to the Public Answered." The violent invectives of the Whig were re-published in the papers of Philadelphia and Boston, while the alarm sounded in Philadelphia by the Sentinel was instantly echoed from the presses of the sister cities; and thus was concentrated the opposition of the three principal cities into an attack more fierce than any which had preceded it.

It is impossible to read many of these publications without a humiliating sense of the infirmity of our nature. If in some, the questions fairly involved are discussed in the spirit of manly argument, in the greater part abusive personalities supply the place of facts, and railing is substituted for reasoning.

Nor is it intended to exempt from this censure many of the publications on the part of the Episcopalians. The American Whig soon found an antagonist under the assumed name of "Timothy Tickler," who followed its successive numbers with what he termed "A Whip for the American Whig," and it must be confessed that his lash is often laid on with merciless severity. There runs through his writings a bitterness of spirit not to be commended, and both these essayists will be laid aside by the candid reader with the feeling that the contest between *them* was, which could call the hardest names.

* These were attributed to Mr. *William Livingston,* already mentioned.

The Sentinel was met in Philadelphia by a gentleman whose talents have seldom been surpassed. Dr. *William Smith*, who for years had been an attentive observer and a prominent actor in the concerns of the American Episcopal Church, came before the public in a series of essays under the title of "The Anatomist." Of all the newspaper productions of that time, this will probably be read with most interest; for though not entirely free from bitterness, it is yet, for the most part, made up of facts and reasoning. There are exhibited a calm self-possession and a coolness of mind which it is obvious were the result of the author's conviction that his cause was good. He is never roused to unbecoming anger, and but seldom stoops to retort abuse. Still these essays are severe, but their severity consists principally in the unanswerable nature of their arguments.

The newspaper essays already mentioned were the most prominent in the controversy; but they were not all. There were "Remonstrants" and "Anti-Sentinels," not remarkable for ability: but for scurrility and vulgar humour the meed of superiority is justly due to "A Kick for the Whipper, by Sir Isaac *Foot*." The author aims at wit, and reaches blackguardism.

It is due to Dr. *Chandler* to say that in all his writings on this subject, he preserved his dignity. In reply to Dr. *Chauncy*, he published "The Appeal Defended," and subsequently, in 1771, "The Appeal Further Defended," in answer to a second production of Dr. *Chauncy*.

Of the arguments urged, nothing remains to be added to what has already been said in the history of the discussion between Dr. *Mayhew* and Mr. *Apthorp*. The reasons for desiring the proposed Episcopate remained unaltered; all that Dr. *Chandler* could say had already been said. He was able only to refer to facts more evidently showing the inconveniences under which the Church laboured,* and to remove prejudice as far as possible.

While the controversies of which we have spoken were at their height, *legislative* interference was not wanting to oppose obstacles to the obnoxious measure. The province of Massachusetts Bay was the first to interfere. At the period of which we are writing, *Dennis de Berdt*, Esq., was agent to the province in London, and to him on the 12th of January, 1768, the House of Representatives addressed a letter, from which the following extract is taken:—

* Shortly before the appeal was written, two missionaries perished in one ship upon the coast of New Jersey, almost in sight of their port, one of whom left a family in N. York dependent upon charity. But one of the most remarkable instances of the inconvenience and risk of obtaining orders in England was furnished in the history of the parish of Hebron in Connecticut. For nearly twenty years that congregation exerted themselves, and without success, to obtain a minister at their own expense. They first sent over Mr. Dean, in 1745, who was admitted to holy orders and appointed their missionary, but in returning he is supposed to have perished, as the ship was never heard of. The next was Mr. Colton, who in 1752 died on his passage from London. The third candidate sent to England by this unfortunate people, was Mr. Usher, who, on his passage in 1757, was taken by the French, and died a prisoner in the castle of Bayonne. The fourth was Mr. Peters, who in 1759, very soon after his arrival in England, was taken with the small pox, and narrowly escaping with his life, to the great joy of his people, at length reached them and officiated as their missionary.—The Appeal Further Defended, p. 127–128.

About one-fifth of all who ever went for orders never saw their homes again.

"The establishment of a Protestant Episcopate in America is also very zealously contended for: and it is very alarming to a people whose fathers, from the hardships they suffered under such an establishment, were obliged to fly their native country into a wilderness, in order peaceably to enjoy their privileges, civil and religious: Their being threatened with the loss of both at once, must throw them into a very disagreeable situation. We hope in God such an establishment will never take place in America; and we desire *you would strenuously oppose it.* The revenue raised in America, for aught we can tell, may be as constitutionally applied towards the support of prelacy as of soldiers and pensioners: If the property of the subject is taken from him without his consent, it is immaterial whether it be done by one man or five hundred, or whether it be applied for the support of the ecclesiastic or military power, or both. It may be well worth the consideration of the best politicians in Great Britain or America, what the natural tendency is of a vigorous pursuit of these measures."

It has already been mentioned that Episcopalians were to be found who, *at this time*, opposed the introduction of bishops into America. The most remarkable instance of this occurred in Virginia, and the Legislature of that province (composed chiefly of Churchmen) has left on record a disapprobation of the measure as decided as that of Massachusetts, though resting on a very different ground.

The circumstances which gave rise to the interposition of the Virginia Legislature were the following:—In the month of April, 1771, the Rev. Mr. *Camm*, at that time the commissary of the Bishop of London for Virginia, by public advertisement, requested a general attendance of the Episcopal clergy at the College of William and Mary, on the 4th of May. At this time there were more than one hundred parishes in Virginia, and most of them supplied. On the 4th of May, a very small number of the clergy assembled, and when the proposition was made to address the king in behalf of an American Episcopate, most of those present desired the commissary to call another meeting and inform the clergy of the nature of the business to be considered.

This was done, and on the 4th of June, twelve clergymen only attended, a number less than that of the former meeting. The first question considered was, whether such a minority of the clergy could be deemed a convention of the Virginia clergy: it was determined (not without opposition) that it was a convention. The proposition to address the king was then considered and determined in the negative. A third question was then proposed, whether the convention should apply to the Bishop of London for his opinion and advice; and in the propriety of this measure there was a unanimous concurrence.

But before adjournment a successful effort was made to reconsider the vote upon the subject of the address to the king, and it was finally resolved on. The grounds taken in opposition were, respect to the Bishop of London, the disturbances occasioned by the stamp act, a recent rebellion or civil war in North Carolina just suppressed, and the general clamour at that time; there does not appear to have been the slightest objection to Episcopacy, as such; but on the contrary, there is a distinct declaration of cordial and conscientious approval of the government of the church by the bishops.

Against the vote determining to address the king, two clergymen of eminence solemnly protested: they were Samuel Henley, Professor of Moral Philosophy, and Thomas Gwatkin, Professor of Mathematics and Natural Philosophy, in the College. The reasons assigned in the protest were:

"First. Because as the number of the clergy in this colony is at least a hundred, we cannot conceive that twelve clergymen are a sufficient representation of so large a body.

"Secondly. Because the said resolution contradicts a former resolution of the same convention, which puts a negative upon the question, *whether the king should be addressed upon an American Episcopate?* and that an assembly met upon so important an occasion should rescind a resolution agreed to and entered down but a few minutes before, is in our apprehension contrary to all order and decorum.

"Thirdly. Because the expression *American Episcopate* includes a jurisdiction over the other colonies; and the clergy of Virginia cannot, with any propriety, petition for a measure which, for aught that appears to the contrary, will materially affect the natural rights and fundamental laws of the said colonies, without their consent and approbation.

"Fourthly. Because the establishment of an American Episcopate *at this time* would tend greatly to weaken the connexion between the mother country and her colonies, to continue their present unhappy disputes, to infuse jealousies and fears into the minds of Protestant Dissenters, and to give ill-disposed persons occasion to raise such disturbances as may endanger the very existence of the British empire in America.

"Fifthly. Because we cannot help considering it as extremely indecent for the clergy to make such an application without the concurrence of the President, Council, and Representatives of this province: an usurpation directly repugnant to the rights of mankind.

"Sixthly. Because the Bishops of London have always hitherto exercised ecclesiastical jurisdiction over this colony; and we are perfectly satisfied with the mild, just, and equitable government of our excellent diocesan, the present Lord Bishop of London, and do think a petition to the crown to strip his Lordship of any part of his jurisdiction but an ill return for his past labours, and contrary to our oath of canonical obedience. We do farther conceive, as it had been unanimously determined by this very convention, that his Lordship should be addressed for his opinion relative to this measure, the clergy ought to have waited for his Lordship's paternal advice before they had proceeded any farther in an affair of such vast importance.

"Seventhly. Because we have particular objections to that part of the resolution by which the committee are directed to *apply*, as it is termed, *for the hands of the majority of the clergy of this colony:* a method of proceeding, in our opinion, contrary to the universal practice of the Christian Church, it having been customary for the clergy to sign all acts of an ecclesiastical nature in public convention: whereas the manner of procuring their concurrence, now proposed, is unworthy the decorum and dignity by which so venerable a body ought ever to be guided."

This matter was deemed of sufficient importance to occupy the attention of the House of Burgesses, and on the 12th of July, they passed the following vote:

"Resolved, *nemine contradicente,* That the thanks of this house be given to the Rev. Mr. *Henley,* the Rev. Mr. *Gwatkin,* the Rev. Mr. *Hewitt,* and the Rev. Mr. *Bland,** for the wise and well-timed opposition they have made to the pernicious project of a few mistaken clergymen for introducing an American bishop: a measure by which much disturbance, great anxiety, and apprehension would certainly take place among his Majesty's faithful American subjects; and that Mr. *Richard Henry Lee* and Mr. *Bland* do acquaint them therewith."

The circumstances which we have just detailed unfortunately produced a coldness between the Episcopalians of Virginia and those of the northern provinces. The clergy at whose request Dr. *Chandler* had prepared the

* The Rev. Messrs. *Hewitt* and *Bland* subsequently protested, or joined in the protest of Messrs. *Henley* and *Gwatkin.*

"Appeal," appointed a committee, who prepared "An Address from the Clergy of New York and New Jersey, to the Episcopalians in Virginia." This was published in 1771, and in 1772 a spirited pamphlet, in reply, was published by Mr. *Gwatkin.*

There is a warmth of feeling betrayed in the Address and in Mr. *Gwatkin's* answer, the more to be lamented because it is obvious that the opinion of both parties was substantially the same on all the points discussed, save one, viz., the expediency *at that time* of making the proposed effort. Mr. *Gwatkin* explicitly declares that the authors of the protest "have not any aversion to Episcopacy in general, to that mode of it established in England, or even to an American Episcopate introduced *at a proper time, by proper authorities, and in a proper manner.*"

The grounds of opposition to an "immediate establishment" are stated to be "a prudential regard to the *practicable*, a desire to preserve peace, heal divisions, and calm the angry passions of an inflamed people."

And on this point of *expediency*, it will probably now be confessed that the clergy of Virginia judged wisely. It certainly was a time when, in addition to all the objections urged on former occasions, there might have been presented the powerful consideration that the people of this country were hostile to the measure on *political* grounds, that they were fast verging to the point when they would not hesitate to resort to arms against the mother country, that the adoption of the scheme would inevitably exasperate the colonies to a forcible resistance in many parts of the continent. All this was known at home, and therefore the application was calculated only to increase the hostility among the colonists, without the slightest prospect of accomplishing any good.

Considerations of this kind seem to have been present to the mind of Dr. *Smith*, for in the concluding sentence of the "Anatomist" (which is terminated abruptly before he had finished the discussion of all the points proposed), he uses this language:

> "But, in truth, from the gloomy prospect that seems gathering against us on the other side of the Atlantic, it might be better for you and for me to cultivate *domestic harmony* for the present, and to suspend the settlement of our remaining differences to a more convenient season."

THOUGHTS

UPON THE PRESENT STATE OF THE

CHURCH OF ENGLAND

IN AMERICA.

[*Written in* 1764,—*Author uncertain.*]

As the Civil, Commercial, and Military States of America are at present under the consideration of his Majesty's Ministers, it is humbly hoped that, as soon as there is leisure to go through this extensive subject, the State of the Church of England in those parts will also be regarded, and the design so often mentioned, and so often misunderstood, of having Bishops appointed and settled in the Episcopal Colonies, will be maturely and impartially considered. The great accession to the British Empire in America calls for due attention to the Episcopal affairs there at this crisis. It cannot be thought presumptuous to revive this subject now with all respect and submission. It would be an omission not to do it, and it seems necessary to determine upon it at this juncture; to reject or to model this Design, which to many experienced wise and good men, conversant in these Countries, appears so desirable for the sake of Government as well as Religion.

The Church of England is established in many Colonies, but without considering it established it seems even from the charters of the Colonies of New England to have an equitable claim to have order settled amongst its members according to its own discipline, as well as every other Persuasion. Protestant Churches, of all Denominations, there, provide a succession of Ministers amongst themselves. This is the case of every Christian Church in the world except the Church of England in America. To supply that Ministry at great hazard and expence, a Voyage to England must be incurred by the natives of America, let them be ever so well qualified; and in consequence of the Difficulties many improper persons are unavoidably sent from hence.

The great New England Colonies were founded by those who fled from the Intolerance of the Church here in the last century; and they enjoy there full and free liberty of conscience, and order in regard to their Ministers and Churches. The Principle is right, that it is not advisable to send Bishops unto those Colonies, nor was it ever meant to disturb the minds of those subjects of his Majesty by such a proceeding, or to infringe upon any one's Liberty in any Colony; but to model everything upon the most extensive

Principles of Toleration. The Church of England is the only one in those parts distinguished by the want of the compleat Exercise of Religion according to its Rites and Ceremonies, whilst it desires that all its fellow Protestants may enjoy the full exercise of their religion without any obstruction, according to their forms in every part of his Majesty's dominions.

Though the Colonies settled with those who dissent from the Church of England are extensive and respectable, yet let it at the same time be considered that there are very great, equally great numbers of Episcopalians in America, who have equally an earnest desire and a fair claim to have the order of their Church completed which hath never been; and from this defect have arisen many inconveniencies and mischiefs; and as the concerns of Great Britain are enlarged, more inconveniencies and mischiefs must consequently arise both to Church and State.

The Bishop of London, by customary usage (which seems to have taken its rise from accidental connexion) hath exercised Jurisdiction by his Commissary in the Plantations. The first mention of it is in 1620. Instructions were given at different times to the Governors that the Clergy and Schoolmasters should have Certificates of their Conformity from the Bishop of London. Accordingly he Ordained and gave Certificates to those that went to America; and in 1685 the Governors are directed to give all countenance to the Bishop of London's Jurisdiction, except in collating to Benefices, granting Licenses for Marriages, and Probates of Wills, which are reserved to the Governors. So passed the Bishop of London's Pastoral care of the Colonies, very imperfectly indeed as to any real benefit to Religion. In 1725, Sir Philip York and Sir Clement Wearg, then Attorney and Solicitor General, in a Report to the Privy Council, declared that the whole Ecclesiastical Jurisdiction was in the Crown; that the Plantations were not part of any Diocese in England, and that no jurisdiction could be exercised there legally but by Commission from the King under the Great Seal. Upon this Bishop Gibson sent out a Commission. Bishop Sherlock who succeeded him in 1748 thought the Commission imperfect and ineffectual, and did not take one out. The last Commissary died sometime before Bishop Sherlock, and none hath been appointed since. The succeeding Bishops of London took out no Commission, and at present there is neither Commission nor Commissary, nor any legal jurisdiction in Ecclesiastical affairs in America but what is vested in his Majesty.

The Bishop of London acts now according to the old usage. But how impracticable is it in him to fulfill his duty as he would wish, in any respect, to any good purpose, even if he had a Commission from the King, as Bishop Gibson had! Some Jurisdiction is necessary, but Inspection is more so. No one who is sensible of the weight that is upon every honest mind in executing the trust of conferring orders, and the expediency of that previous knowledge which every Bishop would willingly have of the character of the candidates; No one who knows the necessity of constant attention to right conduct in the clergy, and to instruction of the youth; No one who has been witness of what may be preserved in order, or put into order by regular Visitations; No one who reflects on the great service which it is to persons of all ages, particularly through the common ranks of Life, with regard to plain knowledge and plain Virtue (which are foundations of the Principles of the

Community) to have education kept in a right method; No one who has seen the general Benefit in the previous steps to Confirmation, and the rational use of it.—No one who has an idea of the just Influence of Residence and Mutual Correspondence of a Bishop with his Clergy, of the Superintendance, the Example, the Assistance of a Man of Character and Discretion at the Head of a Diocese; No one who has any experience or sense of these things can ever say, that the Bishop of London could at any time take any competent care of the Plantations, as a Bishop. Nor did the ablest prelate that ever filled that chair ever think that he could, or ever wish to continue in so irksome and fruitless an office.

It seems equally improbable that a Commission of different Bishops here, or Itinerant Bishops sent there for a time, or a number of Commissaries inhabiting there would do any real service in the present state of America. Dioceses in England, which have been long formed and regulated, do not perhaps require so much attention as those extensive and irregular countries where vast Tracts are without Churches or Ministers, and nothing but the immediate eye of a constant resident Bishop can produce order amongst Instructors, as well as those who are to be instructed in Religion, can watch over the great influx of Foreign Protestants, and by encouraging of worthy persons acceptable to people increase the Establishments of Religion, and secure obedience to Government.

It could not be expected that a Bishop living in England could do anything effectually even in the enlightened state in which America was in the last century and the beginning of this. But the state of America within these last thirty years, and particularly by the late regulations, is so different, so much more known, and so much more valuable, that the subject of Ecclesiastical affairs, as well as all others, is greatly extended in comparison of former times. From the year 1672, when a Bishop was first thought of for Virginia, to 1750, when the subject was dropped in compliance with a Message from his Majesty's Ministers, it does not appear from any of the Papers, that this subject has ever been fully and impartially considered. It now becomes much more important for the service of Religion and Government, and objections may diminish or disappear, when the numbers, dispositions, and circumstances are brought into view in their present state, and the design fairly laid open, as it is here, with the most dutiful and zealous Intentions for his Majesty's service, and firm Resolution of cheerful obedience to his Royal Pleasure whatever he shall in his Royal Wisdom determine.

Upon a review of the numbers in May, 1762, exclusive of the new acquisitions, there were in the American Colonies and the Islands:

Blacks	844,000
Whites	1,260,000
Total of the Inhabitants	2,104,000

Of the whites the Religious Persuasions were thus divided, viz.:

Episcopalians	401,000
Presbyterians, Independants, and Anabaptists	391,000
People of various Denominations, German Sectaries, Jews, Quakers, Papists, &c.	468,000
	1,260,000

This general calculation was formed as exactly as the circumstances would allow upon particular calculations in each Colony by Persons conversant in America. The new acquisitions must increase the number of Inhabitants considerably.

In Maryland the Church of England is established by Charter, and in fact there are forty-two Parishes, though the proprietor was a Papist, and many Papists are now there.

In Pennsylvania all Persuasions are united, and no objections to Bishops arise from thence.

In New England many Independants may object, though perhaps not so many as is imagined, and none can give a reason but what must contradict their own Principles of Liberty, and deny to others an equal claim to such Privileges as they enjoy. If we can judge by the opinions of the chief persons of the established Church of Scotland, or of those who dissent from the Church of England here, the body of Dissenters will not be, as they have no reason to be, offended; though some of the warmest in America might care. Moderation on all sides is more universal. It is owned that order is necessary to every Establishment of Religion, and that religion itself cannot properly be supported without it. Now there is a manifest deficiency in the order and discipline of the Church of England in America, by wanting Bishops; and no objections against supplying it will be made by any one who has a just value for the doctrine of Toleration, and is a sincere well wisher to Piety, Virtue, and good Government: provided the Regulations in settling Bishops are calculated not to offend or disturb those who enjoy their Liberty of Conscience to its full extent.

In this and in all other important subjects there will be different opinions; and perhaps it creates fewer animosities to decide about a proposal upon a sense of its fitness than to seek for a variety of sentiments. Objections arise from different motives, from licentiousness, from a dislike of any inspection, from an undistinguishing aversion to all Church Discipline, from old inveteracy against the Church of England, from prepossession against unseeming novelty, from various views and passions. In the late Reign the fears of disturbing his Majesty's Government, particularly in New England, influenced the Ministers that they not only, perhaps very wisely, hesitated about the Proposal of sending Bishops in America, but finally postponed it. These fears seem to have been carried too far, and probably other reasons were combined in them. But the scene has been so much more in view lately and so much enlarged, that in the opinion of impartial and understanding Persons Government is more likely now to suffer in its tranquillity and stability by the imperfect state of the Church of England in America, which can only be set right by the residence of Bishops there. The Heats too of the most respectable part of the Dissenters are so abated, that in the eye of the most timid Policy apprehension of any considerable uneasiness in that Quarter seems groundless. There does not seem a greater likelihood of reviving Church Parties, and Dissensions, and Controversies by this step than by the Establishment of the Church of England in the new acquisitions. Nor can there be any sort of grounds to foresee consequences of exorbitant Church Power, of any Spiritual Tyranny or Intolerance. The Inclinations and Principles of the chief of the Clergy manifestly do not tend that way; and if ever they should, the proposed regulations may entirely defeat such ideas. It must be owned that the probable consequence will be the increase of the Church of England in America when the present disorder of it is removed; but it should be considered that the Civil Government here may receive great support there from such increase, and that it is no less important, even as a matter of State, that Ecclesiastics should be able to do good, than that they should not be able to do harm.

That there may be some zealous Independants in America, who will cry out at such an appointment, and alarm themselves and others with false suspicions; and even that many persons will not care for any steps taken towards promoting order, is probably true; but it is fitting to be done by his Majesty upon principles of true Religion and sound Policy. The objections of such Persons might be an additional Reason to the State for doing it.

His Majesty's Royal Protection is extended to Protestants of all Denominations, and the Church of England humbly hopes for it in this instance of settling Bishops in America. This appointment is not only useful but necessary to the welfare of that Church, to the regular administration of its offices and purposes of Religion and Virtue which is the end of its establishment. This design appears reasonable in itself, and free from every material Inconvenience or just objection: And if his Majesty, upon a view of the Equity, the Safety, and Advantage of it, thinks fit to give orders for carrying it into execution, the mode must be referred to his Majesty's Determination. However, the following thoughts are humbly submitted for consideration, which occur after reflecting upon it, and which though imperfect may excite better.

Four suffragan Bishops to the See of Canterbury or London may be appointed by the King in conformity to the Statute in the twenty-sixth year of Henry VIII.

Of these none should reside in the Colonies where the Government is in the hands of Dissenters, as in New England. It is only desired that they may ordain clergymen for such Church of England Congregations as are in those Colonies, inspect into the manners and behaviour of the Episcopal clergy there, and confirm such fit persons as may offer themselves for that purpose.

First. The Residence of the four Bishops might be at Burlington in New Jersey, or at New York. His Diocese might comprehend all that is East of the River Delaware.

Second. At William and Mary's College at Williamsburg in Virginia. His Diocese might comprehend all that is west of the River Delaware as far as the Southern Boundary of North Carolina.

Third. At Charlestown in South Carolina. His Diocese might comprehend all from the Northern Boundary of South Carolina to the Gulf of Florida, and also the Island of Jamaica, for the passage to Jamaica is said to be easier from the Continent than the other Islands.

Fourth. At Coddrington College in Barbadoes. His Diocese might comprehend all the Islands, exclusive of Jamaica.

As to the income, it should be suitable to such a character and sufficient to secure a proper respect, and as far as can be judged from the expense of living and extent of the Dioceses, it seems that £1000 sterling per annum is the least that can be allowed, and £1,500 is the most that is requisite.

The people of the Colonies must not be burthened with the maintenance of the Bishops, but the Income may be raised by many ways, some more eligible than others.

There is £3,800 now in the Funds at three per cent. which arose from various Benefactions towards this design, besides £1,000 given by Archbishop Tennison, and £1,000 left by Mr. Fisher this year; and £500 by Bishop Osbaldiston. This might be employed in buying houses, stock, &c., at first, and other Benefactions might come in. But to avoid uncertainty, the Income might be made sure by annexing some great Living in the Diocese to the See of the Bishop, who would also officiate as often as circumstances would allow, in the Parochial Duty of it. Some Prebend, or Sinecure, in England in the gift of the Crown, might be held with the Bishoprick, as some are by Persons in the Universities here; a Salary out of the Revenues of William and Mary College might be added to the Bishoprick of Virginia; and a salary out of the Revenues of Coddrington College to the Bishop of the Islands. Besides this, Lands now unappropriated might be allotted to make up a sufficient Income; or a small part might be granted out of the Quit-Rents, which are said to be capable of great advancement for the King's service.

There has been of a long time £100 allotted out of the Quit-Rents of Virginia to the company there; and £20 has been given by the Crown ever since 1679 as a Bounty to each Minister that goes from hence for his passage to America. There would be a saving in these two articles; and in general the maintenance of the Bishops will not be a difficulty, and may be modelled iu many ways, if it is thought fit to appoint them.

As to the powers. There has been the Difficulty and the stumbling block from a fear of spiritual Courts, without Reason or Distiinction; but if the powers desired here are considered fairly, there is no real ground for objection or Suspicion, or Jealousy. The appointment of Bishops may appear unprecedented in the Colonies, but surely it is as unprecedented to have so many Episcopalian Churches without a Bishop, and to expect the end without the means of Religion. As to the Jurisdiction of the suffragan Bishops, it cannot be justly objected to, as it is no greater than what has been exercised by the Commissary of the Bishop of London. It may be specified to prevent harm, and limited by his Majesty to any Degree in conformity to the statute in the twenty-sixth Henry VIII. No coercive powers are desired over the Laity, but only to regulate the Behaviour of the Episcopal clergy and Clerks of Parishes, and to punish them according to the Law of the Church of England in case of Misbehaviour or Neglect of Duty. The directing and enforcing the Reparation of their Parsonage Houses and Churches, together with a due Provision of all such things as the Laws require for the decent and orderly performance of Divine Service therein, should be also under the Jurisdiction.

Nothing is desired for such Bishops that may in the least interfere with the Dignity, authority, or Interest of the Governor or any other officer of State. Probates of Wills, Licenses for Marriage, &c., are to be left in the hands where they are. Delegates too may be appointed there or here, to whom appeal might be from a Bishop's Jurisdiction, and thereby all irregular extent of power curbed, if ever it should be thought of by him. No share in the temporal government is desired for our Bishops, but every endeavour should be used by them to co-operate with the Governors for the public good, by mutual advice and assistance; and chiefly by sowing the seeds that will insensibly produce right temper and conduct; and by instilling and propagating sound principles in the people, which are the strongest hold in the structure of Government, and the firmest guard to secure obedience. If his Majesty thinks fit the Bishop may be by his office a member of every Council in his Diocese, as the Surveyor General in his Department. This is not desired, except it is thought that it would enable the Bishops to be of more assistance to the Governors and useful to the State.

Many other regulations wiser and better may occur to his Majesty's Ministers in a course of candid deliberation upon this subject; and if the design is likely to be beneficial to the administration of Government in Church and State, and productive of every good end in both, surely there is no reason to stop it for fear of imaginary Dangers or Hierarchical Powers, which can never take effect, when there are real Difficulties which may now be removed, and lasting advantages which may be gained by pursuing it.

If this Proposal is not thought fit to be taken into consideration at this Juncture, there is little reason to hope for it ever succeeding. But the wise and good men in general are convinced from Reason and Experience, that the appointment of Bishops in America would have been at all times of considerable service, and is now become much more necessary for the cultivating Religion and Virtue, for the Propagating Principles conducive to the Quiet of the State, and securing the Allegiance and Loyalty of his Majesty's subjects in those parts; and therefore if unhappily it is thought advisable to lay aside so excellent a design, the Members of the Church of England, both at home and abroad, will receive this Decision with the most serious concern. Yet they will continue their sincere endeavours to carry on every good purpose agreeably to the Principles of their Religion as far as its imperfect state there will allow; and always shew themselves faithful, active and vigilant to the best of their ability in maintaining the Peace and Security of his Majesty's Government in the Colonies.

Archbishop of Canterbury to Dr. W. Smith, of Pennsylvania—1766.

"Good Dr. Smith:

"It is long since I wrote to you; sickness and business have had their shares in preventing me, but the chief hindrance hath been, that I could say nothing determinate concerning our principal American affairs, nor indeed can I now. The beginning of last year we thought an ecclesiastical settlement of Quebec was almost made, on which a Bishop might easily be grafted. But that was opposed by one great man as too favourable, by another as not favourable enough, to the Papists. Then the Ministry changed: we were to begin again; and could get nothing but fair words, though the King interposed for us. Now it is changed once more, and whether we shall fare better or worse for it, I cannot guess. I have begged the Bishop of London to take out a Commission. He is backward; but I hope at length to prevail, and then we may set up our Corresponding Societies. There were no improper expressions in the Address of the Connecticut or of the New York and New Jersey clergy; but they came when both you and we were on fire about the Stamp Act; and so were not presented. But the King was apprised of the contents of them, and desired they might be postponed. The Bishops have expressed their good wishes to Mr. Wheelock's School, but declined contributing to it, as the Society designs to set up one in imitation of it, which Sir William Johnson, who desires to be a member of the Society, presses as peculiarly seasonable. We have sent to ask his advice, and Mr. Barton's, and shall be glad of yours and every Friend's, in what place or places, under what Masters or Regulations, we may best begin the work. I was at first for sending Indians to Mr. Wheelock to be afterwards Episcopally Ordained; but Mr. Apthorp was clear, that they would all turn out Presbyterians. Mr. Whitfield hath got such hold of Lord Dartmouth, who was First Lord of Trade till a few Days ago, that I laboured in vain to oppose his scheme for the Orphan House. But if it be not completed, I hope it may now be altered. I wrote a long Letter to Mr. Duche in December, in answer to one from him about his religious notions. I hope he hath communicated it to you, and hath at least received no harm from it. I considered Mr. Peters as some way superior to the compliment of a Dr.'s Degree; but if you find he would like it, and think it would be useful, I can easily obtain it on your sending me word, where he was educated, what Degree he hath, what age he is, &c. I condole with you on the sad loss of Messrs. Wilson and Giles and your Brother, which I mentioned to the King as one argument for American Bishops. You will have had an account from Dr. Burton of what the Society have done on the occasion, and I hope you will find that sooner or later, such care, as we can, hath been taken, or will be taken, of every thing which you have recommended to us; particularly we shall be mindful of what Mr. Peters and you desire concerning Sussex and Kent Counties. Mr. Neill hath been directed not to give his assistance any longer to Mr. Macclenachan's congregation, as they have made no application to the Bishop of London. The clergy at N. York have been alarmed with a Report, that the American Dissenters are uniting themselves with the Kirk of Scotland, in hopes of obtaining, by their means, some new privileges from our Parliament. I do not apprehend any danger of that sort. Pray write frequently and fully about everything, though I should write seldom and briefly. Yet I will endeavour to mend in that respect, if I am able. But at least be assured, that I shall take much notice of your Information and advice, and that I am,

"With great Regard,
"Your loving Brother,
"THO. CANT."

"Lambeth, August 2, 1766."

[The history of the alienation of the glebes in Virginia from the Church, by the Legislature, is well known. The following memorial will serve to show how manfully our brethren of the laity, of that day, contended for what they deemed their rights:]

"Halifax County, Virginia, July, 1795.

"*To the Honourable the Speaker and other Members of the House of Delegates, sundry Inhabitants of the Parish of Antrim and County of Halifax, beg leave to offer the following Remonstrance and Petition:*

"Relying on the wisdom, the impartiality, and patriotism of the House, we come forward, on the present occasion, to express our sentiments by remonstrating with the most determined firmness against the attacks which are now made on our dearest rights. It is well known to the Honourable House that Petitions have frequently been presented to it by the Baptists and their adherents, praying for a sale of the Glebe lands always in possession of, and now for some considerable time vested by law in, the Protestant Episcopal Church. Concerning Petitions of this kind in general, permit us to observe, that from their origin we have always viewed them with extreme dissatisfaction, conceiving them to be hostile to the peace of the community, and opposed to those principles which give security to property, in every free government. At the late happy revolution, everything was settled on a sure foundation. The great principles of Republicanism were then established, and they have since continued to influence most of our publick deliberations. It was then declared 'That all men are equally entitled to the free exercise of religion;' a privilege which, since that time, we have all equally enjoyed. And the great maxim adopted by our Legislators since the Declaration seems to be, to separate religion, as far as relates to its temporal support or establishment, as much as possible from the political institutions of our country. Accordingly, by the first General Assembly that met, after the formation of our Constitution, in 1776, it was enacted, "That all and every Act of Parliament which renders criminal the maintaining any opinions in matters of religion, forbearing to repair to Church, or the exercising any mode of worship whatsoever, shall henceforth be of no validity or force within this Commonwealth.' In the very next section of the same Act, 'All Dissenters, of whatever denomination, from the Church,' at that time, 'established by law, are totally freed and exempted from all levies, taxes, and impositions whatsoever, towards supporting and maintaining the said Church, as it now is, or hereafter may be, established, and its ministers.' And by the fourth section of the said Act, it is farther enacted, 'That there shall in all time coming be saved and reserved to the use of the Church by law established, the several tracts of Glebe lands already purchased, the churches and chapels already built, and such as were begun or contracted for before the passing of this Act, for the use of the Parishes; all books, plate, and ornaments belonging or appropriated to the use of the said church, &c.; and that there shall moreover be saved or reserved to the use of such Parishes as may have received private donations, for the better support of the said church and its ministers, the perpetual benefit and enjoyment of all such donations.' This Act was generally satisfactory at the time it was passed. It gave the Baptists and other Dissenters all which, at that time, they demanded. It flowed as a consequent from the last article in the Declaration of Rights, concerning Religion; and serves as the basis, next to the Constitution itself, whereon the peace, the prosperity, the security, and independence of all religious societies rest. Therefore, to attempt innovations now with regard to religious affairs, or with regard to the property belonging to any religious society, indicates designs, in our apprehension, highly inimical to the spirit of our Constitution, designs of a threatening and revolutionary aspect, in their consequences pregnant with injustice and persecution, perhaps with tumult and blood, and such as we cannot contemplate in prospect without abhorrence.

"When we address this Honourable House, our duty and our wish is, to use the language of respect. But being sincere, the expression of our sentiments must correspond with our perceptions of the subject. Neither do we wish to weary the attention of this House on a subject which has so often come under its consideration. But we request to be heard with patience, whilst, not only for the foregoing considerations, but also for the following reasons, we remonstrate against all memorials and petitions for the sale of Glebes, either collectively or separately:

"1st. Because we conceive it to be contrary to the Constitution of this country.

"Neither the State nor Federal Constitution, indeed, say anything expressly concerning Glebes, or the property belonging to any religious society. This was unnecessary. They left such property as they found it, and as it always had been, in the possession, and to the use of each society respectively; and doing so, we conceive that it ought still so to remain. But it is not necessary for us in this case to rely on an argument merely negative. For if a law were passed by the Assembly for the sale of the Glebe lands which have been in possession of the Church ever since the first settlement of this country, and been confirmed to her by their own Act nearly twenty years ago, such a law, having an *ex post facto* view, would certainly, in its own nature, be unconstitutional.

"2dly. Because it would destroy that confidence which we and the rest of the community ought always to have in the Legislature.

"The Assembly of Virginia has already pledged its Legislative faith, the most solemn pledge and firmest sanction which a free State can give, that this property shall, 'in all time coming, be saved and reserved to the use of' our church. We are sensible that this Assembly has powers adequate to repeal the law. But should it now be repealed, and the property disposed of, according to the prayer of the Baptists, it would tend to sap the foundation of those rights by which property in general is held, introduce into the Acts of Assembly instability and uncertainty, be a fluctuation in law which we are confident is without precedent in Virginia, and thus would overturn that trust and security which should always be placed in the Legislature. It would also be a violation of right; for we think that the Assembly may, as in the case of escheats, vest landed property in an individual or society, which property cannot be taken away without an equivalent, by a subsequent Assembly, with equal powers, unless at the same time justice and the constitution be disregarded. Should the law simply be repealed, still the property would be held by a certain body of men who were in the rightful possession of it before that law was made. And a question of the greatest magnitude, and involving the highest interests, would arise: whether this property always held and enjoyed by a certain society, and still applied to the use for which it was originally set apart, could be taken from them without trampling on their rights as men and as citizens.

"3dly. Because we conceive that by the Baptists and their abettors, the meaning of the fourth Article of our Declaration of Rights is misrepresented, when they assert, that in conformity to the spirit of that article, the Act vesting the Glebe lands in the Protestant Episcopal Church is unconstitutional.

"That article declares 'That no man or set of men are entitled to exclusive or separate emoluments or privileges from the community, but in consideration of publick services.' Here, as the Glebes are vested in us by law, they would insist that we enjoy 'exclusive emoluments from the community.' If we did, it would be something which the community paid for since the revolution; whereas the community or commonwealth of Virginia gave no new or original grant to the church, for all the Glebes were purchased and paid for before the revolution, and most of them one hundred years prior to that event. The community only pledged itself to guaranty to the Church, not any new property at that time or ever since given her, but the property at that time in her rightful possession, and which has been hers from the beginning. But we do not perceive that the article alluded to has any relation to this question; its object being to prevent hereditary offices in the civil government.

"4thly. Because your Remonstrants, with the rest of the community, are involved in an unnecessary expense.

"Glebes, from their very origin, have been held by Ministers and Vestries, by use, by prescription, by law, by everything that constitutes a sufficient right; and yet to maintain this right we are taxed, and that not only to pay those who advocate its security, but also those who wish to destroy it. But rather than relinquish our right to anything, however trivial that thing may be in itself, and particularly before we will relinquish our right in the property belonging to us as a religious society, we will murmur at no expense incurred for its security.

"5thly. Because by holding this property no superiority or pre-eminence, as is alleged, is conferred on us by law, which indeed would be odious in Republican Government.

"We, as well as the Constitution and Laws of our country, justly abhor distinctions with regard to religious sects, or with regard to the right of holding property; and as we enjoy no superiority above others by law, so we claim none. But the rights and property which are ours already by the Constitution and by law, which were ours before the revolution, during its progress, and ever since, and which were never attempted to be taken from us until very lately, we cannot now be deprived of, without violating the principles of justice, and that principle of equality which they themselves pretend to advocate. For if this property is taken from us at the request of one sect or party, it will create a distinction in favour of that party or sect; and would be one mean of putting it in their power to establish their own religion and tenets on the ruins of those of another.

"For the foregoing reasons, and a variety of others which might be adduced, did we wish to trespass on the patience of this House, we remonstrate against the sale of Glebes in general; and to what has already been advanced, we add the following reasons why we remonstrate in particular against the Petition or Petitions praying for a sale of the Glebe belonging to Antrim Parish, in this County:

"1st. Because should the Glebe of Antrim Parish be sold by the operation of an Act of Assembly, none will deny that the Episcopalians would be entitled to their proportion of the money.

"But the injustice done the Episcopal Society must be obvious in taking their Church property out of their own hands, and appropriating that part of it which would fall to their share, even on the principles of those who petition for a sale, to a public purpose; for the Episcopalians are as able and as willing as any other denomination to pay whatever taxes may be expedient for the support of the Federal and State Governments, or whatever levies may be necessary for the order, the safety, or conveniency of their county, and do not choose that their share of the money arising from the sale of the Glebe, if an equal division is to take place after the sale, should be appropriated to a different purpose. If it be urged that a majority of the people in this county have a right to have the money appropriated according to their wish, yet it should be remembered that neither in a County nor in a State can a majority of the people violate the constitutional rights of the minority. If it be said that the right itself is in dispute, we reply that we and our ancestors have been in possession of this right from the earliest settlement of this country, and under different forms of government; that it is ours by use, by prescription, by law, and that now we cannot be deprived of it, without compelling us to submit to laws, in their own nature having retrospective views, and in their operation involving *ex post facto* circumstances; which would be unconstitutional and oppressive. If it be said that the county, or people in the county, originally paid for the Glebe, or that it was paid for by the State or community at large, and therefore that the State or a majority of the people in this county, have a right to have it sold; yet it should be remembered that the State, and likewise the County, by its representation in the State Legislature, has, in a constitutional sense, 'saved and reserved' it to the religious uses of a certain society. And for the State or County to violate its publick faith, by taking back what it once gave, would be fully as unjust as for one individual to violate a contract entered into with another, or take back what he formerly gave him. Neither is it certain, although it may be so represented to this Honourable House, that it is the wish of a majority of the people in this county to have the Glebe sold; for no fair and equal measures have been adopted to ascertain their sentiments on the subject. It is, in fact, more a party dispute than anything else: and your Remonstrants are very sensible of the disadvantages they lie under in this, that they have it not in their power, except in their present address, to obviate any misrepresentations which may be made, as both the Delegates from this county are decidedly for the sale of our Glebe. We think that the Baptists are, perhaps, the most numerous denomination of Christians in this county at present, and for the most part busying themselves in elections, our candidates and delegates generally embrace the views, and espouse the claims of that party. But we also think that there is a part of the people fully as numerous as they are, who have joined no church, who are very indifferent with regard to affairs of this kind, and particularly with regard to the point in dispute; but who have been prevailed upon by the Baptists and their partizans to sign the petition for the sale of our Glebe, which, had the matter been represented to them in a just point of view, we are confident they would not have done. This House cannot be ignorant of the underhand and unjustifiable means which are often made use of in procuring subscribers to Petitions of this kind, that too often principle is sacrificed to party, and reason to passion. But we trust that this House, sitting as the Guardian of Rights, will not violate the sacred deposit placed in her hands, but that she will, 'without favour, affection, or partiality,' secure to every class and description of men, the privileges and rights which, by the Constitution, and by Law, they now enjoy.

"2dly. Because the Episcopal Society within this county has been at considerable expense in repairing the Churches of the Parish, and taking care of the social property.

"These expenses were cheerfully incurred under the firm belief—a belief which still forms part of their political creed—that the Assembly of Virginia would never grant its approbation to have their Glebe or any part of their Church property disposed of, to gratify the wishes of any sect or any party whatever; and which they conceive it cannot indeed do, consistent with justice and the constitution. But if the Glebe is sold, this money will have been expended, not for their own benefit and use, but that of the Baptists or some other sect, as the Churches will eventually fall into their hands, your Remonstrants being partly deprived of the means of procuring a Minister of their own persuasion. This, indeed, would not be a direct prohibition of the 'free exercise of their religion,' which by the constitution, 'all men are equally entitled to,' though in its effects it would extend that far; and therefore would be unconstitutional, inasmuch as it would do violence to their conscientious principles, either by depriving them entirely of religious ordinances and the means of instruction in that Church which they prefer to all others, or by obliging them to have recourse to some other with which their consciences will not permit them to join. And we expect it will not be denied, that whatever by a natural consequence produces an unconstitutional effect, must in itself be unconstitutional.

"3dly. Because the Incumbent of this Parish, one of your Remonstrants, has been at considerable expense in improving the Glebe lands and repairing the plantation.

"He has occupied these lands for nearly five years. When he received them, the fences were entirely in a ruinous situation; and the repairs and improvements he has made, not only in that respect, but in several others, have far exceeded the profits derived from the plantation, accurate statements of which he can produce. But if the Glebe is sold, agreeable to the prayer of the Petition for that purpose, he will thus have expended the little he had to spare for the benefit of the County at large, to which the Glebe, with its appurtenances and improvements, if sold, would be little more than a mite. It may indeed be represented to the House, that he wasted the Glebe lands by cutting down and selling the timber. Since he has occupied these lands, there has been timber sold off the premises to the amount of thirty-three shillings, all of which, except a few trees, would have been given gratis, as the rest encumbered a few acres intended to have been cleared. But the money laid out in improving the place has far exceeded that amount. Circumstances of this kind, however, are to be judged of by the Vestry of the Parish, and come with no propriety under the cognizance of any others. It may also be represented to this House, that the Incumbent neglects some of the churches in his Parish, and attends only at those where they pay him; to which it is replied, that the Incumbent makes known to the Vestry of the Parish and people at large on what conditions he can officiate at the churches, which conditions they deem reasonable. Where these conditions are complied with, he gives a regular attendance, either at the churches, or anywhere else in the Parish. Where they are not, it is not in his power. And your Remonstrants are astonished that circumstances coming entirely under their notice, as they relate to their own church government and the rules of their sect, should in the least be submitted to the consideration of others, and particularly when they are so represented that, through their medium, the minister may be seen in an unfavourable point of view.

"4thly. Because the petition for the sale of the Glebe of Antrim Parish in this County, strikes, in the most unconstitutional, arbitrary, and persecuting manner, in the first place, at the rights of the Minister and Vestry, and through their medium, those of the whole Episcopal Society within the Parish.

"In the year 1784, an Act was passed to 'empower the Vestry of Antrim, in the county of Halifax, to sell the Glebe of the said Parish, and to lay out the money in purchasing a more convenient one.' The former Glebe has been sold, agreeable to this Act, and the money laid out in purchasing a more convenient one, agreeably to the third section of the said Act, namely, 'That the money arising from the sale of the said Glebe shall be by the said

Vestry laid out and applied towards purchasing a more convenient Glebe for the use and benefit of the Minister of the said Parish for the time being, for ever.' In the year 1784, an Act was passed for incorporating the Protestant Episcopal Church. This Act gave offence, and was repealed in 1786; in consequence of which the several powers of government and discipline in the said Church returned to the members at large, to be freely exercised by them as by any other religious society; for in the 'Act to Repeal the Act for Incorporating the Protestant Episcopal Church, and for other purposes,' there is a clause to the following effect, namely: 'Saving to all religious societies the property to them respectively belonging, who are hereby authorized to appoint from time to time, according to the rules of their sect, trustees, who shall be capable of managing and applying such property to the religious uses of such societies.' We, as a religious society, have appointed trustees, 'according to the rules of our sect, for managing the property to us belonging, and applying it to the religious uses of our society;' and 'according to the rules of our sect,' made in a Convention of the clerical and lay deputies of our church, it is an established Canon among us, 'That no person shall be received into any Parish within this Commonwealth, as a Minister, until he shall have entered into a contract in writing with the Vestry or Trustees on behalf of the society within such Parish, by which it shall be stipulated and declared that he holds the appointment subject to removal, agreeably to the rules and Canons of the Convention of the Protestant Episcopal Church within this State.' Here is a contract entered into, by the Minister on one side, and by the Vestry or Trustees, in behalf of the Society, on the other; and that contract authorized to be made by law, 'according to the rules of our sect.' Your Remonstrants now wish to call the attention of this House to the tenth section of the first article of the Federal Constitution, and will submit it to their judgment, whether a Glebe can be taken from a Minister and Vestry without violating that part of the Constitution; for among the prohibitory clauses in the section just mentioned of the Federal Constitution are the following, viz.: 'No State shall pass any *ex post facto* law, or law impairing the obligation of contracts.' Whereas a contract has been entered into, and is on record in the Vestry Books of this Parish, a contract authorized to be made by law, a contract of the most solemn kind, a contract concerning the use of that property which ever was, and still is ours, by the constitution, and by the common and statute laws of the land; and concerning that kind of service which is the most interesting and important of any. But all these bulwarks of happiness and security, law, prescription, custom, contracts, and constitution, are, by this Petition for the sale of our Glebe, to be prostrated beneath the feet of a party. No. The Assembly of Virginia, the House of Delegates, will never permit it. And even were not the constitution and laws so express on this subject, yet we doubt not but this House will abhor the prayer of any Petition, by whatever hand it is presented, or from whomsoever i comes, which, if it were granted, would disfranchise the citizen of his rights, and turn from house and home many indigent families and many worthy characters who have deserved well of the Republic. The Ministers of the Protestant Episcopal Church would not then have the pleasing prospect before them of living in a land of peace and equal liberty, but all the horrors of proscription and exile; for if in one parish the rights of the Protestant Episcopal Society be violated, so they may be in every parish in Virginia. And the question concerning the sale of the Glebe belonging to Antrim Parish in this county, involves, in fact, the question respecting the sale of the whole.

"5thly. Because to grant the prayer of the Petition for the sale of our Glebe would very much interrupt the peace and harmony of this country, and involve your Remonstrants and many others in much needless altercation and controversy.

"The dispute in itself has too near an affinity to religion not to participate in much of that animosity and rancour, which are the unhappy fruits of religious controversy. It directly militates against that wise and Christian maxim in our Declaration of Rights, which affirms it to be the 'mutual duty of all to practise Christian forbearance, love, and charity towards each other;' and we are confident this House will patronize no attempt that has a contrary tendency. And,

"6thly. We remonstrate against this Petition for the sale of our Glebe, and all others of a similar nature, because in its whole tenor we conceive it to be vexatious, unreasonable, unprecedented, and unjust; because it tends to destroy our political happiness; because it threatens to unnerve our Constitution and laws; and because it can be productive of no publick good, but may be productive of much publick evil.

"These, gentlemen, are the principles on which we remonstrate; they are the principles in which we have lived, which we teach our posterity, and in which we hope to die. And we trust this Honourable House will not, as it tenders the preservation of publick faith and publick peace, encroach on the rights of the peaceable,—rights which a very numerous part of your constituents maintain, and which we, your Remonstrants, hold most sacred and dear.

"And we pray that this House will come to some resolution indicative of its displeasure, at least, declarative of its sense in the most explicit and decisive tenor, respecting any Petition for the sale of a Glebe occupied by a Minister, if the money arising from the sale is to be appropriated to a different purpose; and that it will adopt such other measures as in its wisdom it may deem most eligible for a farther confirmation and security of the rights and property now enjoyed by the Protestant Episcopal Church, and for the prevention of future attempts to invade them. Such measures as these, we are persuaded, would soon put an end to this disagreeable contest, would contribute greatly towards the promotion of peace, piety, and morality, and more effectually diffuse their happy influence over the minds of the people at large.

"And your Remonstrants and Petitioners will, as in duty bound, ever pray."

Address of the Rector of Antrim Parish, Virginia, to the Members of the Church, on the proposed Sale of the Glebes in Virginia.

"Brethren:

"When I solicit your attention to what I have just now to say concerning the sale of the Glebes, I am well aware of the difference of sentiment which exists with regard to the subject. I have only to request of you to lay passion and prejudice aside, and calmly and impartially weigh the arguments I shall offer.

"It is, I believe, generally known, that for several years past, memorials and petitions have been presented to the Assembly by the Baptists for the sale of the Glebe Lands vested by law in the Protestant Episcopal Church in this State. These petitions have still been rejected by the Assembly, and generally by a very considerable majority; the members from the upper counties, where there are but few glebes, and few of the Episcopal profession, voting almost to a man in favour of the Baptist memorial; and those from the middle and lower counties generally opposing it. So long has this struggle continued, so much money has it cost the country, so much offence has it given to sober Christians of all persuasions, and so little prospect is there of its being terminated according to the wish of the Baptists, that even they and their abettors begin to be convinced, that to persist in presenting memorials of that kind will never be productive of the intended effect.

"The attention of the Baptists, therefore, is now turned towards effecting a sale of the Glebe Lands in each county separately. Accordingly a petition has lately been drawn up by , for the sale of the glebe in this parish, which I presently occupy, and sent out among the people, or soon will be, in order to obtain subscribers.

"This is a brief statement of the case, as far as has come within my knowledge. And, on the present occasion, I do not mean to lay before you the variety of arguments which is urged on either side, or to weary your attention by a multiplicity of words. I only design just now to submit a few things not unworthy the consideration, I think, of every impartial and honest man.

"To begin at the source, therefore, of this dispute. You know that before the late happy revolution in this country, the Church of England, the same, except in some points of discipline, with ours at this day, was the established religion in Virginia. But when the British yoke was thrown off, these States became sovereign, free, and independent, not only with respect to civil affairs, but with regard to religious affairs also. Accordingly, in the Declaration of Rights made by the Representatives of the good people of Virginia, met at Williamsburg, in May, 1776, it is said: 'That Religion, or the duty which we owe to our Creator, and the manner of discharging it, can be directed only by reason and conviction, not by force or violence; and therefore all men are equally entitled to the free exercise of religion, according to the dictates of conscience; and that it is the mutual duty of all to practise Christian forbearance, love, and charity towards each other.'

"But this only goes so far as to establish free toleration, by declaring that 'all men are equally entitled to the free exercise of religion.' Still, however, there was a religion established by law, and all other sects were obliged to contribute to the support of the established Church. This was an intolerable grievance, and loudly called for redress. And it was not long before it was redressed. For by the first General Assembly that ever met in Virginia after the formation of our State Constitution, at Williamsburg, in October, 1776, it was enacted, 'That all dissenters, of whatever denomination, from the Church established by law, shall, from and after the passing of this Act, be totally free and exempt from all levies, taxes, and impositions whatever, towards supporting and maintaining the said Church, as it now is or hereafter may be established, and its ministers.' And in the very next section, the glebes and Churches, with their appurtenances, are vested in the church at that time, and ever since, possessing them, in the following words: 'And be it further enacted by the authority aforesaid, that there shall in all time coming be saved and reserved to the use of the Church by law established the several tracts of Glebe lands already purchased, the churches and chapels already built, and such as were begun or contracted for before the passing of the said Act, for the use of the Parishes, all books, plate, and ornaments belonging or appropriated to the use of the said Church, and all arrears of money or tobacco arising from former assessments or otherwise; and that there shall moreover be saved or reserved to the use of such Parishes as may have received private donations, for the better support of the said Church and its Ministers, the perpetual benefit and enjoyment of all such donations.'

"This Act, seemingly, gave universal satisfaction to the Baptists and other dissenters at the time it was passed; but in a few years after, they began to petition to have that part of it repealed which makes over the Glebes and Churches to the Protestant Episcopal Society, and have continued to petition almost every Assembly to have this property sold.

"The principal arguments they make use of to support their plea, are the following:

"1st. As most of the Glebe lands were originally purchased with money levied upon the people at large, they say that in whatever County a majority of the people wish these lands to be sold, they ought to be sold, and the money refunded, or applied to some other use.

"The sentiments of the majority of the people, I allow, are always entitled to much attention; but when they petitioned to have an establishment of religion annulled, as it justly was, almost twenty years ago, then was the time for them to insist also on a sale of the Glebes and Churches. Whereas, in this petition at that time, they prayed for no such thing, although their claim at that day was just as good as it is now. And if in one instance, they petition for money to be given back, which was paid under the British Government, it is equally just that they should do so in every case.

"If they say that the laws were oppressive which compelled them to support a religion from which at that time they dissented, then let them recollect how few were dissenters when the Glebes were originally purchased, and that, even upon their own principles, if a part of the original purchase money is to be given back, it ought to be a part only in proportion to that number who then were dissenters. For if they, from conscientious motives, have dissented from their forefathers, they can with no justice now have any retrospective view or claim to what was done by their ancestors with a good conscience.

"Whatever was then done with respect to religious affairs was done by the authority of those laws and that government under which we then lived. Many of these laws are now repealed, and especially those which had the least respect to an establishment of religion; and that government we wisely rejected for one of our own. And under our present constitution and laws, property of every kind is secured to the individuals and bodies who are the rightful holders thereof, by everything firm and sacred which the laws of God and of our country have devised. Glebes and Churches are held and enjoyed by ministers and vestries, by as good a right as each of you hold your private estates.

"You know that in this country landed property has always been considered in the eye of the law as the most sacred of any, and that she puts forth her hand with reluctance to seize it. And once the Legislative body passes an Act vesting in any individual or society any landed estate, there must be cogent and weighty reasons indeed to move it to rescind a confirmation made of that kind of property which, in its own nature, is the most permanent, and rendered the most fixed and stable of any, by the nature of our laws. We are not now in the heat of a revolution. Everything has been settled on a sure foundation, by a free Convention of the people. Nor do I conceive that any innovations can now take place, at least, until another Convention is called with similar powers. For should the Assembly pass an Act to take away from one society the property it has always enjoyed since the first settlement of this country,—and by their own grant, for nearly now these twenty years,—it would be a fluctuation in law, if not an innovation of right, which, I think, highly inimical to the spirit of our constitution, and, I am confident, is without precedent in Virginia. I allow that principle is not to be regulated by precedent. But if the principle be of suspicious or dubious tendency, it certainly stands in need of the authority of precedent, before it is suffered to be introduced.

"The Glebes did originally belong to the country at large, and they still are for the use of the country at large, agreeable to the purpose for which they were first set apart, for the churches are open to all without discrimination, and the services of ministers are tendered to all on the same terms. But the country at large did, by its representatives, at the commencement of the revolution, vest them in a particular society. And now to petition the Assembly to take back what it has already given, is to petition them to introduce a fatal precedent with respect to the right by which property in general is held,—to trample the rights of one society under their feet, and destroy that confidence which the people ought always to have in the faith of the Legislature.

"2dly. The Baptists urge, that by holding this property, a certain pre-eminence and superiority is conferred on us, which is odious in Republican Governments.

"But the constitution of this country is founded on equality, and abhors distinctions of every kind in its laws. The laws themselves cannot, and dare not, without a violation of right, confer superiority or exclusive privileges on any one denomination of Christians above another. If we enjoy any pre-eminence above them, I am sure it is not derived to us from that quarter.

"But they give out that they are afraid of an establishment, and that they consider the Glebes as the foundation of a religious establishment. But it is impossible there can be any such thing as a religious establishment in America as long as there is a free government. Nor do I believe there are ten men in this county, of any discernment, who wish or expect such a thing. Yet I have often heard it said of the Episcopalians, by those of a different religious persuasion, that they generally wished to have their Church established by law. But the reproach is unjust. This spirit prevails no more among us than it does among others. Our Church can support itself without an establishment; and if it does not, why it ought not to exist. And I do not hesitate to say, that in her present state, she is more pure and perfect as a Church than ever she was under the establishment.

"And as we enjoy no pre-eminence by law, so we claim none; but the rights which are ours already by law, we cannot think of relinquishing; because if these rights are given up at the request of one sect, we cannot tell but we shall be obliged to deliver up others still dearer unto us; and that when they shall have it in their power to deprive the Episcopal society of the property which it enjoys,—they may next proceed to deprive it of the free exercise of its religion, and establish their own upon its ruins.

"3dly. They quote the fourth Article of the Declaration of Rights to support their assertion, that the Act vesting the Glebe lands in the Protestant Episcopal Church is unconstitutional.

"That Article declares, 'That no man, or set of men, are entitled to exclusive or separate emoluments or privileges from the community, but in consideration of publick services.' Here they would insist, that, as we enjoy the Glebes, we enjoy 'exclusive emoluments from the community.' They might as soon say that the Members of the Council and Parish Ministers under the British Government, who are now living in this State, enjoy 'exclusive emoluments from the community.' For the money which partly purchased the estates they now live on, was certainly paid them by the publick. If we enjoyed any 'exclusive emoluments from the community,' it would be something which was paid for by this community since the revolution; whereas the community gave no emolument or new grant to the Church; it only confirmed to her what from the beginning was her's, and has ever since been in her possession. Most of the Glebes were purchased and paid for one hundred years before the revolution; and in many counties, from the frequent migrations to the western country and to other States, it is very questionable whether there be one third of the inhabitants remaining whose ancestors paid for the purchase of a Glebe. So that if they petition for the sale of them because their ancestors paid for them, it will be very difficult, if not impossible, to find out to whom the money is now owing. If they say that the Country or the State first purchased them, and that they are to be given back to the Country or State, then it should be remembered that the State has already pledged its legislative faith, that they shall, 'in all time coming,' remain to the use of one religious society, according to the intention for which they were originally given. And for the State to take back what it once gave, would be fully as unjust as for one individual to take back what he formerly made over to another.

"But it is unfortunate for them, that this article which they quote has not, I think, the smallest allusion to the point in dispute. Its intention is to prevent *hereditary* honours, offices, or emoluments in the civil government. This the connection of the whole Article makes plain—'That no man or set of men are entitled to exclusive or separate emoluments or privileges from the community, but in consideration of publick services; which, not being descendible, neither ought the offices of magistrate, legislator, or judge, to be hereditary.'

"Influenced by these and arguments of a similar kind, the House of Delegates have hitherto negatived the prayer of the Memorial and Petition offered by the Baptists. But an attempt is now made to sell the Glebe lands belonging to this Parish, by a petition from the county ———, which will soon be circulated for this purpose, in order to procure as many subscribers as possible.

"In relation to the sale of this Glebe in particular, permit me to observe a few things.

"This Petition, therefore, for the sale of the Glebe in this Parish, or in any other Parish, let it be signed by ever so many, will certainly be opposed in the House of Delegates, and I am confident will be rejected by a considerable majority, for it involves the main question for the sale of all the Glebes in the State. The Vestry of this Parish hold their glebe lands by the very same right as all other Glebes in the State are held; and if the law is violated in one instance, it may be so in twenty.

"It is true there have been several Glebes sold by Act of Assembly, and the money applied to a different purpose; but it has been in such Parishes only where there was no minister or vestry, or for some other weighty reasons. But that a Glebe should be sold while it was occupied by a Minister, or that a petition should be presented for such a purpose, I know of no instance in Virginia.

"But, behold, here is a petition brought forward for the sale of the Glebe which I occupy; a Glebe which I procured neither by intrigue nor by stealth, but honestly and openly, and on which I have lived without interruption for several years. And what is it now that I have done, that I should be compelled to give up the privileges I have hitherto enjoyed? Have I taken a sixpence from any man by fraud or by oppression? Have I told lies? Am I guilty of robbery, drunkenness, or murder? Or what black and enormous crime am I to be charged with, that I should forfeit the rights of a citizen? On the contrary, has not my manner of life, since I came among you, been sufficiently known? I am not ignorant that on several occasions reports have been whispered prejudicial to my character. But I challenge any man to step forth, if he dare, and say anything in any company, and before my face, which an honest man would blush to own. In the discharge of my office I have industriously avoided all subjects of a controversial and inflammatory nature, though at the same time I have used all freedom in delivering my own sentiments,—a privilege I always will exercise. For as I know not, so I care not, to dissemble. I value the approbation of mine own mind more than that of all mankind.

"The friends of this petition are very confident of having a great majority of the freeholders and other inhabitants of this county as subscribers. I shall not attempt to undeceive them. It is very probable they will. But of the unprejudiced, of those who are averse from contention and discord, of the well-informed and peaceable, I hope they will have very few. The promoters of it also do everything they can to make it interest and agitate the minds of the people at large. But in fact, it is a matter of no such high concernment. It is a matter of small consequence to the county whether the Glebe be sold or not. They, however, have their own views. They know that as long as they are the heroes of the day they will not be forgotten. But if they are truly patriots; if they wish to promote the peace and prosperity of their county, let them abet no partial and party schemes, and gratify one part of its inhabitants at the expense of the other; but let them devise some plan equally beneficial to the whole; let them introduce among us manufacturers, or open to us channels by which we can more easily find a market for the commodities we now have to spare.. These, and such like, are objects more worthy the attention of *Friends to the People*, and would confer on them more deserved and more lasting popularity.

"Those who favour this plan should also consider, that no material advantage can be derived from the sale of the Glebe, either to themselves or to others. You think, perhaps, it would annihilate the Church. If it should, would that be of any advantage to you? or would you wish to give power to one denomination of Christians to trample upon another? They will next trample upon yourselves. Although the Baptists are the most numerous sect in this county at present, they may not be so always. We find that first one sect has its day, and then another. In short, there can be nothing more variable and fluctuating than the state of religious sects with regard to decadency or increase. And in this county, it is a truth too plain and too lamentable, that, notwithstanding the number of preachers, there is not one half of the people at large who are in church communion with any denomination of Christians. They have joined no church. They attend regularly at no place of publick worship, and generally are very indifferent with regard to religious affairs. To these people it is a matter of no concern whether the Glebe be sold or not. They will, when asked, give their voices for it or against it, according to the prevailing opinion in the company where they may be, or in the neighbourhoods where they live.

"You, however, who have the smallest concern for the interests of religion in general and the peace and happiness of our county, but more particularly all freeholders who have a respect for the constitution and laws of our country, and are unbiassed by party views, I would have seriously consider and think what you are called upon to do, when you are solicited to sign these petitions for the sale of the Glebe. You are called upon to give your voice for taking away from one religious society the property they have always possessed, and that without an equivalent, and deprive a fellow-citizen, myself, of his just rights, who has had no other object in view than to promote your dearest interests. This appears so iniquitous and unjust, so arbitrary and persecuting, that I have no doubt it partly excites your righteous indignation as well as mine.

"I have lived on the Glebe since I have been Minister of the Parish, and most of what I have received for my services has been expended in repairing and improving the plantation. These repairs have been of considerable value, and though my word, I expect, will not be doubted by any person present, yet I wish none to take it upon that authority alone. I am willing to submit their value to the determination of a jury. And if the Glebe is sold, I shall thus have expended the little I had to spare for the publick, to whom, when divided among them, it will be little more than nothing.

"For if the Glebe were sold, what would it be to the whole county? It would fetch little more than £200, perhaps not so much in ready money. This would not pay half your County and Parish levies for one year. Indeed, the proportion which would fall to the share of every man is too insignificant, and not worth the attention of any freeholder whatever. And, therefore, to agitate and inflame the public mind concerning a matter of so trivial importance to the county at large, must be done with no other end than to gratify the wishes of a party, or to promote selfish and particular views.

"The Baptists say they do not petition for the sale of the Glebes on account of their value. Neither need we wish to hold them on account of their value, but as a matter of right. The one I occupy has hitherto brought me every year into debt, authentic accounts of which I can at any time produce. If the law, however, which vests the Glebes in us be unconstitutional and oppressive, if it be contrary to the principles pervading Republican Governments and free States, for God's sake let it be repealed. But if it is not; if the law is constitutional; if it secures rights which we hold dear as life and liberty itself; if it is wished to be repealed to gratify the views of one religious sect, then let it stand fast as the pillars of justice, and secure not only to us the rights which we presently enjoy, but to our posterity for ever.

"To the preachers, and other members of the Baptist Church, who are zealous in promoting this Petition, I would take the liberty of observing, that as this, at best, is but a circumstance of a political nature, it seems not with any propriety to come so particularly under the cognizance of those who labour in the vineyard of Christ. Ministers, to be sure, are men; and they have civil rights to defend; but this dispute is too nearly connected with religion not to partake of much of that animosity and rancour which are the unhappy effects of religious controversy. How different is this from the mild spirit of that religion which breathes unanimity, forgiveness, meekness, and peace! When we ourselves make it appear by our conduct, that Christianity has so little power over our hearts, can it be supposed that ever we will recommend it to the esteem of others? The infidel will never believe us, and the libertine will get confirmed in his vicious practices. Alas! we pull down with our own hands that Church of Christ which we ought to build up and defend. We fill the minds of the community, moreover, with 'wrath, hatred, and emulations, envyings, and strife.' How long shall it be before the doctrines of the Son of God have full influence on the minds of men! How long shall this land, the asylum of all nations, be filled with contention? When shall we fully prize the blessings we enjoy? We might now sit every man at peace 'under his own vine, and under that fair Tree of Liberty which we planted.' But, alas! the canker-worm of Jealousy feeds on its foliage; the whirlwinds of discord threaten to root it out for ever.

"On you, however, who are attached to this Church, and who in your respective neighbourhoods must have some influence, I must place my sole dependence for obviating the efforts which are now making to ruin your Church; and particularly that you will be industrious in procuring as many subscribers as possible to the remonstrances which I shall put into your hands. The issue of the affair will not depend on the number of subscribers, though it may be materially affected by it. For me to take an active part, farther than by endeavouring to set it in a fair and just light before the public mind, would be indelicate and improper. This is not so much my business as yours. And unless strenuous exertions are now made, the event may be very unfortunate for your Church. If the Glebe is sold, it will affect neither my reputation nor my property; but if it is, the church in this Parish, and in a great many others in Virginia, will well nigh be ruined. Yes, that Church which I believe in my confidence to be as pure as any at this day on earth, will be left without a vestige of her memory in the land. She will fall, as a bright star from heaven, and be lost in perpetual night. Unfortunate she! she has 'nourished and brought up children, and they have rebelled against her.' Like the sun in an unclouded sky, she was once the light and glory of this land; and shall she set in darkness and rise no more? Forbid it, heaven! forbid it, justice: forbid it, honour.

"I myself, whilst holding the station which I possess, will, I trust, discharge my duty with fidelity. If we are all united and act in concert, the effect we can produce will be considerable. Adversity is the fire which purifieth the Church. Through many such she hath passed, and ours when tried in that furnace will come forth still more pure. That at the present crisis you may act your parts with firmness as her friends, having due regard at the same time to the Christian character, is my earnest recommendation. Providence will thus smile on our labours, and conduct them at length to a happy issue. Conscience will approve of our conduct; and death will introduce us to glory.

"Antrim Glebe, Halifax, June 4th, 1795."

MR. HENDERSON WALKER

TO THE

LORD BISHOP OF LONDON.

"North Carolina, 21st October, 1703.

"May it please your Lordship:

"The great and pious designs of your Lordship towards these American Parts for the Propagation of the Christian Church, of which you are so pious and good a Pillar, imboldens me to lay before your Lordship the present State of North Carolina as to their Christian well-being; and I was the more encouraged to do it by reason that our Lords Proprietors were pleased to write to us concerning Mr. Bray, your Lordship's Commissary, coming to visit us.

"My Lord, we have been settled neer this fifty years in this place, and I may justly say most part of twenty-one years on my own knowledge without Priest or Altar, and before that time, according to all that appears to me, much worse. George Fox some years ago came into these parts, and by strange infatuations did infuse the Quakers' Principles into some small number of the people, which did and hath continued to grow ever since very numerous by reason of their yearly sending in men to encourage and exhort them to their wicked principles; and here was none to dispute nor to oppose them in carrying on their pernicious principles for many years, till God of his infinite goodness was pleased to inspire the Rev. Dr. Bray some time about four years ago to send in some books of his own particular pious gift of the explanation of the Church Catechism, with some other small books to be disposed of and lent as we thought fit, did in some measure put a stop to their growth; and about a year after did send to us a library of books for the benefit of this place, given by the honourable the Corporation for the establishing of the Christian religion, by one Mr. Daniel Bret, a minister appointed for this place. He for about half a year behaved himself in a modest manner, but after that in a most horrid manner; broke out in such an extravagant course that I am ashamed to express his carraige, it being in so high nature. It hath been a great trouble and grief to us who have a great veneration for the Church that the first minister that was sent to us should prove so ill as to give the Dissenters so much occasion to charge us with him. My Lord, I humbly begg you to believe that we do not think that the Rev. Dr. Bray knew any thing of the life and conversations of the man. We did about this time two years, with a great deal of care and management, get an Assembly, and we passed an act for building of churches and establishing a maintenance for a minister amongst us, and in pursuance thereto we have built one church, and there is two more a going forward, and his Excellency Francis Nicholson, Esq., Governor of Virginia, was pleased of his pious goodness to give us £10 to each church, and we sent copies of that act of Assembly to our Lords proprietors to get the same ratified, and likewise a copy to Dr. Bray to entreat his favour with them to obtain a Ratification, which we are in hopes to obtain this shipping, but they not being come we are in a great loss. My Lord, I humbly beg leave to inform you that we have an Assembly to sit the 3d November next, and there is above one half of the Burgesses that are chosen are Quakers and have declared their designs of making void the act for establishing the Church; if your Lordship out of your good and pious care of us doth not put a stop to their growth, we shall the most part, especially the children born here, become heathens. I humbly entreat your Lordship to send some worthy good man amongst us to regain the Flock, and so perfect us in our duty to God, and establish us by his Doctrine, life, and conversation in the fundamentalls of our Christian profession that we in our time and those as come hereafter, may bless God that he has raised up so noble a pillar as your Lordship to regain those who are going astray, and put a stop to the pernicious growing Principles of the Quakers.

"Your Lordship may see the copy of our act by Dr. Bray, and I humbly beg your Lordship's Pardon for giving you this trouble, and take leave to subscribe myself,

"My Lord,

"Your most humble and obedient servant,

"HENDERSON WALKER."

AN ACCOUNT

OF

MR. BLAIR'S MISSION

TO NORTH CAROLINA.

"I WAS ordained in order to go to the Plantations 12th April, 1703, and then received the Queen's Bounty of £20, and soon after my Lord Weymouth's bounty of £50, upon which I lived in England till the 1st October following, which together with my fitting out for such a Voyage and Country consumed the most part of my money. I had likewise £5 sent me by my Lord of London to Portsmouth, and when I landed in Virginia, I had no more than £25.

"I landed in Virginia 14th January, 1703. As soon as I could conveniently travel, I waited on the Governor, and immediately after made the best of my way into the country where I was bound.

"I arrived amongst the Inhabitants after a tedious and troublesome journey on the 24th. I was then obliged to buy a couple of Horses, which cost me fourteen pounds, one of which was for a guide, because there is no possibility for a stranger to find his Road in that Country, for if he once goes astray (it being such a Desart country) it's a hazard if ever he finds his Road again. Besides there are mighty inconveniences in travelling there, for the roads are not only deep and difficult to be found, but there are likewise seven great Rivers in the country, over which there is no passing with horses, except two of them, one of which the Quakers have settled a Ferry over for their own conveniency, and nobody but themselves have the Priviledge of it, so that at the passing over the Rivers, I was obliged either to borrow or hire Horses, which was both troublesome and chargeable, insomuch that in little more than two months I was obliged to dispose of the necessaries I carried over for my own use to satisfy my creditors.

"I found in the Country a great many children to be baptized, where I baptized about one hundred, and there are a great many still to be baptized, whose parents would not condescend to have them Baptized with Godfathers and Godmothers.

"I married none in the Country, for that was a Perquisite belonged to the Magistrates which I was not desirous to deprive them of.

"I preached twice every Sunday, and often on the week days when their Vestries met, or could appoint them to bring their Children to be baptized.

"I called a Vestry in each Precinct, in my first progress through the country, to whom I gave an Account of my Lord Weymouth's charitable bounty, in supporting my Mission among them, and likewise of the good designs the honourable Society had for them, as I was informed by Mr. Amy that they had settled £80 per annum for the maintenance of two Clergymen amongst them. And likewise a proposal that Dr. Bray desired me to make to them upon their procuring good Glebes he doubted not but that there might be a settlement made for the advantage of the Church, such as there is in the Island of Bermudas, viz. two Slaves and a small Stock in each Precinct, and that to be continued good by the Incumbent to his successor, which will be a lasting Estate to the Church.

"They have built in the Country three small Churches and have three Glebes.

"In the three Chief Precincts there is a Reader establisht in each, to whom they allow a small salary, who reads Morning and Evening Prayer every Lord's Day, with two Sermons, and I took care to furnish them with books from the Library before I came away.

"I remained very well satisfied in the Country till their Assembly sat, which was on 1st March, where I expected they would propose a settlement for my maintenance; and they taking no care of it, together with my then circumstances, which were but very indifferent, Discouraged me very much, and occasioned my first thoughts of returning to England, for I was informed before I went thither that there was £30 per annum settled by Law to be paid in each Precinct for the Maintenance of a Minister, which Law was sent over hither to be confirmed by their Lords proprietors; and it being supposed not to be a competency for a Minister to live on, was sent back again without Confirmation, whereof the Quakers took the advantage, and will endeavour to prevent any such Law passing for the future; for they are the greatest number in the Assembly, and are unanimous, and stand truly to one another in whatsoever may be for their Interest, for the Country may be divided into four sorts of people: 1st, the Quakers, who are the most powerful enemies to Church Government, but a people very ignorant of what they profess; 2d sort are a great many that have no Religion, but would be Quakers if by that they were not obliged to lead a more moral life than they are willing to comply to; a 3d sort are something like Presbyterians, which sort is upheld by some idle Fellows that have left their lawful Imployment and preach and baptize through the country without any manner of orders from any sect or pretended Church. A 4th sort, who are really zealous for the Interest of the Church, are the fewest in number, but the better sort of people, and would do very much for the settlement of Church Government there, if not opposed by these three Precedent Sects, and although they be all three of different pretensions, yet they all concur together in one common cause to prevent anything that will be chargeable to them, as they allege Church Government will be if once establisht by Law; and another great discouragement these poor people have is a Governor who does not in the least countenance them in this Business, but rather discourage them.

"Finding it impossible to travel through the Country at that rate I begun I was resolved to settle in one precinct, but the people all alledging my Lord Weymouth's Charity was universally designed for the whole country would not consent to it, which bred some disturbance amongst them, upon which I was advised by some of the best friends of the Church to come over and represent their condition to the Honourable Society, not only of their want of Ministers, but likewise of Inhabitants to maintain them; and their desires, they complying with my necessities, was a powerful argument, considering I was then reduced to my last stake, and knew not where and upon what account to be further supplied. Besides such a solitary, toylsome, and hard living as I met with there, were very sufficient discouragement. I was distant from any Minister one hundred and twenty miles, so that if any case of difficulty or doubt should happen, with whom should I consult? And for my travelling through the Country, I rid one day with another, Sunday only Excepted, above thirty miles per diem in the worst roads that ever I saw, and have sometimes layn whole nights in the woods.

"I will now endeavour to shew you how ineffectual a single Man's labours would be amongst so scattered a people. In the first place, suppose him Minister of one precinct (whereas there are five in the Country), and this precinct as they are all, bounded with two Rivers, and those Rivers at least twenty miles distant, without any inhabitants on the Road, for they plant only on the Rivers, and they are planted in length upon these Rivers at least twenty miles. And to give all these Inhabitants an opportunity of hearing a Sermon, and bringing their Children to be baptized, which must be on the Sabbath, for they want spare time of another day, and must be in every ten miles distance, for five miles is farthest that they will bring their children or willingly come themselves, so that he must, to do his duty effectually, be ten or twelve weeks in making his progress through one precinct.

"You may also consider the distance that the New Colony of Pamtico is from the rest of the Inhabitants of the country, for any Man that has tried it, would sooner undertake a voyage from this City to Holland than that, for besides a Pond of five miles broad and nothing to carry one over but small Perriaugers, there are about fifty miles Desert to pass through without any human creature Inhabiting in it. I think it likewise reasonable to give you an Account of a Great Nation of Indians that live in that Government computed to be of no less than 100,000, many of which live amongst the English, and all as I can understand a very civilized people.

"I have often conversed with them, and have been frequently in their towns. Those that can speak English among them seem to be very willing and fond of being Christians, and in my opinion there might be methods taken to bring over a great many of them. If there was no hopes of making them Christians, the advantage of having Missionaries among them would redound to the Advantage of the Government, for if they should once be brought over to a French Interest (as we have too much reason to believe there are some promoters amongst them for that end) by their late Actions; it would be (if not to the utter ruin) to the great prejudice of all the English Plantations on the Continent of America.

"I have here in brief set down what I have to say, and shall be ready to answer to any Questions the Honourable Society shall think convenient to ask me concerning the Country, and shall be both ready and willing to serve them anywhere upon such encouragement as I can live according to my education, after my Lord Weymouth ceases to lay his commands on me.

"I have made a considerable losing voyage of it this time, both by my troublesome travelling in America and likewise by being taken into France, where I was prisoner of war nine weeks, and was forced to make use of my credit for my sustenance, and have lived in the same circumstances since I came to England, without any manner of relief, which has been very troublesome to me, all which has brought me considerably in debt, near £35, and now in no way to pay it, without my charitable Benefactor or the Honourable Society judge my labours worthy a reward."

www.ingramcontent.com/pod-product-compliance
Lightning Source LLC
LaVergne TN
LVHW010558110826
845149LV00003B/693